Presidential Risk Behavior in Foreign Policy

Presidential Risk Behavior in Foreign Policy

Prudence or Peril?

By
William A. Boettcher III
Assistant Professor
North Carolina State University

PRESIDENTIAL RISK BEHAVIOR IN FOREIGN POLICY
© William A. Boettcher III, 2005.

First published in 2005 by
PALGRAVE MACMILLAN™
175 Fifth Avenue, New York, N.Y. 10010 and
Houndmills, Basingstoke, Hampshire, England RG21 6XS
Companies and representatives throughout the world.

PALGRAVE MACMILLAN is the global academic imprint of the Palgrave Macmillan division of St. Martin's Press, LLC and of Palgrave Macmillan Ltd. Macmillan® is a registered trademark in the United States, United Kingdom and other countries. Palgrave is a registered trademark in the European Union and other countries.

ISBN 1–4039–6854–3

Library of Congress Cataloging-in-Publication Data

Boettcher, William A., 1969–
    Presidential risk behavior in foreign policy : prudence or peril? / by William A. Boettcher III.
        p. cm.
    Includes bibliographical references and index.
    ISBN 1–4039–6854–3
    1. Presidents—United States—Decision making—Case studies. 2. Presidents—United States—Psychology—Case studies. 3. Risk-taking (Psychology)—Political aspects—United States—Case studies. 4. United States—Foreign relations—1945–1989—Decision making—Case studies. I. Title.

JK516.B64 2005
327.73'001'9—dc22   2004058691

Design by Newgen Imaging Systems (P) Ltd., Chennai, India.

First edition: March 2005

10 9 8 7 6 5 4 3 2 1

Printed in the United States of America.

*For my wife, Becky
and our children, Abigail and Andrew*

CONTENTS

PREFACE

Three core questions provide the underlying structure for this book: Why did U.S. presidents frequently engage in anticommunist crusades in peripheral areas (in terms of strategic value) during the Cold War? How can we explain individual decisions that appear to be irrational? How should we apply and test psychological theories of human decision-making based on laboratory experiments? My interest in these questions emerged in the early 1990s as articles by Robert Jervis, Jack Levy, Barbara Farnham, and Rose McDermott introduced "prospect theory" to international relations scholars. Borrowing from the seminal work of psychologists Daniel Kahneman and Amos Tversky, these authors sought to develop explanations for risk-taking decisions that could not be easily explained by expected-utility theory. Prospect theory provided a relatively parsimonious, intuitively compelling, and descriptively accurate challenge to the reigning paradigm. Prospect theory's emphasis on risk-taking, when faced with losses (along with research on the endowment effect, sunk costs, and escalation of commitment), seemed particularly well suited for military intervention decisions that are often fraught with danger. Unfortunately, much of the early research on prospect theory in international relations was focused on straightforward application instead of adaptation and integration. The current wave of international relations research on prospect theory takes account of the critiques leveled at the work of the early pioneers, builds on the latest research in behavioral decision theory, and self-consciously attempts to combine the insights derived from prospect theory with knowledge gained from years of research by international relations theorists.

This book integrates research on reference dependence, personal predispositions, and uncertainty and information accuracy in a "Risk Explanation Framework" (REF) designed to reflect the contextual nuance of the empirical realm of foreign policy decision making. I argue that personal predispositions interact with the characteristics of a situation (including the number and framing of alternatives and the degree of uncertainty and time pressure) to produce choices that could not be predicted by theories of rational state interest or domestic politics. Hypotheses gleaned from the theoretical discussion and critique are tested in six case studies across two presidential administrations (Truman and Kennedy). Throughout these case studies, I am sensitive to the problems of evaluation and testing that have plagued earlier research in this area. I find particularly strong support for the hypotheses regarding reference dependence and uncertainty and information accuracy, while the weaker results for the hypotheses regarding personal predispositions suggest areas for revision and future research.

I would like to thank the people who introduced me to the study of foreign policy decision making, encouraged my interest in political psychology, supplied thoughtful advice and criticism of draft manuscripts, and provided emotional support in times of frustration. Throughout my years in graduate school and my time as an assistant professor, Don Sylvan (my dissertation advisor) pushed me to follow my heart and pursue an independent course. He has not only been a great teacher but also a true colleague and friend. I must also thank Rick Herrmann, Peg Hermann, and Tom Nygren for their patience as I struggled through the early phases of my research. Michael Fischerkeller, Tanya Charlick-Paley, Michael Young, Jack Levy, Yaacov Vertzberger, Jerel Rosati, and Nehemia Geva have provided comments on various chapters and conference papers that greatly improved the quality of the manuscript. Jeffrey Taliaferro has acted as a model colleague: reading multiple versions of each chapter, challenging unexamined assumptions, forcing me to refine weak arguments, and catching both major and minor errors. I owe a great debt to the archivists at the National Archives, National Security Archive, John F. Kennedy Library, and Harry S. Truman Library. In particular, Sam Rushay of the Truman Library went out of his way to assist a young political scientist struggling through his first attempt at archival research. As I prepared the final manuscript for publication, Ekaterina Barachkova meticulously corrected flaws in citations and helped me track down incomplete bibliographic entries. David Pervin, my editor at Palgrave Macmillan, encouraged and supported me throughout the publication process, and his assistant, Heather VanDusen, was instrumental in helping me deal with the minor obstacles that often frustrate authors. I also need to thank the copyediting team at Newgen Imaging Systems for cleaning up a number of flaws in the manuscript (those that remain are the author's responsibility alone). Finally, my wife Becky and our children Abigail Grace and Andrew William have provided love and patience in times of stress.

This project was supported in part by a grant from the National Science Foundation (DIR-9113599) to the Mershon Center Research Training Group on the Role of Cognition in Collective Political Decision Making, by a Graduate Student Alumni Research Award and a Presidential Fellowship from the Graduate School at The Ohio State University, by a research grant from the Harry S. Truman Library Institute, and by financial support from the Department of Political Science and Public Administration and the College of Humanities and Social Sciences at North Carolina State University.

CHAPTER ONE

Introduction

I. Overview

From 1946 to 1950, President Harry S. Truman guided a hesitant country, triumphant in war and prepared to return to peace, onto a new path of global involvement. In Iran, Greece, and Korea, Truman and his advisors forged a policy of interventionism—both military and economic—in areas outside the traditional sphere of influence of the United States. This expansion of U.S. commitments on a massive scale ran the dual risk of entrapment in "wasting wars" in the periphery or escalation and direct conventional (and later atomic) conflict with the Soviet Union. Truman embarked on this new policy despite congressional opposition, public indifference, and military reluctance. The specter of these areas falling to Communist subversion/aggression loomed larger than the very real political, economic, and military risks of engagement. Why would an American president expose the country to such peril to defend states whose loss would result in only minimal shifts in the balance of power between the United States and Soviet Union?

From the spring of 1961 to his death in 1963, President John F. Kennedy had to deal with more domestic and foreign policy crises than many of his full-term predecessors. Immediately following his inauguration, Kennedy was faced with important decisions concerning U.S. intervention in Laos, Vietnam, and the Congo. A decade into the Cold War, Kennedy confronted significant risks from all courses of action/inaction: a series of costly and inconclusive stalemates like Korea, conventional (and possibly nuclear) conflict with the Soviet Union and/or China, opposition from "dovish" Democrats in Congress to military intervention, accusations from "hawkish" Republicans regarding Kennedy's "softness" on Communism, public opposition to large-scale troop commitments, and the economic cost of involvement in or the loss of the areas to Communist subversion/aggression. For Kennedy, the prospect of limited victories over America's Cold War nemesis was tempered by the political, economic, and military risks of engagement. Why would the president who had promised so much in his inaugural address follow the prudent path of incremental policy change?

The behavior of Presidents Truman and Kennedy in these six cases cannot be fully explained by existing theories of foreign policy and international politics. Defensive realism could account for Kennedy's reluctance to intervene in Laos and the Congo, but not for his limited intervention in Vietnam or Truman's bold commitments in Iran, Greece, and Korea. Communist threats to these states would not merit the attention of a great power since their loss would have only a limited impact on the balance of power.[1] Offensive realists have characterized Truman's decisions as responsible balancing against an expansionist Soviet Union, but cannot explain Kennedy's attempts to achieve the neutralization of Laos or his cautious incrementalism in Vietnam. The effort to produce a new Geneva conference on Laos came close to an appeasement policy by the new administration, and the limited expansion of U.S. involvement in Vietnam barely crossed over the boundary between buck-passing and balancing.[2]

Domestic politics explanations of U.S. foreign policy during these periods would focus on the role of congressional and/or public opinion or on important "logrolling coalitions" in favor of imperial expansion (see Snyder, 1991). Electoral constraints would force a democratically elected leader to respond to an agitated and engaged constituency. These theories could explain the Iran, the Vietnam, and even possibly the Greece decisions, but the other decisions were made with little public or congressional involvement. Indeed, in many of these cases, the president attempted to guide or shape the views of a public and congress that was largely uninformed or uninterested in foreign affairs. When there was substantial public, congressional, or interest group pressure in a particular direction, counterpressures were often applied. While both presidents were clearly attentive to and constrained by these domestic forces, they often either perceived a relatively open decision space or so many crosscutting constraints that any course of action ran the risk of alienating an important group.

One of the most significant limitations of extant theories of foreign policy and international relations is their inability to offer an adequate explanation for state or decision-maker risk behavior. States, governments, and individual political leaders operate in an environment plagued by risk and uncertainty. International outcomes are not the result of parsimonious deterministic laws, instead they emerge from complex webs of probabilistic contingencies. Reality as we know it is an unlikely event—lightning strikes, sharks attack, lotteries are won, and wars are lost by seemingly stronger powers. In this environment value trade-offs, stress, time pressure, and uncertainty affect even the most intellectually prepared and technologically sophisticated actors. Without a nuanced understanding of the personal and situational determinants of risk behavior, our theories will at best offer idiosyncratic post hoc explanations and be utterly incapable of reliable prediction.

This book marks an attempt to develop a synthesized model of risk behavior that is sensitive to the empirical domain of presidential foreign policy decision making.[3] Building on research on risk behavior in political science, psychology, economics, business, and sociology, the "Risk Explanation

Framework" (REF) integrates three veins of research (reference dependence, personal predispositions, and uncertainty and information accuracy) in a new conceptual framework for the study of presidential risk behavior in foreign policy. The explanatory power of the hypotheses that compose the REF is evaluated through six case studies from the Truman (Iran 1946; Greece 1947–1948; and Korea 1950) and Kennedy (Laos 1961; Vietnam 1961; and Congo 1962) administrations. These 6 cases are divided into 12 decision periods yielding 53 opportunities to test the 7 hypotheses discussed later. Across the 53 opportunities, the REF hypotheses received "strong support" 30 times, "moderate support" 10 times, and "weak support" 5 times. Evidence counter to the REF hypotheses was found at only eight points in the cases. The relatively strong empirical support for the REF hypotheses demonstrates the utility of this new approach to the study of risk behavior, while the limited number of negative results highlights promising areas of revision and future testing.

II. Risk Behavior in International Relations

The study of state behavior in the face of risk and uncertainty has been an integral part of International Relations research for at least the last quarter century (see Alpert, 1976; Singer et al., 1972). Researchers focusing on the systemic, state, or individual levels of analysis have consistently recognized that states (or individual decision makers within states) operate in a complex and uncertain world where they are forced to anticipate and respond to the actions of enemies and allies. While different research traditions approach the study of risk behavior in markedly different ways, almost every scholar of international relations recognizes that the fundamental foreign policy task facing states/decision makers is to discern order in a disorderly world. In short, states/decision makers worry about the future; and in planning for the future, they must deal with risk and uncertainty.[4]

Two basic approaches have dominated the study of risk behavior in the field of international relations. The first approach recognizes the importance of unit or actor risk propensity, but assumes that risk propensity is consistent across all units or actors within a system. This approach is evident in much of the defensive realist literature (see Keohane, 1986; Waltz, 1979).[5] In defensive realism, it is assumed that the most basic value possessed by every unit within the system is survival. States are forced to be concerned (or even obsessed) with survival because of the anarchic nature of the international system. This concern generally leads to risk-averse behavior by states. Because survival is valued so highly, states require significantly lower risks (or higher stakes) before they will pursue policies that could potentially endanger their existence. Conflict between states is usually the result of the security dilemma and not the result of risk-taking by significant actors.[6] In the event that a risk-taking state does emerge, it is expected that systemic constraints will force that state to recognize the folly of its ways—or perish. All states act as risk-averse security-maximizers, going to war only when survival is at stake or when the mix of risks and potential gains outweighs the fear of extinction.[7]

Waltzian neorealism is designed to be a theory capable of describing systemic trends; it is not designed to make point predictions regarding the behavior of individual states (see Waltz, 1979, p. 72). This lack of predictive power is one weakness that has led other researchers to develop theories capable of explaining foreign policy behavior. Since these theories seek to explain why individual decision makers (or groups of decision makers) behave differently (rather than to reveal behavioral regularities), scholars have focused on the extent to which risk propensities vary across units or actors. This second approach to the study of risk behavior can be further broken down into theories operating at the national level that treat state governments as unified rational actors and theories that operate within the "black box" of state decision making by focusing on individual decision makers or groups of decision makers.

Theories that treat state governments as unified rational actors generally develop mathematical models based on the expected-utility tradition (see Alpert, 1976; Bueno de Mesquita, 1981, 1985; Bueno de Mesquita and Lalman, 1992; Morrow, 1987). The expected-utility tradition (see Savage, 1954; von Neumann and Morgenstern, 1947) suggests that actors are risk-acceptant, risk-neutral, or risk-averse. The difficulty for scholars of international relations lies in determining a state government's risk propensity. The main indicator that has been used to infer a state government's risk propensity is its willingness to trade security for autonomy as indicated by its alliance commitments (Morrow, 1987, pp. 435–436).[8] Risk propensity thus modifies the utility curves of state governments (regarding war initiation decisions), introducing concavity or convexity. Unfortunately, this method of inferring a state government's risk propensity suffers from a fundamental flaw: inferring risk propensity at time t from behavior at time $t - 1$ borders on tautology. State governments are assumed to be risk-takers if they behave like risk-takers; there is no attempt to identify the factors contributing to a state government's risk propensity. As Bueno de Mesquita notes, his "indicator of risk taking will therefore be several stages removed from a direct measure and so will be crude and error prone" (1981, p. 123).

Theories that operate within the "black box" of state decision making seek to identify the origins of individual or group risk propensities. Pioneering work in this area was undertaken by Hannes Adomeit (1982), Robert Jervis (1976), Alexander George (1980), and Alan Lamborn (1985). This vein of research has been furthered by recent advances in psychology and economics. Kahneman and Tversky's (1979) *prospect theory* has provided a new and intuitively compelling explanation of how situational factors affect individual risk propensity. The recent introduction of prospect theory to the study of foreign policy decision making has led to a surge in research regarding risk behavior. Numerous empirical studies have offered prospect theory-based explanations for risk-taking and risk-aversion,[9] while other analyses have discussed the implications of prospect theory (and other decision theories that deal with risk) at the theoretical level.[10] Unfortunately, this marked growth in empirical research has proceeded ahead of careful reflection on the theoretical side.

Theories generated in other disciplines (economics and psychology) have been transported across disciplinary boundaries without ample attention to the data requirements of the theories or differences between the foreign policy decision-making milieu and the domains in which the theories were generated. In particular, issues of definition (what is meant by terms such as *risk, uncertainty*, and *risk propensity*?), measurement (can we measure utilities and probabilities and distinguish frames/reference points in "real world" cases?), validity (can we generalize from laboratory studies involving medical or gambling decisions?), and evaluation (what are the various alternative explanations for the choices under examination?) are often discussed, but seldom resolved.

Regardless of the theoretical position adopted by the scholars listed above, each recognizes that the risk propensity of the decision maker plays an important role in almost any foreign policy decision made by an individual or group. Any issue requiring a decision maker to arrive at a conscious choice between policy options will be affected by that decision-maker's risk propensity. Of course, we should not overstate the importance of decision-maker risk propensity. Knowing a policy maker's risk propensity will not tell us what options will be considered, or how estimates of risk and uncertainty are made. Knowing a decision-maker's risk propensity will, however, contribute to our understanding of why a given option will be chosen over another. The study of risk behavior supplements work on the inputs to the decision-making process by focusing on the decisional procedure by which inputs are translated into foreign policy choices.

The study of risk behavior has important implications for the study of war initiation, war termination, deterrence, international military and economic cooperation, bargaining, and military intervention. (This is by no means an exhaustive list, see Jervis, 1992, pp. 192–199; Levy, 1992b; Stein and Pauly, 1993.) The risk propensities of key decision makers will affect decisions to go to war, and their commitment to achieving certain goals (*reference points*) will affect the degree to which they persevere in the face of losses. Deterrence will more often fail against risk-acceptant adversaries or decision makers who are committed to the belief that the status quo is unacceptable. International military and economic cooperation will be more likely, when each side fears the losses (outcomes below the reference points) that will result if agreements are not reached. In bargaining, the advantage will be held by states attempting to reach or remain at certain goal levels. Finally, risk-acceptant decision makers may be more willing to intervene militarily, particularly when they fear the potential losses they might face if they do not decide to intervene. In each of these substantive issue areas, our knowledge about the relevant actors' risk propensities will affect our predictions regarding the outcomes of international interaction.

This book adopts the "inside the black box" perspective on the study of risk behavior. By focusing solely on presidential decisions, it avoids the difficulties experienced when attempting to aggregate individual risk propensities into group orientations toward risk. It builds on previous work in this research tradition, developing a new conceptual framework for the study of risk behavior that includes personality factors (which are often ignored in the international relations literature). It breaks new ground by examining more recent advances in behavioral decision theory and by examining the significant literatures on risk behavior in business, economics, and sociology. Finally, it raises and deals with a number of conceptual and methodological issues that have not been resolved by the extant literature.

III.   Theoretical Foundations

The REF is based on three broad theoretical traditions. From behavioral decision theory it adopts the notion of *reference dependence*, from personality theory it adopts the view that *personal predispositions* affect individual risk propensity, and from the foreign policy decision-making tradition it adopts a concern regarding *uncertainty and information accuracy*.

Reference Dependence

Prospect theory (developed by Daniel Kahneman and Amos Tversky, 1979; see also Tversky and Kahneman, 1992) and SP/A theory (developed by Lola Lopes, 1987, 1990, 1995; see also Lopes and Oden, 1999) are two psychological theories of individual decision making under risk that develop the notion of reference dependence to explain preference reversals exhibited by subjects in laboratory experiments. In these experiments, subjects demonstrated that they were not concerned so much with final asset positions (as would be suggested by expected-utility theory), but rather with departures from an initial position or "reference point." In the language of Kahneman and Tversky, subjects think in terms of "gains" and "losses," and their risk propensities vary from one "frame" to the next. *Thus, individual risk propensity is dependent on the reference point that the subject adopts at the beginning of the choice problem.*[11]

The "reference point" adopted by a decision maker may be conceived of in a number of ways. In the Kahneman and Tversky experiments, the reference point is provided for the subjects by the experimenters. Kahneman and Tversky suggest, however, that in "real world" decision making the reference point adopted may represent the status quo or some "aspiration level" sought by the decision maker (1979, p. 286). Lopes (1987, p. 277) uses the term aspiration level to represent the decision maker's situational judgments regarding what can (or must) be obtained in a particular choice problem. March and Shapira (1992, p. 172) discuss situations in which the aspiration level becomes a "survival level" that identifies the absolute minimum that must be obtained in a choice problem. The usage of these various terms suggests that the notion of a reference point is closely related to the view that decision making is goal-directed behavior (see Anderson, 1984; Heath et al., 1999). A foreign policy decision maker may hope to simply maintain the status quo, may wish to achieve some aspiration level, or may feel compelled to at least reach a survival level. In each of these cases, the decision maker identifies a landmark value that affects perceptions of utility, which in turn may alter that individual's risk propensity. Outcomes above the reference point are perceived as possessing added value, while outcomes below the reference point are viewed more negatively. Generally, it is helpful to think of a reference point as a threshold that affects the interpretation of outcomes.

In the REP, the term "aspiration level" denotes the president's minimum level goal (or goals) during the decision process. The president's aspiration level acts as a situational constraint that precludes the consideration of options that are viewed as incapable of achieving the minimum goals in a particular case. The aspiration level also serves as a yardstick by which the outcomes associated with the remaining options are evaluated. We may conceive of the aspiration level as including the decision maker's immediate goal, constraints on the means available for achieving the immediate goal, and commitment to achieving or surpassing the immediate goal.

The decision maker's immediate goal subsumes the traditional notion of a reference point as a particular point on a utility curve. In cases of foreign policy decision making, the decision maker's immediate goal may be to crush a communist insurgency, alleviate starvation caused by a famine, or prevent a particular country from acquiring nuclear, biological, or chemical weapons. These immediate goals are specific manifestations of broader goals such as contain communism, end hunger, or prevent weapons proliferation. As suggested by Kahneman and Tversky (1979), each alternative discussed by decision makers should be at least partially evaluated on its ability to achieve or surpass the immediate goal.

In generating alternatives capable of achieving or surpassing the immediate goal, foreign policy decision makers must also consider certain constraints on available means. In the laboratory experiments, subjects are presented with two prospects developed by the experimenter; the set of alternatives is limited but available. In the "real world," foreign policy decision makers must creatively generate alternatives, and they are often faced with the realization that certain alternatives may or may not be feasible. The president and his advisers do not consider the immediate goal in isolation, but rather as part of a set (or portfolio) of desired states that may be interdependent. This captures the impact of external actors on foreign policy decisions and also allows for capability calculations.[12] Presidents, operating in a multilateral context, must consider the potential reactions of adversaries at home and abroad. In the laboratory, outcomes are not contingent on the decisions of others. Presidents must also consider whether certain alternatives are "realistic." In the laboratory, subjects seldom wager their own money and so are always capable of paying for "losses."

A final element of the aspiration level is a focus on the decision maker's commitment to achieving or surpassing the immediate goal. This may be the most significant part, since understanding an actor's level of commitment will shed light on the extent to which risks will be taken to achieve the immediate goal. As noted above, March and Shapira (1992, p. 172) discuss situations in which the aspiration level becomes a "survival level" that identifies the absolute minimum that must be achieved (see also Levy, 1994, 1996). As decision makers approach the survival level from above, they may accept certain small losses in order to avoid the risk of falling below the survival level. But once it appears that further certain losses will result in outcomes below the survival level, decision makers might take excessive risks in the hope of returning to a point above the survival level. In foreign policy decision making, certain factors may make the president more or less committed to achieving or surpassing his immediate goal. In many Cold War cases of U.S. military intervention, fears of falling dominoes and perceptions of weakness strengthened U.S. commitments to its smaller allies. Unfortunately, few prospect theory-based studies of foreign policy decisions have explicitly examined the depth of the decision maker's commitment to a reference point (exceptions include Levi and Whyte, 1997; Vertzberger, 1998).

Personal Predispositions

The link between personality traits and risk behavior has been investigated extensively since the 1950s. In attempting to explain risky choice, theorists from this tradition have examined such diverse independent variables as subjects' need for achievement (Atkinson, 1957; Bueno de Mesquita, 1975; McClelland, 1961); self-efficacy, self-worth, perceived parental expectations, and sex (Wyatt, 1989); emotional arousability, conformity, moral reasoning, empathy, psychopathy, and sensation seeking (Levenson, 1990); and neuroticism, extraversion, openness, agreeableness, and conscientiousness (Kowert and Hermann, 1995). Other studies (see Slovic, 1972) have simply attempted (often unsuccessfully) to establish cross-situational consistency in observed risk-taking behavior. Personality theorists directly address the person–situation debate in psychology and political science.[13]

The vast literature that focuses on personal predispositions and risk behavior may be divided into two separate research traditions. The first vein of research focuses on risk as a physical sensation. The term "sensation seeking" is generally used to describe physical risk-taking—skydiving, bungee jumping, cigarette smoking, binge drinking (Bromiley and Curley, 1992, p. 94). A more relevant (for political scientists) segment of research focuses on risk-taking in games of skill/chance, everyday life decisions, and business decisions (see Atkinson, 1957; Kogan and Wallach, 1964; March and Shapira, 1987; and McClelland, 1961). This dichotomy suggests that different personality traits contribute to different types of risk-taking behavior. The personality characteristics that contribute to my presidential risk-predisposition index (discussed below) are carefully selected to measure the latter form of risk behavior.[14]

While a number of researchers have studied the link between personality traits and risk behavior, Lopes (1987, 1990, 1995; Lopes and Oden, 1999) is one of the few who has attempted to describe the process through which personal predispositions are translated into risk-acceptant/avoidant choices (see also Kowert and Hermann, 1995). She suggests that the "security" or "potential-motivation" of a decision maker affects the processing of relevant information. Security-motivated individuals tend to engage in "bottom-up" processing—a focus on worst-case outcomes and maximum losses. Potential-motivated individuals tend to follow the "top-down" method by focusing on best-case outcomes and maximum gains (see Lopes, 1995, p. 202).[15] This marked difference in attentiveness to certain aspects of the decision problem results in different rank-orderings of alternatives and thus differences in risk behavior. A "worst-case" focus *generally* produces risk-aversion while a "best-case" focus tends to produce risk-taking.

The REF attempts to build a bridge between dispositional and situational explanations of risk behavior by proposing testable hypotheses regarding the impact of individual personality on information processing. As noted above, the literature on reference dependence lacks a theory of framing, but clearly acknowledges that subject personality undoubtedly plays a role. Lopes' (1995) best-case/worst-case dichotomy allows us to move beyond the simple argument that consistency in risk behavior equals proof of the impact of personality and develop a more complex understanding of how personality might alter the process of foreign policy decision making. In the REF, security/potential-motivated presidents (operationally defined later) are expected to follow this general worst-case/best-case pattern of information processing in making a foreign policy decision. A special exception to this general rule applies in cases where there is a dearth of options. If there is only one alternative capable of achieving the aspiration level, that alternative may be selected regardless of its level of risk.

Uncertainty and Information Accuracy

The study of "cognitive biases" that influence decision making in the face of uncertainty is well established.[16] George (1980, pp. 35–47) describes the myriad ways in which American presidents deal with perceived information inadequacy or inaccuracy. More recently, Vertzberger has recognized the extent to which issues of uncertainty and information accuracy can influence perceptions of risk. He identifies four ideal typical criteria for information validation: epistemic-based, person-based, belief-based, and situation-based (1995a, pp. 352–353). Vertzberger proposes that increased uncertainty and the perceived lack of valid information causes heightened vigilance regarding feedback after a decision has been made. Conversely, he argues that increased certainty and confidence in the validity of information "reduces alertness to warning cues and may generate premature cognitive closure and conservatism regarding risk estimates" (1995a, p. 354). Similarly, George (1980, p. 37) suggests that presidents faced with high uncertainty, inaccurate information, and time pressure may become "hypervigilant." George also considers other psychological and cognitive aids that a president can use to deal with these problems.

"Bolstering" and "incrementalism" are two types of defensive avoidance strategies that presidents have used to deal with uncertainty, inaccurate information, and time pressure. Bolstering is defined as the "psychological tendency under certain conditions of decisional stress to increase the attractiveness of a preferred (or chosen) option and doing the opposite for options which one is inclined to reject (or has rejected)" (George, 1980, p. 38). Incrementalism is simply the strategy of selecting "policy alternatives that differ only slightly from existing policies and aim at securing marginal rather than dramatic improvements" (George, 1980, p. 40).[17] Incrementalism is viewed as a conservative strategy that allows for risk-avoidance (although over-cautious strategies can involve their own risks). Of course, when presidents do not perceive acute time pressures they may simply delay the decision in order to reduce uncertainty and collect more valid information (see George, 1980, pp. 35–36).

In the REF, I follow George (1980) and propose that presidential perceptions of high uncertainty and the lack of valid information will interact with presidential risk predispositions and affect the output of the decision process. If time pressures are not acute, both security-motivated and potential-motivated presidents are likely to delay the moment of decision in order to reduce uncertainty and collect more valid information. If time pressures are acute, security-motivated presidents are likely to engage in incrementalism, while potential-motivated presidents are likely to engage in bolstering.

IV.   Hypotheses

The three theoretical traditions briefly discussed earlier suggest the following testable hypotheses regarding presidential risk behavior. Hypotheses 1 and 1a are drawn from the literature on reference dependence. Hypotheses 2, 3, 4, 5, and 6 are derived from the "personal predisposition" research tradition. Finally, hypotheses 7, 7a, 7b, and 7c are gleaned from the work of researchers focusing on uncertainty and information accuracy.[18] Together, these hypotheses sketch the outline of my REF.

H1: Presidents tend to evaluate outcomes relative to an aspiration level rather than an overall value level.

> **H1a**: The president's aspiration level (acting as a situational constraint) is likely to preclude the consideration of options that are viewed as incapable of achieving (or surpassing) the aspiration level in a particular case.

H2: Security-motivated presidents tend to engage in "bottom–up" processing—(i.e., focusing on worst-case outcomes and maximum losses).

H3: Potential-motivated presidents tend to engage in "top-down" processing—(i.e., focusing on best-case outcomes and maximum gains).

H4: Security-motivated presidents are likely to behave in a risk-averse manner.

H5: Potential-motivated presidents are likely to behave in a risk-acceptant manner.

H6: If there is only one alternative capable of achieving the aspiration level, that alternative is likely to be selected regardless of its level of risk.

H7: Presidential perceptions of high uncertainty and a lack of valid information will interact with presidential risk predispositions and affect the output of the decision process.

> **H7a**: If time pressures are not acute, both risk-averse and risk-acceptant presidents are likely to delay the moment of decision. (The rationale is that the presidents will use this added time to reduce uncertainty and collect more valid information.)
>
> **H7b**: If time pressures are acute, risk-averse presidents are likely to engage in incrementalism.
>
> **H7c**: If time pressures are acute, risk-acceptant presidents are likely to engage in bolstering.

V.   Methods

This research project employs the structured, focused, comparative case study method (as described by George, 1979, 1982 and Bennett and George, 1997a,b, 2001; also King et al., 1994; and Snyder, 1984/1985, 1988) and data collected by others following the personality assessment-at-a-distance technique (as developed by M. Hermann, 1980a,b). The evaluation of the hypotheses put forth above is facilitated through six case studies from the Truman and Kennedy administrations. The personality data assists in the coding of the dispositional variable capturing security/potential-motivation.

Structured, Focused, Comparative Case Study

The major method employed in this project is the structured, focused, comparative case study method (as described by George, 1979, 1982 and Bennett and George 1997a,b, 2001; also Gerring, 2004; King et al., 1994; and Snyder, 1984/85, 1988). George's formulation of the structured, focused, comparative case study is viewed as one of the most rigorous elaborations of the case study method. He discusses the numerous ways in which case studies may be used to uncover causal relationships. I plan to follow his "process-tracing" procedure of within-case explanation. George suggests that, in many cases, the less demanding congruence procedure (which simply attempts to establish covariation between the independent variables and dependent variable in a theoretically predicted direction) reveals relationships that are spurious in nature. Process-tracing goes beyond the identification of covariation and "attempts to identify the intervening steps or cause-and-effect links between an independent variable and the outcome of the dependent variable" (George, 1982, p. 19; see also Gerring, 2004, p. 348). Despite its extensive use of historical data to reconstruct a particular case, "process-tracing" is not a theory-free method. As George notes, "Historical explanation and process-tracing are not purely descriptive, they make use, often only implicitly, of generalizations of one kind or another to support each step in the causal sequence" (1982, p. 19). The testing of the REF hypotheses involves "process verification" or "testing whether the observed processes among variables in a case match those predicted by previously designated theories" (Bennett and George, 1997a, p. 5). Process-tracing allows us to deal with the problem of equifinality by illuminating the "repertoire of causal paths that lead to a given outcome and the conditions under which they obtain" (Bennett and George, 1997a, p. 6).

In "Case Studies and Theory Development: The Method of Structured, Focused Comparison," George (1979, pp. 54–55; see also Bennett and George, 1997b, 2001) proposes five tasks for designing process-tracing comparative case studies: (1) the specification of the research problem and the research objectives of the study, (2) the specification of the variables that will enter into the controlled comparison, (3) the selection of "appropriate" cases, (4) the consideration of how the variables can best be described to further theory development, and (5) the formulation of the general questions to be asked of each case study. I have briefly touched on several of the tasks in this chapter and will more fully address each task in chapter two.

Personality Assessment-at-a-Distance

Hermann's (1980a,b) personality assessment-at-a-distance technique uses content analysis of spontaneous interviews to assess a leader's beliefs, motives, decision style, and interpersonal style. Through this technique, a researcher may obtain measures of a leader's: nationalism, belief in ability to control events, need for power, need for affiliation, conceptual complexity, distrust of others, self-confidence, and task emphasis. The *New York Times* and the *Public Papers of the Presidents* are basic sources for interview responses. These may be supplemented by transcripts from television interview shows, such as "Meet the Press," "Face the Nation," or "This Week." A minimum number of interview responses is required before an individual can be coded for the various personality traits (Hermann suggests 15 or more, 1980a, p. 15). In the case of U.S. presidents, the amount of material may be excessive and a sampling procedure may be used (Hermann suggests coding every fifth interview response, 1980a, p. 15). The coding of interview responses is facilitated through the use of the Personality Assessment-at-a-Distance Concordance computer program and a high-resolution document scanner.[19]

The contemporary literature on personality and risk behavior usually relies on various personality inventories to measure subjects' personality characteristics. Researchers interested in studying presidential foreign policy decision making can seldom hope to administer such tests to the subjects of their inquiry. I have, therefore, adapted data collected by others following Hermann's personality assessment-at-a-distance technique to the study of risk behavior.

Employing Hermann's personality assessment-at-a-distance technique, M. Hermann and J. T. Preston have developed a data set that includes scores for eight key personality characteristics for a number of U.S. presidents (see Hermann, 1984; Preston, 2001). I have obtained the codings for six presidents: Truman, Eisenhower, Kennedy, Johnson, Bush (41), and Reagan. A number of the personality characteristics identifiable through this technique may be associated with security/potential motivation, particularly: belief in ability to control events, need for power, need for affiliation, task emphasis, and conceptual complexity. Plax and Rosenfeld suggest that the "personality pattern of the high risk-taker characterizes a dynamic task oriented leader: aggressive and manipulative, independent and radical—an individual who moves others about as if they were objects placed before him to satisfy his own personal needs" (1976, p. 417). This description suggests an individual with a strong belief in ability to control events, need for power, and task emphasis; and a low need for affiliation. I further assume that conceptually complex individuals are less ideological and more sensitive to environmental cues. Individuals low in conceptual complexity are more likely to exhibit cross-situational consistency in risk behavior.[20] A president is coded as *potential-motivated* if he scores high on an index of belief in ability to control events, need for power, and task emphasis, and low on an index of need for affiliation and conceptual complexity. *Security-motivation* is associated with the opposite pattern. Of course, high and low are relative terms—the overall index score for a president is compared to the index scores of the other five. Kennedy and Bush lie on the security-motivated end of the index, while Truman lies at the potential-motivated end.[21] The Kennedy administration was selected over the Bush administration due to the similarity between their index scores and concerns regarding document availability.

VI. Case Selection

The potential pool of cases for this study was limited to considerations of military intervention by U.S. presidents. I only considered cases where the president contemplated (but did not necessarily approve) one or more proposals to deploy/employ U.S. military forces to deal with the situation at hand. The demanding nature of the process-tracing case study limits my ability to extend this study to a large number of cases. Limiting the scope of the study to cases of potential military intervention clearly limits the generalizability of its results, but it also enhances the plausibility of the results for this specific type of decision problem. Further, the study of presidential considerations of military intervention, from Johnson's Vietnam decisions to Reagan's Lebanon policies, is an established research focus of scholars

Table 1.1   Potential cases by case selection criteria

	Level of presidential involvement	Adversary perceived to be controlled by Soviet Union and/or China	Multiple options considered by president	Stakes for United States as perceived by president	Level of prior U.S. commitment
Iran	High	Yes	Yes	Moderate	Moderate
Greece	High	Yes	Yes	Moderate	Moderate
China	High	Adversary was Chinese communists	Yes	High	High
Berlin 1948	High	Adversary was Soviet Union	Yes	High	Moderate
Korea	High	Yes	Yes	Moderate	Moderate
Bay of Pigs	High	Yes	Yes	Moderate	High
Laos	High	Yes	Yes	Moderate	Moderate
Berlin 1961	High	Adversary was Soviet Union	Yes	High	High
Vietnam 1961	High	Yes	Yes	Moderate	Moderate
Congo	High	Yes	Yes	Moderate	Moderate

Note: The judgments presented above are based on a brief survey of the secondary literature on each case. Since an analysis of the primary sources for every case was not conducted, these judgments should be viewed with caution. I feel confident in using them for case selection, but willingly admit that they are rough estimates.

interested in theories of foreign policy decision making. Finally, the significant stakes and risks involved in this type of decision make this an almost ideal issue context in which to study presidential risk behavior.[22] I chose to study U.S. presidents because they act as the final authority in determining U.S. foreign policy and their decisions are often of high substantive importance. As the sign on Harry Truman's desk read: "The Buck stops here."

I initially considered a pool of ten cases[23] for this study.[24] The final six cases, across two presidential administrations, were selected through five basic criteria (see table 1.1): the high level of presidential involvement in decisions, the fact that the adversary was perceived to be controlled by the Soviet Union and China, multiple options were considered by the president, the perceived stakes for the United States were moderate, and the level of prior U.S. commitment was moderate.

The criterion regarding the role of the Soviet Union and China is used to enhance the comparability of the cases selected. The criteria regarding level of presidential involvement, the number of options considered by the president, the perceived stakes for the United States, and the level of prior U.S. commitment not only contribute to the comparability of the cases, but they were also selected because of theoretical concerns. A high level of presidential involvement is required in each case in order to justify the application of an individual-level theory of risk behavior. Presidential consideration of multiple options is required so that hypotheses 1–5 can be tested. Finally, the perception of moderate stakes for the United States and moderate prior commitment are required because it has been suggested that extreme stakes or commitment may affect the applicability of the theories from which hypotheses 1 and 1a are drawn (see Levy, 1992a,b). A consequence of this selection process was the selection of cases that fit within an even more restrictive issue area: potential Cold War regional military interventions in opposition to revolutionary Communist movements. While this happily increases the comparability of the cases, it should not necessarily limit the applicability of the results of this study to potential military interventions of this type alone. These further restrictions are not expected to bias the results of this study in any way.

In selecting the Truman and Kennedy administrations, I have attempted to vary presidential risk predisposition in a manageable fashion—through the use of the personality assessment-at-a-distance technique and my presidential risk-predisposition index. For the Truman period, I examine the decision to back the Iranian Post-War regime in 1946, the decisions resulting in the Truman Doctrine regarding Greece in 1947–1948, and the decision to intervene in Korea in June of 1950. For the Kennedy administration, I examine the decision making regarding the Laos Crisis in the spring of 1961, the decisions regarding Vietnam in response to the Taylor mission report in November of 1961, and the decisions regarding the Congo in 1962.

VII.   The Plan of the Book

Chapter one has provided a brief introduction and theoretical and methodological overview of the book. Chapter two includes a much more in-depth discussion of various concepts, such as risk and uncertainty, and presents and defends the definitions that I will follow throughout this study. It also contains an extensive review of the various literatures on risk behavior in political science, psychology, economics, business, and sociology; as well as a critique of these literatures organized around issues of measurement, validity, and evaluation. Finally, it provides a more complete (and critical) discussion of the REF and the methods employed in this book. Chapter three reports the results for the three Truman case studies, while chapter four reports the results for the three Kennedy case studies. Finally, chapter five discusses the theoretical implications of the case studies, suggests potential revisions of the REF, and proposes a research agenda for the future study of presidential risk behavior.

CHAPTER TWO

Clarification, Critique, Framework Construction, and Research Concerns

I. Introduction and Overview

The study of how human beings make decisions has evolved in the last century, as the classical expected-utility (EU) model (developed by D. Bernoulli, 1967 [1738]) was refined by von Neumann and Morgenstern (1947) and then modified by Savage (1954). Savage's model of subjective expected-utility (SEU) has since served as the primary theory guiding research on decision making in the social sciences. While the normative strength of EU and SEU is often accepted, the descriptive accuracy of the Bernoullian family of theories has been seriously questioned. The failure of SEU to explain the behavior of significant numbers of experimental subjects and real world decision makers has led to further revisions and the development of generalized EU theories that have the ability to explain some (if not all) of these anomalies. All of these theories attempt to explain, at least in part, decisions under risk—where outcomes are not certain, but the chances of the outcomes occurring follow a known probability distribution. Recently, skepticism regarding the descriptive accuracy of EU and SEU has crossed disciplinary boundaries from psychology and economics to political science, sociology, and business. In particular, researchers in political science studying foreign policy decision making have begun to examine alternatives to the Bernoullian models.

In this chapter, I first consider the myriad ways in which the concepts of *risk, uncertainty*, and *risk propensity* have been interpreted by social scientists, and the implications of adopting one set of definitions rather than another. In section II, I put forth and defend the definitions that I will follow throughout this study. Section III focuses on the various literatures from political science, psychology, economics, business, and sociology that inform this study. Section IV raises issues of measurement, validity, and evaluation, constructing a critique that provides the foundation for the theory and research design explicated in sections V and VI. In section V, I propose a "Risk Explanation Framework" (REF), discussing the theoretical and empirical roots of each hypothesis. Finally, section VI focuses on the research methods used in this study, providing a more complete and critical examination of the methods introduced in chapter one (sections V and VI).

II.   Conceptual Clarification

The concept of *risk* is commonly used in discussions of private and public decisions. Individuals may decline to engage in a particular activity (e.g., skydiving) because they are unwilling to "take the risk." The president may describe a particular policy as entailing "risks that we are willing to bear." The commonality of the notion of *risk* is exemplified by the diversity of fields in which literatures on risk and risk-taking have proliferated: political science, psychology, economics, sociology, business, health sciences, systems engineering (and others). Unfortunately, the extensive study of risk across numerous disciplines has also resulted in a proliferation of perspectives regarding the concepts under study. Aside from cross-disciplinary confusion, a further problem emerges when research based on one set of perspectives (and resultant definitions) is used to support elements of research based on other perspectives (and definitions).

The classical definition of risk emerges from decision research in psychology and economics. In this tradition, *risk* describes choice problems where the various outcomes associated with potential actions are probabilistic, and the probabilities and utilities associated with the outcomes are known by the decision maker. Risk is thus differentiated from *uncertainty*, which is used to describe similar choice problems where the probabilities and/or utilities associated with outcomes are not known by the decision maker (and the potential set of outcomes may be unknown as well). Betting on whether a fair coin will land on its "head" or "tail" involves risk (the probability of each outcome is known to be .50). Betting in April that the Boston Red Sox will win the World Series in October involves uncertainty (the probability of this outcome is not known—it may be .8, .5, or more likely 0). "Uncertainty" suggests a broad range of probabilities that may be associated with any outcome, although the range may be limited through the acquisition of knowledge, it can seldom be reduced to a single numerical probability. Much of behavioral decision theory rests on experimental results produced through confronting subjects with decisions that involve risk (see Kahneman and Tversky, 1979; and Lopes, 1987, 1990), while some recent advances have incorporated uncertainty into the standard research design (see particularly Lopes and Oden, 1999; Tversky and Kahneman, 1992).[1]

While the classical definition was developed in the clarity of the experimental laboratory, the use of *risk* in business, sociology, and political science is more empirically oriented. In these disciplines, definitions of risk are often adapted to reflect the reality of the domain under study. Thus, in business, risk has been associated with "exposure to a chance of loss" (MacCrimmon and Wehrung, 1986, p. 9). Losses may either be defined as movement from a preexisting asset level (i.e., the status quo) or as "opportunity losses," which are obtained through the selection of sub-optimal decisions. In sociology, risk often "denotes the possibility that an undesirable state of reality (adverse effects) may occur as a result of natural events or human activities" (Renn, 1992, p. 56). A burgeoning literature, therefore, focuses on environmental and technical risks for society and how risks should be distributed across different groups/regions (see Renn, 1992; Sjöberg, 1980; Teuber, 1990; and Vlek and Stallen, 1980). In political science, risk has been described as "the likelihood of the materialization of validly predictable direct and indirect consequences with potentially adverse values, arising from events, self-behavior, environmental constraints, or the reaction of an opponent or third party" (Vertzberger, 1995a). As Adomeit notes in his discussion of the study of risk in international relations: "Risks, in the mind of the political scientist, refer to conditions which are more or less likely to result in war" (1982, p. 17). The common thread that runs through each of these definitions is a focus on adversity or loss (i.e., negative outcomes) and uncertainty.

The study of risk (at least in business, sociology, and political science) is evolving away from the traditional focus on probability and utility, and moving toward a focus on loss and uncertainty (see Yates and Stone, 1992). Risk "has entered politics and in doing so has weakened its old connection with technical calculations of probability . . . The idea of risk in itself was neutral; it took account of the probability of losses and gains . . . now *risk* refers only to negative outcomes . . . The language of risk is reserved as a specialized lexical register for political talk about the undesirable outcomes" (Douglas, 1990, p. 3, italics in original). Uncertainty is included as an "integral element" of risk in order to account "for the predecisional state of knowledge and its impact on the incentive to take or avoid risk" (Vertzberger, 1995a, p. 350). This redefinition of risk results from a frustration with the traditional use of the term and its inability to reflect the reality of the domain under examination. "Risk must be approached in a nontechnical manner, and hence the common distinction between risk and uncertainty is neither realistic nor practical when applied to the analysis of nonquantifiable and ill-defined problems, such as those posed by important politico-military issues" (Vertzberger, 1995a, p. 349).

A key concern at this stage in the study of risk and decision making has to be the implications of this redefinition of the concept under examination. It is important to note that, while Vertzberger advocates a new approach (sociocognitive) to the study of risk that is based on his rethinking and reconceptualization of the concept, his discussion of problem-framing and risk estimation relies on a number of psychological studies that subscribe to the traditional definition of risk (1995a, pp. 361–369). Simply put, the results obtained by these researchers may not apply to decisions under risk as defined by Vertzberger. In fact, the terms risk-seeking and risk-aversion have vastly different meanings depending on your definition of risk. In terms of Vertzberger's definition, risk-seeking and risk-aversion are functions of the relationship between "real risk," "perceived risk," and "acceptable risk" (1995a, p. 357). This view of risk propensity is quite different from the traditional view that risk propensity is related to the EU of the outcomes under examination.[2] Obviously, empirical studies based on the traditional view of risk and risk propensity uncover behavioral regularities that may not occur in situations fitting the new definitions. The fundamental logical assumptions underlying the classical and adaptive definitions are so different that it is questionable whether the same phenomenon is being examined.

A further implication of the redefinition of risk is a focus on threats to the neglect of opportunity. The focus on "adverse values" and "negative consequences" in political science has resulted in a number of studies of decision making in the domain of losses (see Elms, 2004; Fanis, 2004; Farnham, 1992; Jervis, 1988; Levy, 1987; McDermott, 1992; McInerney, 1992; and Stein and Pauly, 1992), but few in the domain of gains (to follow the language of Kahneman and Tversky, 1979).[3] Foreign policy decisions that involve risks of the type that may result in "opportunity loss" (MacCrimmon and Wehrung, 1986, p. 10) are seldom examined. This redefinition of risk reduces the scope of the study of risk in foreign policy decision making and may contribute to the status quo bias found in so much of the current international relations literature.[4]

For the purposes of this project I shall speak of the domain of foreign policy decision making as being characterized by *subjective risk under uncertainty*. It is important to recognize the differences between the foreign policy and gambling domains, but we should not attempt to reconcile these differences by simply redefining our concepts. Viewing foreign policy decision making as *subjective risk under uncertainty* allows us to retain the content of the classical concepts while adapting them for use in the foreign policy domain. Subjective risk under uncertainty describes occasions for decision where the complete set of potential outcomes (gains and/or losses) and outcome probabilities are not fully known, forcing decision makers to develop subjective estimates of potential outcomes, the values of those outcomes, and the probabilities associated with the occurrence of those outcomes. By adopting this viewpoint, we may continue to speak of *risk* in a consistent and meaningful manner, and we may also consider how subjective estimates of the elements of risk are formed, as well as how uncertainty regarding these estimates affects the decision process. In effect, we can recognize the special character of the foreign policy decision-making domain without rejecting the concepts developed to explain decisions under risk elsewhere. By maintaining a connection with the classical definition of risk, we may avoid the equation of risk with solely negative outcomes. By characterizing the foreign policy decision-making domain as *subjective risk under uncertainty*, we may define a new area of study for which the classical literature on risk is not well-suited.

This project chooses to reject the definitions of risk-aversion and risk-seeking developed in Vertzberger (1995a, pp. 355–357). The notion of *acceptable risk* is certainly plausible, but the distinction between *real risk* and *perceived risk* is difficult to discern outside of the laboratory setting. Vertzberger's

(1995a, p. 356) notion of *real risk* runs counter to his depiction of the foreign policy decision-making domain under conditions of uncertainty. If the dominating characteristic of the domain under study is uncertainty, how can the researcher expect to identify *real risk* any better than the subjects under study? This is not so much a phenomenological as a practical view.[5] Recall that, in the EU tradition, risk-seeking occurs when an option is chosen with (a) a higher probability of a negative outcome, and (b) equal or lower EU; while risk-aversion occurs when an option is chosen with (a) a lower probability of a negative outcome, and (b) equal or lower EU. An alternative formulation focuses on variation in the potential range of outcomes, probabilities associated with negative outcomes, and the validity of subjective estimates (see March and Shapira, 1987). For the purposes of this project, comparatively riskier options are characterized by: (a) more numerous and extremely divergent outcomes, (b) the perception that extreme negative outcomes are at least possible,[6] and (c) recognition that estimates of potential outcomes and the probabilities associated with the occurrence of those outcomes are potentially flawed and may, in fact, be totally incorrect. This formulation of riskiness retains the comparative nature of the classical view, and yet also reflects the difficulties in measuring utilities and probabilities discussed below. It not only reflects the character of the domain as discussed by Vertzberger (1995a), but also indicates a descriptive rather than normative perspective.[7]

III.   Extant Theory and Empirical Research

As mentioned at the outset of this chapter, the classical study of risk behavior is usually traced to Daniel Bernoulli's introduction of EU theory in 1738. Scholars of this era had been wrestling with Nicholas Bernoulli's "St. Petersburg Paradox" since 1713. The "paradox" challenged the intuitive plausibility of the then–dominant expected-value (EV) theory. N. Bernoulli posed a simple question: "Suppose that a fair coin is tossed until tails first appears, at which point the player is paid a sum equal to $\$2^n$, where n is the number of the toss on which tails appears. How much should a person be willing to pay for a single play of the game?" (quoted in Lopes, 1995, p. 179). According to EV theory,

$$EV = \sum_{i=1}^{n} p_i(v_i)$$
$$EV = \frac{1}{2}(\$2) + \frac{1}{4}(\$4) + \frac{1}{8}(\$8) + \cdots + \frac{1}{n}(\$2^n)\ldots$$
$$EV = 1 + 1 + 1 + \cdots + 1\ldots$$
$$EV = \infty$$

where p_i is the probability of tails appearing on the *i*th toss, and v_i is the value of tails appearing on the *i*th toss, so the value of the game is infinite. As Lopes notes: "Though intuition whispers that the game is worth no more than a few dollars, expected value demands that one give all one has or hopes to have in exchange for a single play" (1995, p. 179). D. Bernoulli solved the problem by developing the notion of "moral value" (utility) (1967 [1738]).

The Bernoullian Tradition

D. Bernoulli's EU theory is based on the notion that "rich men value given increments of wealth less than poor men" (Lopes, 1995, p. 180). Rather than view increases in wealth as a monotonic function, Bernoulli posited that individual perceptions of utility might be represented by negatively accelerated utility curves. Lopes solves the St. Petersburg paradox by positing a utility curve that decreases logarithmically and finds that the game is worth approximately $4 (1995, p. 180). Bernoulli's negatively accelerated utility function introduced the concept of risk-aversion: ceteris paribus, most individuals prefer certain outcomes to gambles. This simple theoretical advance provided the foundation for the next two centuries of research on human risk behavior.

EU theory was modernized in the 1940s and 1950s. Von Neumann and Morgenstern (1947) provided an axiomatic procedure for measuring *cardinal utility* (similar to Bernoulli's *subjective value*), altered the interpretation of the utility function so that it summarized rather than caused preferences, and suggested that utility maximization applied to single choices as well as to iterated decisions (see Lopes, 1995, p. 181). In 1948, Friedman and Savage suggested that: if utility functions summarize preferences, it is possible that they may have both concave and convex regions (allowing for risk-aversion and risk-seeking). Finally, Savage (1954) introduced SEU theory. SEU "challenged the idea of probability objectivity by replacing measured or stated probabilities by their subjective counterparts" (Lopes, 1995, p. 181). In SEU, the perceptions of the individual decision maker were finally taken into account, but the challenge of estimating subjective probability opened a "Pandora's box."

Much of the work on risk behavior in political science is based on the Bernoullian tradition. The revised specification of EU theory proposed by von Neumann and Morgenstern (1947) provides the foundation for researchers who use game theory to explore strategic decision making.[8] Morrow (1994, pp. 16–50) details the manner in which EU theory has been (and can be) applied to political decision making. Bueno de Mesquita has based an entire research program on EU theory (see 1975, 1981, 1985; Bueno de Mesquita and Lalman, 1992; Bueno de Mesquita et al., 2001). These authors have proposed alternative measures of national risk attitudes that can be entered into the EU calculus (Bueno de Mesquita, 1985; Morrow, 1987). They clearly recognize the challenges to EU theory discussed below, but they argue that "their proponents have not yet demonstrated their general importance to the construction of social theory based on individual choice" (Morrow, 1997, p. 49).

Preference Reversals

The axiomatic specificity of the newly modified EU theory had the unintended consequence of highlighting its weaknesses. In the late 1950s and 1960s, scholars (in such fields as experimental psychology and economics) began to conduct strict empirical tests of these axiomatic relations. One vein of research introduced the notion of *preference reversals* (for a review of this research see Slovic and Lichtenstein, 1983; Tversky et al., 1990). These studies focused on the fact that "models of rational choice assume a principle of procedure invariance, which requires strategically equivalent methods of elicitation to yield the same preference order" (Tversky et al., 1990, p. 204). Thus, asking for a preference between gambles while also asking for a buying or selling price for the gambles should yield similar preference relations. If one prefers bet A to bet B they should also value bet A more than bet B. These studies found just the opposite, hence the term *preference reversal*. In one of the pathbreaking studies, Slovic and Lichtenstein (1968) found that "both buying and selling prices of gambles were primarily determined by the payoffs, whereas choices between gambles (and ratings of their attractiveness) were primarily influenced by the probability of winning and losing" (Tversky et al., 1990, p. 204). The empirical results of the early studies were supported by a rigorous (and skeptical) series of replications reported in Grether and Plott (1979). These economists proposed no less than 12 alternative explanations for the preference reversal phenomenon (including "experimenters were psychologists") and yet found that "the preference reversal phenomenon which is inconsistent with the traditional statement of preference theory remains" (1979, p. 634). Buoyed by this persuasive evidence of the empirical weakness of EU theory (and combined with the paradoxes discovered by Allais (1979 [1952]) and Ellsberg (1961)), many psychologists and economists began to develop new theories of choice that sacrificed theoretical simplicity in exchange for descriptive accuracy (see Kahneman, 2000, p. ix).

A number of significant modifications of the basic EU model have been proposed in the last 25 years. Kahneman and Tversky's prospect theory (1979; Tversky and Kahneman, 1992) has received the most attention from political scientists and will be the focus of our concern, but others have also had some influence. Machina's (1987) "fanning out" hypothesis, Neilson's (1992) "mixed fanning" hypothesis, Yaari's (1987) "dual theory" of choice, and Loomes and Sugden's (1982) "regret theory"[9] are all promising revisions that have been empirically tested against EU theory (see Harless and Camerer, 1994). Despite the modest success of several of these theories, they are seldom employed by political scientists because their mathematical innovations are difficult to translate into "real world" behavioral observations. I feel that the interest of political scientists in prospect theory is the result of its intuitively plausible hypotheses, supportive experimental results, and apparent simplicity and relevance. In particular, I feel that International Relations theorists are also attracted by its focus on risk-taking in the face of "losses" or threats.

Prospect Theory

Prospect theory, as developed by the aforementioned Kahneman and Tversky, was formally introduced in a 1979 *Econometrica* article and popularized through a number of more descriptive pieces in other publications (see Kahneman and Tversky, 1982, 1984; Tversky and Kahneman, 1981). Prospect theory is viewed by many as the dominant *weighted-utility* theory in psychology and economics.[10] Kahneman and Tversky hoped to modify the standard SEU model in order to account for the preference reversal phenomenon as well as the Ellsberg paradox (which introduced the notion of nonlinear subjective probability).[11] While SEU has been described as a normative theory of choice, prospect theory is a descriptive theory based on extensive laboratory testing (Quattrone and Tversky, 1988, p. 720). The most compelling (and oft cited) finding of Kahneman and Tversky's experiments is their explanation for the preference reversal phenomenon. Kahneman and Tversky's subjects were not concerned so much with final asset positions (as would be suggested by EU theory), but rather with departures from an initial position or "reference point." Thus, subjects think in terms of "gains" and "losses" (decision frames) and their preferences are actually variable (as opposed to the invariance predicted by standard SEU models; see Quattrone and Tversky, 1988, p. 727) as they shift from one frame to the other. This observed shift in preferences also involves a shift in risk propensity.

Tversky and Kahneman "use the term 'decision frame' to refer to the decision-maker's conception of the acts, outcomes, and contingencies associated with a particular choice" (1981, p. 453). The framing of any decision is not simply the result of "objective" elements of the problem, it is also shaped by the "norms, habits, and personal characteristics of the decision-maker" (1981, p. 453). This goes beyond the simple notion of subjectively defined probabilities and utilities and suggests that people experience similar combinations of probability and utility in markedly different ways. Tversky and Kahneman posit that due to "imperfections of human perception and decision . . . changes of perspective often reverse the relative size of objects and the relative desirability of options" (1981, p. 453). Thus, *weighted-utility* theories (like prospect theory) must be developed to account for these perceptual distortions.

Despite the wide scope of Tversky and Kahneman's definition of framing, its application has been more narrowly focused. Indeed, in the experimental work that provides the foundation for prospect theory, only the outcomes associated with alternatives are directly framed. People "die" or are "saved," money is "won" or "lost," but no verbal modifier attempts to frame contingencies (probabilities) or acts (alternatives). It is unclear how contingencies and acts would be framed (possibly "lousy chance of 35%," or "advisers' most preferred option—B") and whether this type of framing would yield similar preference reversals. It is also unclear that subjects would similarly frame ambiguous decision problems without the explicit guidance of the experimenter. Kahneman and Tversky (1979) openly admit that they lack an adequate theory of framing and attempts to develop such a theory have met with little success (see McDermott, 2004a,b on the need for a theory of framing and Bueno de Mesquita and McDermott, 2004 on the need for a theory of the origin of preferences). Fischhoff offered three alternative framings of a civil defense problem and asked subjects to rate their "naturalness"—they were judged "equally attractive" (1983, p. 107).

The above observations led to the following hypothesis regarding human decision-making behavior: "risk aversion in the positive domain is accompanied by risk seeking in the negative domain" (Kahneman and Tversky, 1979, p. 268). Subjects tended to prefer the *less* risky option when the problem was framed as a gain, and the *more* risky option when the problem was framed as a loss.[12] This "reflection effect" and the correspondent sensitivity to the way a problem is framed, are the main findings that have been utilized by political scientists.

Prospect theory "distinguishes two phases in the choice process: an early phase of editing and a subsequent phase of evaluation" (Kahneman and Tversky, 1979, p. 274). The editing phase is discussed, but not formally modeled.[13] The most significant element of the editing phase is "coding"— subjects "perceive outcomes as gains and losses . . . Gains and losses, of course, are defined relative to some neutral reference point" (1979, p. 274). The subject's current reference point is usually assumed to be the status quo, although it may also be associated with some previous or anticipated reference point. The evaluation phase is explicitly modeled. Kahneman and Tversky note, "Following the editing phase, the decision maker is assumed to evaluate each of the edited prospects, and to choose the prospect of highest value" (1979, p. 275). The value of the prospects, V, is expressed through a modified EU equation. This modified utility equation includes a decision weight, π, and a value function, v. The decision weight measures "the impact of events on the desirability of prospects" (1979, p. 280); it essentially introduces a measure of the subjectivity involved in interpreting probabilistic information. The value function introduces a measure of the subjectivity involved in interpreting values as deviations from the reference point. It captures loss aversion as well as the diminishing marginal utility of gains.

The general design of the Kahneman and Tversky (1979) experiments involved presenting subjects with gambling prospects. Subjects were presented with two prospects, framed as either gains or losses. The prospects include an outcome (a monetary gain or loss) and an associated numerical probability. The values of outcomes and the probabilities associated with the occurrence of outcomes are varied so that one prospect can be viewed as more "risky" than the other while the EU of each prospect is roughly equivalent (allowing the elimination of SEU as an alternative explanation for subject choice).[14]

International relations theorists have interpreted the Kahneman and Tversky findings in such a way as to increase the applicability of prospect theory to the study of foreign policy decision making. In the original experiments (1979), framing was more a characteristic of the prospects rather than the situations. In the more recent international relations applications, the decision maker is viewed as being in a certain domain (gains or losses) and the focus is often on the decision maker's frame of the situation rather than the manner in which options are framed (see Farnham, 1992; Huth et al., 1992; McDermott, 1992). This is an important difference, and yet this new interpretation has not been subject to extensive empirical testing (see Boettcher, 2004a).

Process Models

A promising alternative to the Bernoullian family of decision-making theories is the *process* approach described by Lopes (1995). This research tradition has rejected the normative character of EU theory, instead focusing on "the question which logically ought to come first—how do people actually go about making decisions in gambling situations?" (Edwards, 1953, p. 351). These studies have examined risk dimensions and duplex bets (Slovic and Lichtenstein, 1968), intransitivity and lexicographic semiorders (Tversky, 1969), responses to histograms and multioutcome distributions (Coombs, 1975; Lopes, 1987), choice boards and eye movement (Payne et al., 1990; Rosen and Rosenkoetter, 1976), and verbal protocols (Payne et al., 1980). The process approach hopes to achieve descriptive accuracy and appears to be more easily adaptable for use in the study of presidential foreign policy decision making.

Despite the sharp conceptual contrasts between the Bernoullian, and process traditions, the fundamental intuitions that underlie the models are often similar. As Lopes notes, the Bernoullian (algebraic) and process models "can be easily reconciled by recognizing that algebraic models describe patterns of preferences across option sets, whereas process models describe the sequence and content of comparison processes that underlie individual acts of choosing" (1995, p. 213). Lopes (1987, 1990, 1995) has attempted to develop a model of risky choice that builds on both traditions.

SP/A Theory

Numerous decision theorists have attempted to explain the observed behavioral departures from SEU theory. One such research tradition is known as "rank dependent value modeling." These theorists hypothesize that "decumulative probability values are shrunk systematically as a function of the rank position of the outcome value . . . Decumulative probabilities attached to the worst outcomes in the distribution are shrunk proportionally little or not at all while probabilities attached to the best outcomes are shrunk proportionally much more" (Lopes, 1990, p. 276). The manner in which decumulative probabilities are transformed yields functions whose shapes depict risk-avoidance and risk-seeking (or a combination of each, see Lopes, 1990, p. 278). This notion of transforming decumulative probabilities is the rank dependent value modeling parallel to prospect theory's weighting function.

A promising variation on the rank dependent value modeling tradition is SP/A theory as developed by Lola Lopes (1981, 1987, 1990). Lopes (1987) attempts to construct a theory of risk behavior that captures individual dispositions toward risk, in accord with the motivational literature on risk behavior (see Atkinson, 1957; McClelland, 1961), and the impact of situational factors on risk-taking/risk-aversion. The dispositional factors are described as "security motivation" and "potential motivation," while the situational factor is termed "aspiration level" (Lopes, 1987, pp. 276–277). Simply put, "security motivation corresponds to weighting the worst outcomes in a lottery more heavily than the best outcomes, and potential motivation corresponds to the opposite"(Lopes, 1987, p. 276).[15] "Aspiration level" is intended to capture the opportunities and constraints facing the decision-maker.[16] The crucial differences between the weighting functions of SP/A theory and prospect theory are (1) factors posited to affect the weighting functions: security/potential motivation and aspiration level in SP/A theory, coding in terms of gains and losses in prospect theory; (2) in SP/A theory the weights are joint functions of the magnitudes of probabilities and the magnitudes of outcomes, in prospect theory the weighting of probability and value is independent; and (3) in SP/A theory, weights do not reflect perceptions of probabilities or values—"the fact that a person chooses . . . to minimize the likelihood of a bad outcome does not imply either that (subjectively) he underestimates the value of good outcomes or that he overestimates the probability of bad outcomes" (Lopes, 1987, p. 276).[17]

Like prospect theory, SP/A theory is a descriptive theory of choice based on experimental observations. Lopes' (1987) method is slightly different than Kahneman and Tversky's (1979) however, as she presents subjects with choices between lotteries with similar expected utilities but differing levels of risk. While the domain of choice continues to be gambling problems, presenting subjects with multi-outcome prospects is viewed as a closer approximation of "real world" decisions (Lopes, 1987, pp. 264–265). Lopes' results are particularly interesting because of her use of protocol analysis. This method allows subjects to directly report their rationales for choosing one lottery over another. The researcher is provided with direct insight as to which aspects of the decision problem receive the most weight.[18]

While Lopes (1987, 1990, 1995) describes the process through which personal predispositions are translated into risk-acceptant/avoidant choices, she provides little guidance regarding the personal characteristics that contribute to security/potential-motivation. Lopes' experimental method allows her to observe behavioral evidence of security/potential-motivation, but she does not correlate this evidence with the personality traits of her subjects. Her reluctance to proceed to this obvious next step may stem from her recognition of the complex and indeterminate results obtained by researchers attempting to associate personality characteristics with risk-taking propensity.

Personality Theory

The term "personality theory" is used here to describe the conglomeration of theories that focus on the personality traits of individual decision makers. Research in this tradition has focused on the intuitively attractive (but seldom supported) assumption that some people are risk-takers while others are not. For years, other theorists have questioned the relevance of the personality traits of the decision maker. In decision theory (especially in economics), individual differences have often been ignored. Kowert and Hermann (1995, pp. 3–4) note: "That these subjects have been ignored is unproblematic in a field such as economics which ordinarily concerns itself with the modal behavior of utility maximizers in markets. But for students of international politics, no such oversight is permissible when the behavior of a single leader, shaping military or economic policy, often has dramatic consequences."[19] Personality theorists have begun to concentrate on developing a critique of prospect theory, which focuses on the exigencies of the situation or makes generalizations about decision-maker risk propensity without addressing the personality characteristics of the decision maker.[20]

A significant portion of this research focused on the question of whether a general trait of risk-taking propensity exists. The negative results obtained by Slovic (1964, 1972) provided empirical support for a more situational perspective, but a broader study by Kogan and Wallach (1964) produced somewhat more optimistic results. Kogan and Wallach included two moderator variables—defensiveness and test anxiety, and found that subjects high on both of these variables "tended to show greater regularity of risk taking across situations" (Bromiley and Curley, 1992, pp. 118–119). Despite this weak support for an overall trait relating to risk propensity, more recent studies have supported a more individual-by-situation perspective (see Keyes, 1985; MacCrimmon and Wehrung, 1986). These studies suggest that individuals are at times consistent in their risk propensities, but usually only within a limited range of situations. By employing Lopes' (1987, 1990, 1995) SP/A theory, the REF explicitly adopts this individual-by-situation perspective.

Despite the often confusing and contradictory results produced by the experiments discussed above, researchers have begun to trace the outline of the personality traits that may contribute to security/potential-motivation. A number of scholars have focused on "belief in ability to control events" as a significant personality trait associated with risk propensity (March and Shapira, 1987; Plax and Rosenfeld, 1976; Slovic, 1964; Vertzberger, 1995b, pp. 4–5). Individuals with an internal locus of control belief tend to view situations involving risk and uncertainty as games of skill, while subjects with an external locus of control belief tend to view the same situations as games of chance. March and Shapira (1987, p. 1413) note that business managers distinguish between taking risks and "gambling," at least in part "because their experience teaches them that they can control fate." Plax and Rosenfeld (1976, pp. 416–417) describe the attributes that their experiments led them to associate with a "dynamic task oriented leader" (potential-motivated): "aggressive and manipulative, independent and radical—an individual who moves others about as if they were objects placed before him to satisfy his own personal needs." We may consider how these findings may be adapted to describe the prototypical potential-motivated president (see section VI later).

Uncertainty and Information Accuracy

The study of decision-maker responses to the stress inherent in making important decisions is grounded in the seminal work of Irving Janis and Leon Mann (see Janis and Mann, 1977; Mann, 1992; and for a review of their pathbreaking book, Kinder and Weiss, 1978). Their "conflict model" of decision making served as the foundation for later studies of foreign policy decision-maker behavior in the face of uncertainty, time pressure, and information of questionable accuracy (see George, 1980; Vertzberger, 1995a). The coping patterns and mechanisms for dealing with conflict that they identify in their research suggest that we may expect to observe marked deviations in the foreign policy decision-making process of presidents dealing with uncertainty and decisional stress.

Janis and Mann (1977) identify five main coping patterns that decision makers use to deal with difficult choices. The first two, *unconflicted inertia* and *unconflicted change*, involve little conflict and stress. The former involving the belief that risks from "staying the course" are slight, the latter involving the belief that a new policy entails little risk. *Defensive avoidance, hypervigilance*, and *vigilance*, are associated with situations where the decision maker perceives serious risks, no matter what course of action is selected (Mann, 1992, p. 208). In these situations, the decision maker is expected to experience conflict and stress.

Hypervigilance and vigilance describe extremely different coping patterns by decision makers. Hypervigilant decision makers approach a level of panic in the decision-making process. Symptoms associated with this coping pattern include an acute awareness of time pressure, a focus on threats, impulsivity, vacillation, emotionality, reduction in memory span, and simplistic and repetitive thinking (Mann, 1992, p. 210). Vigilance, conversely, is associated with only moderate levels of stress, optimism, painstaking information search and assimilation, and careful evaluation of alternatives (Mann, 1992, p. 210). Clearly, vigilance may be associated with traditional notions of "rational" decision making, while hypervigilance is expected to produce highly "irrational" behavior.

Each of these coping patterns is observable in the laboratory setting, but George notes that "while hypervigilance is relatively rare, defensive avoidance is a highly pervasive tendency that is encountered in many different types of decisions whether in business, family affairs, or in politics" (1980, p. 37). Of course, much of the research presented above would also seem to indicate that vigilance (i.e., perfectly rational decision making) is a relatively rare response to uncertainty and the perceived lack of accurate information. Thus, our focus here will be on defensive avoidance strategies as developed by Janis and Mann (1977) and then modified by George (1980) and Vertzberger (1995a).

Janis and Mann (1977) proposed three basic defensive avoidance strategies: procrastination, buck-passing, and rationalization. Procrastination (or George's "rational" procrastination, 1980, pp. 36–37) is most likely to occur when the decision maker does not perceive that time pressure is acute. It involves delaying the decision until further information can be collected and analyzed. This strategy involves the implicit belief that a better decision can be reached at some point in the future.[21] Rationalization, or the more familiar "bolstering," is the "psychological tendency under certain conditions of decisional stress to increase the attractiveness of a preferred (or chosen) option and doing the opposite for options which one is inclined to reject (or has rejected)" (George, 1980, p. 38).[22] Bolstering allows a decision maker to reach closure by reducing (or eliminating altogether) the perception of uncertainty.

Building on these psychological strategies of coping with decisional stress, George lists a number of "cognitive aids" that may assist the decision maker (1980, pp. 39–47). Of these, *incrementalism* appears to be the most relevant—particularly when defensive avoidance strategies are linked to decision-maker risk predispositions (see section V). Incrementalism is simply the strategy of selecting "policy alternatives that differ only slightly from existing policies and aim at securing marginal rather than dramatic improvements" (George, 1980, p. 40). Incrementalism is viewed as a conservative strategy that allows for risk-avoidance (although over-cautious strategies can involve their own risks). In section V, I discuss how these different strategies of defensive avoidance are integrated into my "Risk Explanation Framework."

IV.   Methodological Issues

As noted above, the study of risk behavior in political science has generally focused on algebraic models of decision making—particularly the Bernoullian family of EU theories. These models, from Bernoulli (1967 [1738]) to von Neumann and Morgenstern (1947) to Savage (1954) to Kahneman and Tversky (1979), share a number of flaws that limit their applicability within the study of foreign policy decision making (see Boettcher, 2004a). When taken together, the following issues suggest the need for significant theoretical adaptation and innovation.

Measurement

The Bernoullian theories, being models of mathematical expectation, require the exact measurement of estimates of utility and probability. While the models vary in terms of the objectivity vs. subjectivity of judgment, they all need inputs that are expressed numerically in order to accurately test their propositions. This presents problems for researchers attempting to evaluate these theories in the domain of foreign policy decision making. Levy (1992b, 1995), Jervis (1992), Vertzberger (1995a), and others (Boettcher, 1995; Freudenburg, 1992; Sjöberg, 1980) have written extensively on the difficulties inherent in attempting to measure utilities and probabilities outside the laboratory setting. In foreign policy decision making, values are attached to soldier's lives, "national interests," prestige, reputations, domestic political welfare, and a host of other tangible and intangible factors that resist exact measurement. The researcher is often forced to roughly aggregate different factors into a single estimate of positive or negative utility associated with the success or failure of particular options. This rough aggregation makes comparisons between the values of the options difficult. These problems have led to a distinct lack of rigorous, replicable, and valid utility measurement strategies in the foreign policy decision-making literature.[23]

Vertzberger (1995a) and Boettcher (1995, 1996) address the difficulties that researchers face when trying to determine the probabilities that are attached to outcomes by decision makers. Vertzberger notes that "in using subjective probabilities, decision makers use symbolic descriptions of numbers ('highly likely, probably') that express categorical and ordinal relations with certain focal or bounding landmark values" (1995a, p. 366). Simply put, decision makers seldom communicate in explicit numerical probabilities, but instead rely on verbal expressions of probability. Budescu, Weinberg, and Wallsten comment on the irony of the fact that "the numerous decision models that assume numerical representation of uncertainty are in sharp contrast with the fact that people generally prefer to express their beliefs by means of natural language"(1988, p. 281). Experiments have even shown that while consumers of probabilistic information prefer to receive numerical estimates, providers of information prefer to communicate probabilistic estimates in verbal terms.[24]

The extent to which foreign policy decision makers communicate probabilistic information in words rather than numbers will hamper researchers' attempts to accurately measure perceived risk.[25] Verbal expressions of probability mean different things to different people; certain terms may cover probability ranges of 20 percent or more (see Clark, 1990). A further problem is the fact that individuals often rely on nonprobabilistic expressions such as "good chance" or "never" or "usually" (Clark, 1990, p. 231). The indeterminate nature of these expressions results in probability estimates that cannot easily be entered into the standard EU equation. Vertzberger adds that "even when likelihoods are described in numerical terms, they are actually treated as names of landmarks . . . The use of subjective probabilities in this form does not allow for multiplication and addition operations or for measuring errors and biases as distances from the correct values" (1995a, p. 367). Thus, even numerical expressions of probability may not be easily manipulated as they are in the laboratory.

A third measurement problem is encountered when researchers using Kahneman and Tversky's (1979) prospect theory attempt to identify the frame or reference point adopted by a decision maker. The notion of framing is undoubtedly the single most important contribution of Kahneman and Tversky's (1979) prospect theory, however, the editing phase is neither explicitly tested nor modeled numerically. As Levy (1992b, 1995), Jervis (1992), and others have suggested, the foundation of a prospect theory-based explanation of a foreign policy decision lies in determining the manner in which the decision maker is framing the problem, and yet Kahneman and Tversky's (1979) seminal article offers no theoretical guidance as to why a particular frame is selected. Levy notes that "the difficulty of determining empirically how an actor defines her reference point is particularly troubling . . . If we cannot establish the reference point, and do so independently of the behavior we are trying to explain, then prospect theory and its key hypotheses . . . cannot be tested and have no explanatory power"(1995, p. 17). A number of works have attempted to empirically identify the framing of a problem confronting a decision maker (see Farnham, 1992; Huth et al., 1992; McDermott, 1992, 1995; McInerney, 1992; and Stein and Pauly, 1993), but only Farnham (1992), Taliaferro (1994), and McDermott (1992) have developed theoretical explanations as to why one frame was chosen over another (in the first case—affect, in the latter—analogical reasoning).[26] Of course, it is no small task to empirically identify the framing of a particular decision in a post hoc analysis, simply because the manner in which a decision is framed may often be open to issues of interpretation (see Taliaferro, 1998, p. 109). Without a great deal of empirical evidence, we cannot be confident about the plausibility of a researcher's subjective interpretation.[27]

The indirect identification of a decision maker's framing of a situation seems to take either (or both) of two forms—the "hedonic tone" of the problem and its expected implications itself suggests a "natural" frame, or past outcomes regarding the same or other issue have placed a decision maker "in" a domain of gains or losses. For a number of researchers, certain types of problems are expected to invoke different frames. Thus, the notion of framing moves away from semantic manipulation and the manner in which specific outcomes are described by decision makers and their advisers. Instead, these studies suggest that particular problems, by their very nature, have to impose losses on decision makers and are interpreted as such (see Berejikian, 1992, 1997; McInerney, 1992; Pauly, 1993; Weyland 1996, 1998). These researchers tend to focus on changes in the status quo that should be viewed as losses by the decision makers who have earlier expressed (or can be assumed to possess)[28] certain goals (identifiable reference points). These applications of prospect theory are somewhat odd, since they suggest a "natural" or "objective" interpretation of the problem while they are using an inherently "subjective" theory of decision making. However, I would argue that of the indirect frame identification methods, this is clearly the best.

A less persuasive indirect method for ascertaining the frame employed by a decision maker focuses on recent events that put a decision maker "in" a particular domain. As McDermott argues:

> For purposes of prospect theory, framing in domain is restricted to a sense of whether the actor perceives himself to be acting from a position of gains or losses. Gains or losses can be defined by objective criteria, such as public opinion polls . . . congressional indicators, such as the number of overrides on vetoes; economic indicators, such as the stock market index and inflation or unemployment rates; newspaper editorials; and world public opinion as manifested through diplomatic channels. (1998, pp. 37–38)

This perspective is suspect for three reasons—first, the notion of a decision maker "acting from a position of gains or losses" is quite different from examining the semantic manipulation of outcomes; second, the notion of "objective criteria" suggests that perceived gains or losses on one value dimension may affect decisions regarding other value dimensions (a halo/hangover effect); third, the objective value dimensions identified by the researcher may not be salient to the decision maker.[29] An obvious spin-off from this vein of research has focused on the diversionary war thesis (see Downs and Rocke, 1994; Richards et al., 1993) tying losses on the domestic front to risk-taking internationally (see DeRouen, 1995; Huth et al., 1992).[30] This work is quite interesting and potentially opens up another area of international relations research to prospect theorists, but it clearly expands the concept of framing beyond the bounds understood and tested by psychologists.[31]

The issue of measuring utilities and probabilities is less difficult than it may initially appear. If we accept the notion (discussed below) that it may be impossible to show that prospect theory (or some other behavioral decision theory) is demonstrably superior to EU theory using classic criteria, then we may reject the view that promotes competitive testing against EU theory in the traditional manner. Thus, I advocate less concern about exact measurement of probabilities and utilities and a greater focus on examining the process of decision making. We can then focus on how estimates of utility and probability enter into the decision process (if at all) and how they are discussed by the decision makers.[32] This type of design shifts the focus from simply predicting different outcomes to suggesting different underlying processes that are associated with observed outcomes.[33]

The identification of the frame or "aspiration level" adopted by the decision maker is indeed a difficult task. While it is clearly tempting to follow one of the "indirect" methods, the "objective" determination of a "natural" frame does not fit with the subjective nature of prospect theory, and the notion of a decision maker being "in" a particular domain suffers from the criticisms discussed above. This project attempts to directly identify the aspiration levels adopted by Presidents Truman and Kennedy. While the data requirements are extensive, the task can be accomplished through painstaking archival research and a careful reconstruction of the decision-making process.

Validity

Concerns regarding the internal validity of the Bernoullian family of theories have been discussed extensively in the psychological literature on decision theory (see Budescu et al., 1988; Budescu and Wallsten, 1990; Hershey and Schoemaker, 1980; Lopes, 1990, 1995). Political scientists critical of the application of prospect theory to international relations have focused more on issues of external validity (see Jervis, 1992; Kowert and Hermann, 1995; Levy, 1995, 1992b; Shafir, 1992). A number of issues arise including: the artificiality of the experimental designs, the data requirements of the theories that make empirical testing outside the laboratory difficult (as discussed above), and the applicability and generalizability of certain behavioral observations.

The experiments performed by researchers from the Bernoullian tradition are usually rather simple, and yet ingenious. Of course, in the laboratory, the researcher has almost total control over the content of the information included in various choice problems.[34] The stakes in the problems are usually money, lives, unemployment or inflation rates: carriers of value measurable on an interval scale and easily converted into measures of utility. Probabilities are expressed numerically to ensure that the EU of each prospect can be compared. When prospect theory is tested, the framing of the reference point is inherent in the language of the choice problems: money is won or lost, people die or are saved. There is little ambiguity and subjects are assumed to adopt the frame given. The frames are also always pure: prospects are never mixed between losses and gains.

As table 2.1 shows, few of the conditions mentioned above are met in the domain of foreign policy decisions where: frames are often mixed and difficult to discern; the stakes of the decision may be prestige, domestic political welfare, reputation or some other value that is not easily quantifiable; and decision makers often communicate in verbal probability expressions. In the laboratory, potential outcomes associated with the prospects under consideration are not dependent on the behavior of an adversary or ally. The multilateral and interactive nature of the foreign policy arena might elicit different behavioral regularities. Finally, experimental subjects are often forced to make a single choice without the benefit of feedback. In the "real world," decision makers may make a series of iterated decisions that allow for feedback, learning, and adaptation.[35]

The applicability and generalizability of the results produced in these experiments, is hampered by the fact that the observed behavioral regularities are never exhibited by an entire subject pool. In the Kahneman and Tversky experiments, approximately 20–40 percent of the subjects fall in the "off" cells (Levy, 1992b, p. 305). For the economist studying mass behavior

Table 2.1 Differences between gambling (in experimental setting) and foreign policy domains

Characteristics	Gambling domain	Foreign policy domain
Types of frames	Pure, discernable	Mixed, ill-structured
Stakes of decisions	Lack of value complexity—no comparison between different types of stakes	Value complexity—different types of stakes
	Money, lives, unemployment or inflation rates—easily converted into measures of utility	Prestige, political welfare, reputation—resistant to exact measurement
Estimates of probability	Expressed numerically—easily entered into expected-utility calculus	Expressed verbally or treated as numerical landmarks—difficult to translate into point numerical estimates
Strategic context	Unilateral—outcomes independent of other actors behavior	Multilateral—outcomes depend on behavior of allies and adversaries
	Single shot	Iterated—usually part of an interactive series of decisions

across a number of decisions, this is not so much of a problem, but for the analyst examining a limited number of choices by individuals or small groups, this is a point of great concern. Who falls in those "off" cells and why they fall there, becomes an important question (as discussed above).

A final concern relating to generalizability is the issue of group versus individual choice. Shafir notes: "Prospect theory is a theory of *individual* decision-making . . . It is based on specific assumptions regarding people's anticipated pleasure over gains as compared to their pain over losses . . . All this may be significantly different for groups of individuals" (1992, p. 313, italics in original).[36] The extensive literature on small group behavior (see Clark, 1971; Kameda and Davis, 1990; Levi and Whyte, 1997; Maoz, 1990; Paese et al., 1993; Seibert and Goltz, 2001; Vertzberger, 1997, 1998; and Whyte, 1998) suggests that group risk propensity cannot simply be determined by aggregating individual attitudes toward risk. As McDermott (1992) shows, the framing of a problem may involve competition between advisers with different policy preferences. This dynamism is seldom achieved in the laboratory setting. When foreign policy decisions are made by groups, the researcher must be sensitive to the special character of the group context and take care in applying theories developed to explain individual behavior.[37] While this is clearly not an insurmountable task, we must be careful to embed the insights derived from prospect theory in theories like the REF that fill in the broader elements of the situation confronting decision makers.[38]

By focusing on process rather than solely focusing on outcome, I hope to discern the extent to which the REF hypotheses are applicable to the domain of presidential foreign policy decision making. Concerns regarding the "off cells" of the behavioral decision theories have been addressed through the construction of my presidential risk predisposition index. The issue of group versus individual choice is addressed through careful case selection and limitations in the scope of this research design and the potential applicability of some of its findings.

I have attempted to select cases where historical interpretations and "conventional wisdom" indicate that the president was actively involved in the decision process. As Vertzberger (1997, p. 297) notes "in a presidential system the constitutional lines of accountability eventually lead directly to the president, no matter how many others participate in the decision making or are consulted." As the sign on Truman's desk read "The Buck Stops Here" (McCullough, 1992, p. 481). I have carefully selected cases where the president made the final decision. I recognize that a number of the inputs to the decision process and the aspiration level for the problem itself may have been provided by presidential advisers, but I am less concerned with how options and reference points are developed than I am concerned with how options are compared and a choice among options is made by the president.[39] Despite my restricted focus in this project, I recognize the importance of group inputs and have pursued research into group processes (see Boettcher, 2001, 2004a).

Evaluation

The central purpose of many research endeavors is the elimination of alternative explanations for the results obtained through experimentation, large-N statistical studies, or case studies. Careful research designs are constructed in order to pit hypotheses against one another. When testing a theory of decision, a standard cost–benefit EU model usually serves as the null hypothesis. It is also commonly accepted that the theory being tested should provide "a *better* explanation of that behavior than does expected-utility theory" (Levy, 1992b, p. 297, italics in original). Others argue that the new theory should be capable of explaining the cases previously explained by EU theory and should also be able to explain cases that are not predicted by simple cost–benefit calculations (see Lakatos, 1968). Thus, Levy (1992b, 1995) maintains that the burden of proof lies on prospect theory to perform in cases where EU theory fails. In the laboratory, the Kahneman and Tversky (1979) design is "set up in such a way that expected-utility theory and prospect theory predict different choices, so that it is relatively straightforward to interpret the results of most of these experiments" (Levy, 1995, p. 17). Unfortunately, it is often difficult to replicate this degree of control in the foreign policy domain.

Levy (1992b) and Boettcher (1995) highlight the problems that McDermott (1992) experiences in attempting to eliminate alternative explanations. Her own data may be used to construct an explanation of President Carter's behavior (in the case of the Iranian hostage rescue mission) that is perfectly consistent with EU theory. She avoids this conclusion by challenging Carter's revealed estimates of utility and probability. She writes: "even if he didn't think of the rescue mission as risky, he knew that objectively it was *more* risky than other options that were available to him"; and "while Carter may not have believed that the costs associated with the mission were high, he was wrong objectively" (1992, pp. 260–261, italics in original). McDermott's concern with what Carter "knew" instead of what he "thought" raises the issue of whether prospect theory is an objective or subjective theory of choice. If it is truly a subjective theory, then researchers should not rely on distinctions between perceptions and reality.

McDermott's findings may simply be the product of the measurement problems discussed above, or they may also result from the special character of the foreign policy domain. I have argued elsewhere (Boettcher, 1995) that it may be impossible to demonstrate that prospect theory can succeed where EU theory fails in the "real world."[40] It is important to recall that prospect theory relies on a value and a probability weighting function to reflect risk-seeking in the domain of losses and risk-aversion in the domain of gains (see Kahneman and Tversky, 1979; Levy, 1992a). Subjects are not making "irrational" decisions in Kahneman and Tversky's (1979) experiments, they are simply modifying the probabilities and utilities that are "given" in the choice problems. In the laboratory, "objective" probabilities and utilities are easily identifiable and potentially distinguishable from the subjects' frame-weighted perceptions. In the foreign policy setting, the researcher is unable to demonstrate whether the decision maker has adopted some frame-weighted perception or has remained true to "objective" probability and utility estimates. Thus, decisions like Carter's choice to attempt the hostage rescue mission may appear "rational" in the EU sense only because the researcher measured frame-weighted estimates of probability and utility.[41] In short, the pre-intervention (i.e., pre-framing) estimates may be inaccessible.

In light of the methodological issues discussed above, I have argued (Boettcher, 1995) for a revision of the "standard" evaluation criterion. I propose that we turn to a focus on process, rather than outcome. We should not assume that, since a theory accurately predicted an outcome, that theory's hypotheses regarding the process leading to the outcome are accurate. This is not to say that we should ignore outcomes altogether, but only that we should evaluate theories based on their ability to plausibly characterize the process of decision making (as well as accurately predict outcomes). As noted above, we should not allow theories to avoid careful scrutiny by simply resorting to the "as if assumption" defense (see Friedman, 1953).

The strategy of qualitative "process" validation has frequently been utilized by political scientists concerned with the study of foreign policy decision making. Two particular research traditions immediately come to mind—simulation research and computational modeling. Simulation researchers like Harold Guetzkow and Charles F. Hermann attempted to evaluate the plausibility of their person–machine models both through "outcome" and "process" validation, suggesting that multiple validation strategies provided a more comprehensive understanding of the strengths and weaknesses of various simulation designs (see Guetzkow and Valadez, 1981; Hermann, 1967). Computational modelers such as Donald A. Sylvan, Ashok Goel, and B. Chandrasekaran have also emphasized the multi-criterion approach, arguing that their complex and well-specified models are often best evaluated by qualitative rather than quantitative techniques (1990, pp. 96–98).[42] These researchers performed literature reviews, expert interviews, and counterfactual analysis to check the "process" validity of their model of Japanese energy decision making. In short, the notion of "process" validation has a significant history in the study of foreign policy decision making and clearly provides an appropriate alternative (or supplemental) criterion for evaluating the plausibility of models of presidential risk behavior.

V. A Risk Explanation Framework

Having explored much of the extant theoretical and empirical literature dealing with risk behavior (and having examined the methodological limitations of these approaches), we may now consider how the various veins of research discussed above may be combined into a synthesized model of presidential risk behavior in foreign policy. My REF attempts to draw on the most current and compelling research with careful attention to the implications inherent in crossing disciplinary boundaries. In essence, I have tried to "mine the gems" of each research tradition—separating the truly original and innovative hypotheses from the sometimes cumbersome intellectual frameworks that have limited their applicability to the domain of foreign policy decision making. In this manner, I hope to develop a framework for the explanation of presidential risk behavior that is truly sensitive to the domain of foreign policy decision making.

Figure 2.1 depicts the model of presidential risk behavior in foreign policy suggested by the REF. Following much of the literature on decision making, both within political science (e.g., Voss, 1998) and in other disciplines as well (e.g., Kahneman and Tversky, 1979), I divide the framework into a *representation* or *framing* stage and an *option selection* or *evaluation* stage. In the first stage, an *aspiration level* is constructed and options are generated. Also in this stage, the president first forms perceptions regarding relevant *situational constraints*: particularly the level of uncertainty, the degree to which time pressures are acute, and the extent to which incoming information is accurate.[43]

In the second stage, options are evaluated relative to the aspiration level and options are eliminated that are incapable of achieving (or surpassing) the aspiration level. Also in this stage, I expect to observe the impact of *personal predispositions* upon information processing. Finally, a presidential decision is reached that reflects the interaction of presidential risk propensity and situational constraints. At this point we may observe the selection of one option out of several (influenced by presidential risk predisposition),

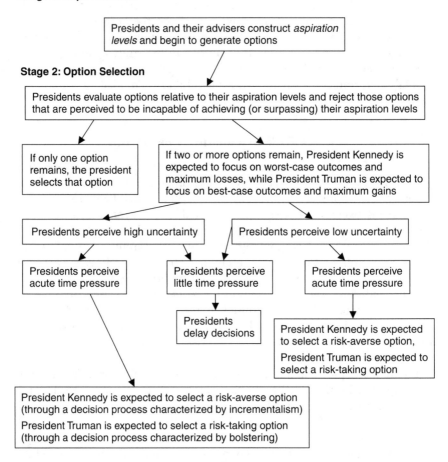

Kennedy–*Security-Motivated*–Scores high on need for affiliation and conceptual complexity

Truman–*Potential-Motivated*–Scores high on belief in ability to control events, need for power, and task emphasis

Stage 1: Representation

Presidents and their advisers construct *aspiration levels* and begin to generate options

Stage 2: Option Selection

Presidents evaluate options relative to their aspiration levels and reject those options that are perceived to be incapable of achieving (or surpassing) their aspiration levels

If only one option remains, the president selects that option

If two or more options remain, President Kennedy is expected to focus on worst-case outcomes and maximum losses, while President Truman is expected to focus on best-case outcomes and maximum gains

Presidents perceive high uncertainty

Presidents perceive low uncertainty

Presidents perceive acute time pressure

Presidents perceive little time pressure

Presidents perceive acute time pressure

Presidents delay decisions

President Kennedy is expected to select a risk-averse option,

President Truman is expected to select a risk-taking option

President Kennedy is expected to select a risk-averse option (through a decision process characterized by incrementalism)

President Truman is expected to select a risk-taking option (through a decision process characterized by bolstering)

Figure 2.1   Ideal decision-making process suggested by REF

the ratification of the only option capable of achieving the aspiration level, or an attempt to delay the decision altogether. If the president perceives high uncertainty, inaccurate information, and acute time pressures, the option selected may represent *incrementalism* (by risk-averse presidents) or *bolstering* (by risk-acceptant presidents). If the president perceives high uncertainty, inaccurate information, but little time pressure, we may expect him to *delay* the decision altogether.

Stage 1: Representation

The representation stage of the REF is grounded in the reference dependence literature in psychology (Kahneman and Tversky, 1979; Lopes, 1987, 1990, 1995; Tversky and Kahneman, 1992) and business (March and Shapira, 1992), and the problem representation literature in political science (Beasley, 1996; Sylvan, 1998; Sylvan and Thorson, 1992; Voss, 1998). Each of these research traditions suggests that the manner in which a decision maker "represents" or "frames" a problem has a significant impact on the eventual solution he or she selects. In foreign policy decision making, presidents must develop these representations because, in general, the problems they face are "ill-structured." That is, they do not have "well-defined initial states, goals, constraints, and/or means to reach the goal" (Voss, 1998, p. 5). While a president's representation of a foreign policy problem may be quite rich, my focus here will be on the minimum level goals identified by the decision maker.

The work of Kahneman and Tversky (1979), Lopes (1995), and March and Shapira (1992) suggests decision makers are not so much concerned with overall asset levels as they are with departures from crucial "reference points." These reference points may be interpreted as the decision maker's minimum level goals (see Lopes, 1995). While much of the experimental literature focuses on a decision maker with a single goal (i.e., achieving a particular monetary payout in a gambling problem), it should now be obvious that presidents, making foreign policy decisions, often have multiple goals in mind. Thus, in the REF, the president's aspiration level is expected to comprise a set (or portfolio) of minimum level goals that the president hopes to achieve or surpass. The aspiration level may include an *immediate goal*, imperatives that *constrain the means available* for achieving the immediate goal, and other interests that *reinforce the president's commitment* to achieving or surpassing his immediate goal.

Stage 2: Option Selection

It is in stage 2 where I first expect to observe the main effects of the president's aspiration level. The following hypotheses emerge from the research traditions concerned with reference dependence and problem representation:

H1: *Presidents tend to evaluate outcomes relative to an aspiration level rather than an overall value level.*

　H1a: *The president's aspiration level (acting as a situational constraint) is likely to preclude the consideration of options that are viewed as incapable of achieving (or surpassing) the aspiration level in a particular case.*

Also at this stage I expect to observe the impact of presidential predispositions on risk behavior. In particular, Lopes' work (1987, 1990, 1995) suggests the impact of risk predispositions on information processing. Her security/potential-motivated decision makers are expected to process information in observably different ways, yielding the following hypotheses:

H2: *Security-motivated presidents tend to engage in "bottom-up" processing—(i.e., focusing on worst-case outcomes and maximum losses).*
H3: *Potential-motivated presidents tend to engage in "top-down" processing—(i.e., focusing on best-case outcomes and maximum gains).*

Further, these differences in information processing are expected to affect option selection. The following hypotheses establish the link between risk predispositions and risk behavior (i.e., option selection):

H4: *Security-motivated presidents are likely to behave in a risk-averse manner.*
H5: *Potential-motivated presidents are likely to behave in a risk-acceptant manner.*

Of course, there are certain circumstances where these hypotheses might not apply (see Lopes, 1987, pp. 281–282). A dearth of alternatives may mitigate the role of presidential risk predispositions, resulting in a choice affected by the aspiration level alone. Thus, the following hypothesis:

H6: *If there is only one alternative capable of achieving the aspiration level, that alternative is likely to be selected regardless of its level of risk.*

At the conclusion of the option selection stage I leave open the possibility of observing the effects of perceptions of uncertainty, information inaccuracy, and time pressure. Following, Janis and Mann (1977) and George (1980) I offer the following hypothesis:

H7: *Presidential perceptions of high uncertainty and a lack of valid information will interact with presidential risk predispositions and affect the output of the decision process.*

In particular, I expect presidents to follow the defensive avoidance strategies discussed above (see section III). I propose the following hypothesis for situations where a president perceives high uncertainty and inaccurate information, but does not perceive acute time pressure:

H7a: *If time pressures are not acute, both risk-averse and risk-acceptant presidents are likely to delay the moment of decision. (The rationale is that the presidents will use this added time to reduce uncertainty and collect more valid information.)*

In situations where presidents perceive high uncertainty, inaccurate information, and acute time pressure, I expect the defensive avoidance strategy followed by the president to fit with his personal risk predisposition. Thus, the following hypotheses:

H7b: *If time pressures are acute, risk-averse presidents are likely to engage in incrementalism.*

H7c: *If time pressures are acute, risk-acceptant presidents are likely to engage in bolstering.*

VI. Operationalization and Measurement Strategies

Structured, Focused, Comparative Case Study

Of the five tasks for designing case studies proposed by George (1979, pp. 54–55; also Bennett and George, 1997b, 2001), the most significant (and daunting) may be the formulation of the general questions to be asked of each case study (see also King et al., 1994).The researcher must take care to develop reliable measurement strategies *in advance of undertaking the proposed research.* Of course, as data collection proceeds the researcher may see fit to refine the questions that are posed in each case study, but he or she should be careful to retain the overall structure and integrity of the original research design. Prior to the initiation of my field research, I developed the questions that are presented in figure 2.2.

The questions to be posed in each case study may be divided into the representation and option selection stages. In the representation stage, the questions focus on the identification of the president's aspiration level. In the option selection stage, the questions focus on the manner in which options are evaluated; the degree to which the president perceives uncertainty, inaccurate information, and acute time pressure; and the characteristics of the "choice" that is reached.The answers to these questions guide the evaluation of the plausibility of the hypotheses that compose the REF.

In order to provide a more subtle (and honest) evaluation of the REF hypotheses, I differentiate between instances in which the available evidence provides *strong, moderate,* or *weak* support.These judgments are based on both the quantity and quality of the evidence available to the researcher. During some decision periods the evidence of presidential decision making is quite complete—memoranda, meeting minutes, oral histories, and memoirs all point in the same direction. Direct evidence of the president's thought processes are available and clearly supportive of the REF hypotheses. These instances are labeled "strong support" in the case summaries. In other decision periods, the quantity of evidence is more limited, there is a higher percentage of indirect evidence regarding the president's thought processes, and/or all the evidence does not run in the same direction. In these circumstances, while I still feel confident that the evidence provides support for the REF hypotheses, I must note that the evidence is neither complete nor overwhelming. These instances are labeled "moderate support" in the case summaries. In a third set of decision periods, direct evidence of the president's thought processes may be scant or fragmentary and/or some of the evidence available is inconclusive or runs against the REF hypotheses. In these situations, I remain convinced that the evidence supports the hypotheses, but my decision is based on inferences and interpretation.These instances are labeled "weak support" in the case summaries.

Stage One: Representation
– What is the president's aspiration level that describes acceptable/desirable outcomes in a case?
  – the aspiration level is not an initial point but rather an end state that the president wishes to reach
  – look for discussions of goals, desires, hopes, needs, requirements in this case
– Is the aspiration level viewed as maintenance of the status quo or does it encompass a positive change from the current state of affairs? How firmly is the aspiration level held: are outcomes below the reference point viewed as undesirable or unacceptable?
  – look for description of commitment to goals, discussion of failures as unacceptable, evidence of "win at any cost" mentality

Stage Two: Option Selection
– What are the options under consideration? How are costs/benefits and estimates of success/failure discussed? How are options discussed, compared, evaluated?
  – identify options being examined by president by examining, memoranda, position papers, minutes of meetings, secondary sources, memoirs
  – are numerical estimates of probability discussed? If yes, how are they used by the president? Does the consideration of options approximate procedural rationality? Are trade-offs between values recognized and resolved? Are notions of expected value considered?
  – are options evaluated relative to the president's aspiration level?
  – are options rejected out of hand because the president perceives that they are incapable of achieving or surpassing the aspiration level?
  – is there a recognizable pattern in the manner the president processes information regarding the options? Does this pattern approximate Lopes' top-down or bottom-up processing?
  – how is the final option selected? what does this process look like? Do explicit considerations of relative risk enter into the process?
– What are the president's perceptions relating to uncertainty, information accuracy and time pressure?
  – does the president express reticence because of a concern over inadequate information, flawed estimates, or incomplete analysis?
  – does the president refer to time as an issue affecting the consideration of options?
– What are the characteristics of the option selected relative to the other options under consideration? Are outcomes more numerous and extremely divergent? Does the president perceive that extreme negative outcomes are at least possible? Does the president recognize that estimates are flawed and may in fact be incorrect?
  – is the option selected viewed as "risky" or "cautious" or some similar language?
  – is concern expressed over the extensive range of potential outcomes associated with certain options?
  – is the option selected one of many, or simply the ratification of the only option under consideration?
  – does the option selected represent incrementalism or bolstering?
  – does the president avoid making a decision? Does he encourage his staff to develop more options, provide better information and/or reevaluate the aspiration level?

Figure 2.2   Questions to be posed in each case study

Fortunately, of the 45 instances identified as "supportive" in the case summaries, 30 (67 percent) were labeled "strong," 10 (22 percent) were labeled "moderate," and only 5 (11 percent) were labeled "weak."

Archival Research[44]

In attempting to reconstruct the process that led to the presidential decisions in these cases (and answer the questions posed in figure 2.2), I undertook both primary and secondary case research. Prior to embarking on my archival research, I attempted to survey the best secondary sources on each case. (These sources include, but are not limited to, *Foreign Relations of the United States* [FRUS], various volumes; Acheson, 1969; Byrnes, 1947; Cumings, 1990; Foot, 1985; George et al., 1971; Hilsman, 1967; Jones, 1955; Kuniholm, 1980; Lefever, 1967; Paige, 1968; Paterson, 1989; Schlesinger, 1965; Sorensen, 1965; Weissman, 1974.) Having developed a more sophisticated understanding of my cases, I then visited the John F. Kennedy Library, the Harry S. Truman Library, the National Archives, and the National Security Archive. At these various archives, I examined presidential papers, personal papers, institutional record groups, and oral histories. I took notes from or photocopied minutes of meetings, departmental memoranda, personal notes, personal correspondence, and other forms of primary documents.

Despite the breadth of my research, I was unable to analyze every document dealing with the cases under examination. Instead, I followed a directed search strategy based on the questions to be asked of the cases and the overall objectives of the research project. In this manner, I hope to have examined or obtained the *key* documents that are the *most relevant*, given the questions at hand.

Personality Assessment-at-a-Distance

As noted in chapter one (section V), the final method employed in this project is the personality assessment-at-a-distance technique as developed by M. Hermann (1980a,b; see Rasler and Thompson, 1980, for a critique of Hermann's seminal article). This technique is used to aid in the coding of the dispositional variable capturing security/potential-motivation. Unfortunately, Lopes (1987, 1990, 1995) provides little guidance regarding the personality characteristics that might be associated with this motivational variable. I have, therefore, attempted to adapt Hermann's personality measurement technique to the study of risk behavior. A number of the personality characteristics measured by Hermann may be associated (either positively or negatively) with decision-maker risk propensity (and thus, security/potential-motivation). In particular, "belief in ability to control events," "need for power," and "task emphasis" may all be positively associated with risk-taking (potential-motivation); while need for affiliation and conceptual complexity may be positively associated with risk-aversion (security-motivation).

Employing Hermann's personality assessment-at-a-distance technique, M. Hermann and J. T. Preston have developed a data set that includes scores for eight personality characteristics for a number of U.S. presidents (see Hermann, 1984; Preston, 2001). This data set allows me to construct an index of presidential risk predispositions. Table 2.2 presents the scores on the five key personality characteristics across six presidents: Reagan, Bush, Johnson, Kennedy, Eisenhower, and Truman. High positive scores on the

Table 2.2   Presidential risk predisposition-index scores

	BACE	Power	Task Emph.	Aff.	Con. Comp.	Total (Raw)	Total (Rank)
Reagan	.390[a]	.400	.760	−.110	−.350	1.09	2
M. H. 1981	(3[b])	(1)	(6)	(5)	(6)	(21)	(2T)
Bush	.330	.440	.470	−.180	−.540	.52	6
M. H. 1991	(1)	(2)	(1)	(3)	(3)	(10)	(6)
Johnson	.394	.731	.621	−.216	−.452	1.078	3
J. T. P. 1994	(4)	(6)	(5)	(2)	(4)	(21)	(2T)
Kennedy	.339	.635	.563	−.175	−.639	.723	5
J. T. P. 1994	(2)	(3)	(2)	(4)	(1)	(12)	(5)
Eisenhower	.494	.639	.602	−.314	−.634	.787	4
J. T. P. 1994	(6)	(4)	(3)	(1)	(2)	(16)	(4)
Truman	.433	.663	.618	−.062	−.420	1.232	1
J. T. P. 1994	(5)	(5)	(4)	(6)	(5)	(25)	(1)

Note: M. H. 19—indicates coding performed in that year by M. Hermann, J. T. P. 19—indicates coding performed in that year by J. T. Preston.

[a] Standardized score.
[b] Rank of standardized score (6 = highest, 1 = lowest).

index indicate potential-motivation, while low (or negative) scores indicate security-motivation. Both standardized scores and comparative ranks were summed to yield a cumulative ranking. President Truman lies at the extreme potential-motivated end of the index, while presidents Bush and Kennedy lie on the security-motivated end of the index (regardless of the method of measurement—rank versus standardized scores). The Kennedy administration was selected over the Bush administration due to the similarity in their index scores and concerns regarding document availability.

The validity of the risk-predisposition index is somewhat supported by biographical data suggestive of Truman and Kennedy's personal orientations to risk.[45] President Truman is described (by Paige) as possessing a "confident willingness to accept responsibility for decision" (1968, p. 22). Indeed, the "President's advisers greatly admired his ability to make crucial decisions without tormenting afterthoughts" (Paige, 1968, p. 24). Truman once noted that "I have to take things as they come and make every decision on the basis of the facts as I have them and then go on from there; then forget that one and take the next" (quoted in Paige, 1968, p. 24). According to a close adviser, there "was no wavering, doubt, or timidity on the part of President Truman" (quoted in Paige, 1968, p. 335). Truman's willingness to make tough choices was combined with an idealism that promoted "courage in the face of politics and other risks when he knew or thought he knew he was right" (Jones, 1955, p. 113). Dean Acheson, one of Truman's closest advisers and confidants, suggests that the president "was unmoved by, indeed unmindful of, the effect upon his party's political fortunes of action that he thought was right and in the best interest of the country, broadly conceived. A doctrine that later became fashionable with presidents, called 'keeping all options open' (apparently by avoiding decision), did not appeal to Harry S. Truman" (1969, p. 411). Truman's detractors also focus on his personal predispositions, noting that Acheson's "president was impatient with ambiguity, and possessed, as Robert Donovan delicately put it, 'an appetite, too much of a one, really, for unhesitating decision.' His penchant for historical analogy usually left him wide of the mark, but it seemed to gird his loins and underpin his confidence, almost as if Walter Mitty sat in the oval office, plumbing 'history' for guidance" (Cumings, 1990, p. 630). In fact, Stephen Pelz suggests that Truman "indulged in bravado" in order to "compensate for his own weakness" (1983, p. 101). These characterizations suggest that Truman's placement at the potential-motivated end of the index is appropriate.

Unlike Truman, President Kennedy is described by admirers as "cautious," "self-disciplined," and "highly-controlled" (see Rostow, 1964, pp. 139–141). In making foreign policy decisions, Kennedy encouraged dissent and "wanted all the pros and cons laid out" (Taylor, 1964, p. 30). Walt Rostow observed a "counterpoint" in Kennedy's character, "between a voracious enjoyment of life and people set off against this sense of the possibility of failure and tragedy" (1964, p. 140). The President tended to "set his goals as high as he could. But he was also awfully conscious of the other side of it; which was the long, difficult, grubby, painstaking, frustrating business it would be to bring the grand objectives to life" (Rostow, 1964, p. 141). Kennedy's detractors fault his pragmatism and note that his tendency "to 'preserve his options' provided too facile a rationalization for postponing unpleasant decisions on major issues where results would not be immediately apparent" (Ball, 1982, p. 168). For his critics, Kennedy's foreign policy lacked direction, and the "extremism" of his caution "was responsible for some of the tottering, the ambiguity, and the blind alleys of American diplomacy" during his administration (Weissman, 1974, p. 192). Indeed, Kennedy often attempted "to compromise internal differences even when these differences were uncompromisable on the level of external reality" (Weissman, 1974, p. 192). Bruce Mazlish views Kennedy as a "Hamlet-like figure" that "continually reversed himself," "vacillated," "evaded responsibility," "permitted events to overtake him," and "could not stay the course" (1988, p. 30). The characterizations presented above suggest that Kennedy's placement at the security-motivated end of the index is appropriate.

Scope Conditions

Before delving into the more empirical chapters of this book, it is important to consider the potential scope of the results it will produce. This study is intended, first and foremost, to be an initial test of the hypotheses that compose the REF. In this regard, any results should be viewed as *suggestive* rather than *generalizable*. I simply hope to demonstrate that it is *possible* to at least partially explain presidential risk behavior through the use of the REF. The study of presidential risk behavior is clearly a complex subject, and the

REF will undoubtedly require further refinement. The research design has also been limited in order to allow for a modicum of control over several exogenous variables, thus reducing the *suggestiveness* of its results to the realm of considerations of potential military intervention within a particular context. I would also be reluctant to extend its results much beyond the two administrations studied here. And yet, despite the modesty of its empirical claims, I feel that the conceptual and theoretical advances embodied in the REF more than make up for any flaws or limitations in this research design.

VII. Conclusion

In this chapter, I first considered the diverse ways in which the concepts of *risk*, *uncertainty*, and *risk propensity* have been interpreted by social scientists and the implications of adopting one set of definitions rather than another. I then put forth and defended the definitions that I follow throughout this study. Section III focused on the various literatures from political science, psychology, economics, business, and sociology that inform this study. Section IV raised issues of measurement, validity, and evaluation, constructing a critique that provided the foundation for the theory and research design explicated in sections V and VI. In section V, I provided a detailed description of my REF, discussing the theoretical and empirical roots of each hypothesis. Finally, section VI focused on the research methods used in this study, providing a more complete and critical examination of the methods introduced in chapter one (sections V & VI). The next two chapters are more empirically oriented: evaluating the REF through case studies from the Truman and Kennedy administrations.

CHAPTER THREE

Truman Case Studies

I. Introduction and Overview

The Cold War between the United States and the Soviet Union began
during the Truman administration. The World War II alliance, cobbled
together by the personal diplomacy of Franklin Roosevelt, fell apart as the
victors squabbled over the postwar settlement. The tensions that emerged
between Truman and Stalin during the Potsdam conference would result
in disagreements over the composition of governments in almost every
liberated area. The threat that held the allies together during the war was
replaced by the perceived opportunity to reshape the world in one's own
image and secure access to economic resources and global markets. The
decisions made by the Truman administration between 1945 and 1951
would shape U.S. foreign policy for the next 45 years.

The three cases examined below trace the origins of the Cold War.[1] First
in Iran and Greece and later in Korea, the Truman administration would
contain and then attempt to roll back the communist "menace."[2] In each of
these cases, Truman and his advisers were confronted with deteriorating
situations under seemingly novel circumstances. Truman was forced to balance alliance and treaty commitments with U.S. interests and declining
military power. His choice to move from cooperation to confrontation
involved decisions with significant elements of risk. In each case, President
Truman considered various levels of U.S. military intervention. Truman's
decision making in these cases is fairly well documented, providing an
excellent opportunity for evaluating the hypotheses that compose the Risk
Explanation Framework (REF).

The Iran, Greece, and Korea case studies all follow the same structure.
First, an overview narrative of the case provides important contextual
information. Then, the various elements of the REF are evaluated through
discussions relating to the president's aspiration level, perceptions of uncertainty and time pressure, consideration of alternatives, and final decision.
A concluding section of this chapter considers the implications for theory
of the results obtained. Throughout each case study, an attempt is made to
remind the reader of the relevant elements of the REF that are being evaluated

in each section. I strive to marshal a "critical mass" of data supporting my observations and conclusions, but I recognize and point out areas where the documentary evidence is thin and certain hypotheses cannot be evaluated in a rigorous manner.

II.   Iran 1946

Overview

One popular interpretation of the events in northern Iran during 1946 argues that U.S. resolve in the face of Soviet intransigence produced the first American victory of the Cold War (Sheehan, 1968, pp. 27–34). A second interpretation, based on extensive archival research, suggests that public confrontation combined with back room negotiation and appeasement resulted in a brief respite for Iran in its efforts to retain its sovereignty in the midst of a great power competition over its strategic resources (Herrmann and Fischerkeller, 1996; Kuniholm, 1980). As a participant in this case, President Truman clearly favored the first interpretation (Truman, 1956, pp. 93–96), while more recently the scholarly community has come to accept the latter. As the following discussion suggests, I trust the historical accuracy of the recent studies, but am more interested in the processes that produced the "lessons" that President Truman and his advisers gleaned from these events. For the major lesson of Iran—that U.S. resolve could contain and even rollback Soviet aggression—shaped the future of the Cold War and presaged interventions in Greece, Korea, Laos, and Vietnam. Iran in 1946 marked the end of cooperation between the World War II allies and opened the era of confrontation between the United States and Soviet Union.

For some time prior to World War II, Iran was the arena where British and Russian imperial ambitions clashed (see Van Wagenen, 1952, pp. 6–16). But as World War II began, the Iranian government proclaimed its neutrality in the hopes of maintaining a mutually beneficial trading relationship with Germany (Lenczowski, 1968, p. 167). This arrangement was successful until June of 1941—when Germany attacked the Soviet Union. As Britain allied itself with the Soviet Union against the Nazis, the significance of Iran as a path for British aid to the Soviets rose rapidly. Thus, Iran's close relationship with Germany was highlighted as evidence of partiality. In August, British and Soviet diplomatic notes demanded "the expulsion of a large number of Germans" (Lenczowski, 1968, p. 168). When the Iranians rejected the allies' notes and defended their neutrality, they were invaded by Soviet troops from the north and British troops from the south. On August 28, the Shah appointed a new Iranian premier who immediately ordered the Iranian army to "cease resistance" (which had been quite weak, Lenczowski, 1968, p. 169). In September, the allies coerced Shah Reza into abdicating, he was replaced by his son—Mohammed Reza Pahlavi (Lenczowski, 1968, p. 174). By the late fall of 1941, the Iranian government was in control of only two cities—Teheran and Meshed.

On January 29, 1942, Britain, the Soviet Union, and Iran signed a "Tripartite Treaty of Alliance" to provide a legal basis for the allied occupation. This treaty allowed the allies to maintain troops on Iranian soil to "defend Iran from aggression on the part of Germany or any other power" (Lenczowski, 1968, p. 175), but the troops were not to be viewed as an "occupation" force. The allies were also given unlimited access to transport and communication facilities in Iran to facilitate the flow of material aid to the Soviets (Van Wagenen, 1952, p. 17). Despite the fairly one-sided character of this agreement, the allies did agree to "respect the territorial integrity, sovereignty and political independence of Iran" (quoted in Lenczowski, 1968, p. 175). They also specified that "the forces of the Allied Powers shall be withdrawn from Iranian territory not later than six months after all hostilities between the Allied Powers and Germany and her associates have been suspended by the conclusion of an armistice or armistices, or on the conclusion of peace between them, whichever date is the earlier" (quoted in Van Wagenen, 1952, p. 17). It was the withdrawal clause of this treaty that would later cause interpretive disagreements.

The U.S. role in Iran began to increase after the allied occupation. In 1942 Dr. Arthur C. Millspaugh was asked by the Iranian government for assistance in managing its public finances. Though Millspaugh was not an employee of the U.S. government, he actively conferred with State Department officials. By 1943 Millspaugh was able to "fill responsible positions in the Iranian government" with over a dozen Americans (see Lenczowski, 1968, p. 264). Also in 1943, Colonel H. Norman Schwarzkopf was sent to Iran to aid in the reorganization of the *gendarmerie* (provincial police). Schwarzkopf's five years of service in Iran were termed an "outstanding success," he was probably the most influential of U.S. advisers in Iran during this period (Lenczowski, 1968, p. 272). Again, during 1942–1943, some 30,000 U.S. troops were deployed to Iran to "speed up supplies to Russia" (Lenczowski, 1968, p. 273). These troops provided technical assistance in the British zone: maintaining and constructing harbors, highways, railways, and airports. While British troops provided security, the U.S. Persian Gulf Command (PGC) constructed the infrastructure that allowed massive quantities of material to reach the Soviet Union (Lenczowski, 1968, p. 273). Clearly, by 1943 the United States had become the third major power in Iran.[3]

The increasing U.S. role in Iran was publicly affirmed in the "Declaration on Iran" signed in Teheran by Roosevelt, Churchill, and Stalin in November of 1943. The United States was not a signatory to the original tripartite treaty (discussed above), so the declaration on Iran was the first public statement of U.S. support for the 1942 agreement (Van Wagenen, 1952, p. 19). By signing this declaration, the United States "reaffirmed Iran's independence, sovereignty, and territorial integrity" (Lenczowski, 1968, p. 176). This statement was undoubtedly a partial reward for Iran's recent (September) declaration of war against Germany, but it also acted as a "moral obligation" guiding U.S. policy in 1946 (Van Wagenen, 1952, p. 19). The "Declaration on Iran" later provided the foundation for U.S. support of Iran in the United Nations.

A preview of the events of 1946 took place in the fall of 1944. As World War II began only two foreign oil concessions were in effect: the Anglo-Iranian Oil Company (AIOC, a joint Iranian-British group) operated a concession in southwestern Iran, while the Kavir-i-Khurian Company (a joint Iranian-Soviet group) operated a concession in northern Iran (Lenczowski, 1968, p. 216). In the spring of 1944, Standard Vacuum Oil and Sinclair Oil (both U.S. companies) began to negotiate with the Iranian government for an oil concession in Baluchistan (southern Iran). The Iranians hired two U.S. petroleum geologists to "survey the oil reserves in various parts of the country" (Lenczowski, 1968, p. 216). Fearful of being excluded from these negotiations, the Soviets sent the People's Commissar for Foreign Affairs Sergei I. Kavtaradze to Teheran to negotiate a new concession for northern Iran. In order to avoid a political dispute over the concessions, the Iranian government announced in October that it would "terminate all negotiations until after the war" (Van Wagenen, 1952, p. 20). The Kavtaradze mission was not satisfied with this outcome, and sought to discredit the Iranian government, suggesting that "British and American influence stood behind Iran's refusal" (Lenczowski, 1968, p. 221). In the face of this pressure, the Sa'ed government fell on November 8 and a new government led by Morteza Quli Bayat was expected to give in to the Soviet demands. In order to prevent this concession, Majlis (Iranian Parliament) member Dr. Mohammed Mossadegh introduced a law prohibiting cabinet members from negotiating foreign oil concessions without previous Majlis approval (Lenczowski, 1968, p. 222). On December 2, Mossadegh's law was adopted by the Majlis, and on December 9, Kavtaradze left Teheran in protest. On his departure, Kavtaradze "told the press that Iran would some day repent of this decision not to negotiate" (Van Wagenen, 1952, p. 20). Despite Mossadegh's clever maneuvering, the oil concession issue would achieve great significance in the events of 1946.

As the tension over the oil "crisis" of 1944 died down, the Iranian government began to draw attention to incidents of Soviet interference in Iranian internal affairs (see FRUS, 1969a, pp. 359–361). At the same time, the importance of Iran as a supply path to the Soviet Union was declining (starting in November of 1944 the Black Sea was open to Allied shipping, Lenczowski, 1968, p. 284). Thus, at the Yalta conference in February of 1945, the issues of troop withdrawals and oil concessions were raised by the United States and Britain during the "Foreign Secretaries" meetings (FRUS, 1969a, p. 362). Given the diminishing importance of Iran for the European war effort, British Foreign Secretary Anthony Eden proposed that "Allied troops begin withdrawal from Iran *pari passu* (at an equal rate) before hostilities ended" (Kuniholm, 1980, p. 215). Despite U.S. support for the Eden proposal, V. M. Molotov, People's Commissar for Foreign Affairs of the Soviet Union, refused to discuss these issues and kept Iran off the agenda of the "Big Three" (FRUS, 1969a, pp. 362–363).

While the German army was desperately defending Berlin and the European war was coming to an end, the Iranian government continued to protest Soviet restrictions on Iranian troop movements (see FRUS, 1969a, pp. 367–368). On May 19, eleven days after V-E day, the Iranian government sent notes to the U.S., British, and Soviet ambassadors requesting the withdrawal of allied troops based on the "spirit" of the Tripartite Treaty of 1942 (FRUS, 1969a, pp. 370–372; Kuniholm, 1980, p. 271). In reply to the Iranian note, the British again put forth the proposal for a *pari passu* withdrawal (FRUS, 1969a, p. 377). The Soviets ignored the British plan, and so at Potsdam Eden suggested a three-stage withdrawal: first from Teheran, then from all of Iran except for a British enclave around Abadan and a Soviet zone in northern Iran, and finally from all of Iran (Kuniholm, 1980, p. 272). Stalin rejected the full withdrawal of Soviet troops before the deadline set by the 1942 treaty,[4] but accepted a limited withdrawal from Teheran and agreed to the consideration of the troop withdrawal issue at the London Council of Foreign Ministers meeting set for September (FRUS, 1969a, p. 388; Kuniholm, 1980, p. 273). At the close of the discussion on Iran at Potsdam, Stalin is reported to have told Truman: "So as to rid the United States of any worries we promise you that no action will be taken by us against Iran" (quoted in Kuniholm, 1980, p. 273). Obviously, the Iranians were less than satisfied with the outcome of the Potsdam meetings (see FRUS, 1969a, p. 389).

In late August of 1945, the Iranian government was given another cause for concern. An armed uprising in Azerbaijan, although of limited duration, was supported by Soviet propaganda and protected by Soviet troops (see FRUS, 1969a, p. 400; Kuniholm, 1980, pp. 274–275; Lenczowski, 1968, pp. 286–287). This period also witnessed the creation of the "Democratic Party of Azerbaijan" led by Ja'afar Pishevari. Pishevari had played a role in various communist enterprises in the Middle East during the 1920s, returning to Iran in 1936 (Lenczowski, 1968, p. 224). This "Democratic Party" absorbed the Tudeh party in northern Iran, forming a left-leaning Azeri-nationalist party with pro-communist sympathies (FRUS, 1969a, p. 407; Kuniholm, 1980, p. 274). Frustrated by Soviet interference, the Iranian government again requested the withdrawal of allied troops. On September 9, seven days after the end of the war with Japan, the Iranian minister for foreign affairs stressed that all allied troops must be withdrawn from Iran by March 2, 1946 (FRUS, 1969a, pp. 408–409). At the London Council of Foreign Ministers meeting, Molotov rejected a British proposal for an early withdrawal, but agreed that March 2, 1946 was the date set by the provisions of the 1942 treaty (FRUS, 1969a, pp. 413–415). The Iranian government now looked forward to the return of its sovereignty (FRUS, 1969a, pp. 408–409).

The situation in Iran erupted on November 19 when the "Democratic Party of Azerbaijan" took control of the province (see FRUS, 1969a, pp. 430–431; Kuniholm, 1980, pp. 278–280; Lenczowski, 1968, pp. 288–289). When Soviet authorities refused to allow the movement of an Iranian force to put down the uprising, the issue of allied troop withdrawals gained even greater importance (Kuniholm, 1980, p. 279). After numerous Iranian appeals for assistance, a U.S. note was delivered to Molotov detailing the U.S. government's understanding of the situation and suggesting that "it would be in the common interest for all Soviet, British, and American troops to be withdrawn immediately from Iran" (FRUS, 1969a, p. 449). The Soviets replied that the U.S. interpretation of the situation did not "correspond to reality," and that the Soviets had restricted the movement of Iranian troops to preserve order and assure the "security of Soviet garrison" (FRUS, 1969a, p. 468). The Soviets refused to reconsider the deadline for troop withdrawals and the stage was set for a contentious ministerial conference in Moscow (Kuniholm, 1980, p. 282). By the time U.S. Secretary of State James F. Byrnes left for Moscow, a "National Assembly" dominated by the "Democratic Party of Azerbaijan" had named Pishevari as the new premier of the autonomous "Republic of Azerbaijan" (Kuniholm, 1980, p. 282).

From December of 1945 to December of 1946, President Truman and his advisers faced two major decision periods affecting U.S. policy toward Iran. During the initial period of December 1945 through May 1946, the president and his advisers decided to support Iran's efforts to secure the withdrawal of allied troops in accordance with the Tripartite Treaty of 1942. During the period from the departure of the last Soviet troops from northern Iran in late May to December of 1946, the president and his advisers decided to support Iran's efforts to eliminate the Pishevari-led resistance movement in Azerbaijan. During the first decision period, U.S. efforts were limited to diplomatic bluster and small-scale gunboat diplomacy. During the latter decision period, U.S. efforts were extended to confidential assurances of U.S. support, should the Soviets intervene, and to a decision to sell a limited amount of military material to the Iranian army. The discussion that follows highlights the attributes of the situation that constrained the U.S. response in the first decision period, and reinforced the U.S. commitment in the latter period.

Aspiration Level

As noted in chapter two, the president's "aspiration level" is expected to comprise a set of minimum level goals that the president hopes to achieve or surpass. In order to evaluate hypothesis 1 (*presidents tend to evaluate outcomes relative to an aspiration level rather than an overall value level*), we must infer the elements of President Truman's aspiration level (regarding Iran) from the documentary record. We need to find descriptions of acceptable/ desirable outcomes/objectives in this case. Thus, we need to find relevant documents that address Truman's goals, desires, hopes, needs, and/or requirements in this case.[5]

Based on the evidence presented below, I believe that President Truman's immediate goal in Iran was to secure the withdrawal of the allied (particularly Soviet) troops and end the autonomy movement in Azerbaijan, thus reestablishing Iran's sovereignty in accordance with the Tripartite Treaty of 1942 and the Declaration on Iran of 1943. The means available for achieving this goal were constrained by the fear of potential Soviet reactions to U.S. initiatives and a concern regarding the resolve of the Iranian government. The president's commitment to achieving or surpassing his immediate goal was reinforced by his desire to demonstrate that the World War II Allies would not trespass on the rights of smaller states; by his fear that communist success in Iran would lead to the fall of Turkey or Greece; and by his desire to prevent the Soviets from dominating Iran's strategic resources (particularly oil). This complex combination of goals and constraints formed the aspiration level that guided Truman's decision making in this case. President Truman's aspiration level was well articulated and the documentary evidence supports REF hypothesis 1.

President Truman's immediate goal in Iran was based, in part, on his desire to eliminate the spheres of influence that had dominated the Middle East prior to World War II. At the end of 1944, the State Department advocated a number of "political objectives of the United States in the Middle East" including the preservation "of the right of peoples to choose and maintain for themselves the types of political, social and economic systems they desire" (FRUS, 1969a, p. 34). By the end of 1945, Loy Henderson, director of the Office of Near Eastern and African Affairs (NEA), provided a background memorandum for the President detailing a "more active" U.S. policy emphasizing the promotion of Western democratic traditions (FRUS, 1969a, p. 11). And yet ironically, just prior to the uprising in Azerbaijan, President Truman "agreed that there was no reason for a conflict between Russia and the United States" in the Middle East (FRUS, 1969a, p. 16). As long as the Soviets lived up to their treaty commitments, the president was willing to accept a Soviet role in the region.

Clearly, the president's immediate goal was also derived from the "moral obligation" of the 1943 Declaration on Iran (Van Wagenen, 1952, p. 19). In that agreement Roosevelt, Churchill, and Stalin voiced their "desire for the maintenance of the independence, sovereignty and territorial integrity of Iran" (quoted in Lenczowski, 1968, p. 323). The president was reminded of Roosevelt's commitment by the Shah in a letter presented to Truman on November 29, 1945 (see FRUS, 1969a, pp. 405–406). One week later, Secretary Byrnes "reiterated America's pledge to observe the Declaration Regarding Iran" (Kuniholm, 1980, p. 281). This public support for the Declaration on Iran was mirrored in the diplomatic correspondence between Ambassador Averell Harriman and Molotov. The U.S. note of November 23, 1945 stated: "This Government has entire confidence that the Governments of the Soviet Union and Great Britain are just as zealous as the Government of the United States meticulously to abide by the assurances contained in this declaration" (FRUS, 1969a, p. 449). The U.S. government would not accept the division of Iran. Having succumbed to Soviet pressure regarding Eastern Europe and the Balkans, President Truman and his advisers concluded by the end of 1945 that they could "compromise no more" (Kuniholm, 1980, p. 298).[6]

While the documentary record suggests that President Truman's immediate goal was to preserve the territorial integrity and sovereignty of Iran, it
also reveals that the means available for achieving this goal were constrained
by the fear of potential Soviet reactions to U.S. initiatives and a concern
regarding the resolve of the Iranian government. Despite President
Truman's desire to secure the withdrawal of the Soviet troops in northern
Iran, his in-theater military capabilities to deal with the situation were
almost nonexistent. By December of 1945, the U.S. ambassador notified the
secretary of state that some 75,000 Soviet combat troops were in northern
Iran, compared to 5,000 British "and less than 6,000 non-combat Americans
in southwestern Iran" (FRUS, 1969a, p. 482). These Soviet troops had
spent five years fortifying their positions and developing defense plans.
Indeed, during the height of the "crisis" in Iran (roughly March 2–April 4,
1946), somewhere between 200 and 500 Soviet tanks along with cannons,
anti-aircraft guns, and hundreds of trucks entered northern Iran (see
Kuniholm, 1980, p. 319; Rossow, 1956, pp. 20–21). While Secretary Byrnes'
initial reaction to the Soviet troop movements was "now we'll give it to
them with both barrels" (FRUS, 1969b, p. 347), Charles Bohlen (Acheson's
Special Assistant) advised against a forceful confrontation. Bohlen argued
that "the United States was in no position to confront the Soviet Union in
Iran" and that "the Soviet Union would consider any strong action a bluff"
(Kuniholm, 1980, p. 322). It was during this latter time period that Stalin
and Molotov reportedly told the Iranian Premier (Qavam), "We don't care
what US and Britain think and we are not afraid of them" (FRUS, 1969b,
p. 352). Even after the withdrawal of Soviet troops in late May, a State
Department policy paper stated that U.S. "military policy does not at this
time contemplate the use of force to achieve our objectives in Iran" (FRUS,
1969b, p. 508). In the spring of 1946, the United States was not in a position to physically compel the Soviets to withdraw from northern Iran.

A second constraint on the means available for achieving the president's
immediate goal was a concern regarding the resolve of the Iranian government. Throughout the period under examination, a delicate diplomatic
game was played between the United States and Iran. On their part, the
Iranian government expressed a determination to stand firm "so long as it
can count on American and British support" (FRUS, 1969a, p. 491).
Particularly as they prepared their case for the UN Security Council meeting in London, the Iranian government sought concrete assurances of U.S.
support (FRUS, 1969b, pp. 292–293). The United States, on the other hand,
expressed a concern that the Iranians would not persevere in their efforts in
the face of Soviet pressure. This concern increased when Qavam Saltaneh
became the new Iranian premier on January 27, 1946 (see Lenczowski,
1968, p. 295). Qavam hoped to settle the situation through direct negotiation. Against the advice of the U.S. ambassador, Qavam personally led
the Iranian delegation to Moscow (FRUS, 1969b, p. 331). Upon his return
to Teheran without an agreement, Qavam alternately conferred with the
Soviet and U.S. ambassadors. It was during this period of intense pressure

that "the prime minister's determination to press his case wavered, first in one direction and then another" (Kuniholm, 1980, p. 327). The inconsistency of Iranian resolve was also highlighted by a split between the Iranian ambassador (Hussein Ala) and Qavam. Ala, directly influenced by the U.S. delegation to the UN,[7] continued to press the Iranian case in late March while Qavam used an apparent split with his interpreter (Muzaffar Firuz) to confuse his position in Teheran (Kuniholm, 1980, p. 327). Finally, in a complex analysis of the situation in Iran, U.S. Ambassador Wallace Murray argued that Qavam's proposed concessions to the Soviets were acceptable because neither government (Iranian or American) possessed the resolve to push the Soviets further (FRUS, 1969b, pp. 373–375). In essence, the United States was not willing to be "more Iranian than the Iranians." Since the battle over Soviet troop withdrawal was largely fought through public diplomacy and public opinion, President Truman and his advisers could not take the matter further without Iranian support.

In considering the factors reinforcing Truman's commitment to achieving or surpassing his immediate goal, we must first examine the president's desire to demonstrate that the World War II allies would not trespass on the rights of smaller states. In discussing the events regarding Iran in his memoirs, President Truman wrote: "What perturbed me most, however, was Russia's callous disregard of the rights of a small nation and of her own solemn promises. International co-operation was impossible if national obligations could be ignored and the U.N. bypassed as if it did not exist" (1956, p. 95). Indeed, in requesting U.S. assistance after the uprising in Azerbaijan, the Iranian charge d'affaires noted that:

> If the United States Government remains quiescent while the Soviet Union carries out what seems to be a carefully laid plan to deprive Iran of its independence or to infringe upon its integrity, *no small country in the world can in the future have any confidence in promises made by the Great Powers. There is no small country which has been given more assurances with regard to its independence by responsible Great Powers than Iran. If these promises are not lived up to, there can be little hope for world stability.* (FRUS, 1969a, p. 435, emphasis added)

This sentiment was also expressed in the U.S. notes to the Soviets on November 23, 1945 and March 6, 1946 (see above discussion; FRUS, 1969a, pp. 449–450; FRUS, 1969b, pp. 340–342). By early 1946, the president had come to the conclusion that the Soviets could not be trusted to live up to their treaty commitments. In a letter to Secretary Byrnes on January 5, the president detailed recent "outrages" in Eastern Europe and indicated that he was "tired of babying the Soviets" (quoted in Kuniholm, 1980, p. 297).[8] Iran would become a test of the durability of the World War II alliance and of UN mechanisms for protecting the rights of smaller nations (Hess, 1974, p. 129).

A second factor reinforcing Truman's commitment to achieving or surpassing his immediate goal was his fear that communist success in Iran would lead to the fall of Turkey or Greece. Of the three U.S. interests in Iran that President Truman discussed in his memoirs, "one was the security of Turkey" (1956, p. 95). The president wrote that: "Russia had been pressing Turkey for special privileges and for territorial concessions for several months. The Turks had resisted all these demands, but their position would be infinitely more difficult if Russia, or a Russian puppet state, were able to outflank her in the east" (1956, p. 95). In Truman's January 1946 letter to Secretary Byrnes, the president stated: "There isn't a doubt in my mind that Russia intends an invasion of Turkey and the seizure of the Black Sea Straits to the Mediterranean. Unless Russia is faced with an iron fist and strong language, another war is in the making. Only one language do they understand—'how many divisions have you?' " (quoted in Kuniholm, 1980, p. 297). While the president was not yet fully seized by the "domino thinking" that would affect U.S. policy toward Greece (see section III later), he was surrounded by advisers who were slowly developing that perspective. George Kennan's famous "long telegram" was received on February 22, 1946, immediately prior to the "crisis" period in Iran. Kennan stressed that "wherever it is considered timely and promising, efforts will be made to advance official limits of Soviet power" (FRUS, 1969c, p. 701). He argued further that the "Soviets are still by far the weaker force" and that they "can easily withdraw . . . when strong resistance is encountered at any point" (FRUS, 1969c, p. 707).

Ambassador Ala in December of 1945 had suggested to Dean Acheson that "Azerbaijan was only the first move in a series which would include Turkey and other countries in Near East" and might prove to be the "first shot fired in third world war" (FRUS, 1969a, p. 508). As Soviet troops poured into Azerbaijan in early March of 1946, it appeared as if Ala's prediction might prove to be accurate. The U.S. vice consul at Tabriz (Robert Rossow) barraged the State Department with reports of Soviet activities, suggesting that the "Soviets are preparing for major military operations" (FRUS, 1969b, p. 343). A map prepared by the State Department's NEA Office revealed that the Soviet troops were not only heading for Teheran, but also toward Turkey and Iraq (see Kuniholm, 1980, p. 322). After delivering a strong U.S. protest to the Soviets on March 9, Kennan tried to calm some of the fears that he had inspired with his "long telegram." He argued that "there is not sufficient evidence here for concluding that present Sov military preparations in northern Iranian sector envisage an immediate attack on Turkey" (FRUS, 1969b, p. 363). He offered a complex analysis of Soviet strategic and tactical thinking, suggesting that they would not "blunder casually into situations" that were "not thought through" (FRUS, 1969b, p. 364). The day following the receipt of Kennan's cable, Ambassador Ala brought Iran's case before the United Nations while Premier Qavam was negotiating with the Soviet Ambassador in Teheran. While Kennan appeared to be correct in his interpretation of immediate Soviet intentions, Stalin's long-term ambitions regarding Turkey and Greece remained a great concern for President Truman (see Kuniholm, 1980, p. 334; Truman, 1956, p. 96).

The final factor reinforcing Truman's commitment to achieving or surpassing his immediate goal was his desire to prevent the Soviets from dominating Iran's strategic resources (particularly oil). In writing his memoirs, President Truman was quite frank in assessing the importance of oil to his administration's policies toward Iran:

> The second problem was the control of Iran's oil reserves. That Russia had an eye on these vast deposits seemed beyond question. If the Russians were to control Iran's oil, either directly or indirectly, the raw-material balance of the world would undergo a serious change, and it would be a serious loss for the economy of the Western world. (1956, p. 95)

Loy Henderson was particularly concerned with emphasizing the strategic and economic significance of Iran. Henderson stated in his oral history interview that Iran's "independence and territorial integrity were . . . of vital importance, not only to the Western world but to all the peoples who looked to Middle Eastern oil as the source of their energy" (1973, p. 54). Henderson also noted that both Secretary of War Robert D. Patterson and Secretary of the Navy James V. Forrestal agreed that the United States should safeguard its oil supplies (1973, p. 56). Indeed, it appears that Qavam felt that U.S. acceptance of his deal with the Soviets could be bought by oil concessions. On March 23 (1946), he assured the U.S. ambassador that the remainder of the unallocated oil reserves of Baluchistan would go to U.S. companies (FRUS, 1969b, p. 373). Secretary Byrnes forwarded an indignant reply stating bluntly that the United States would not accept a *quid pro quo* agreement of this type.

In the fall of 1946, a Joint Chiefs of Staff (JCS) study reiterated the strategic importance of Iran. Commissioned by the State Department in a "high priority" request (see FRUS, 1969b, p. 515), the report was based on the "assumption that a war with Soviet Russia is a possibility" (FRUS, 1969b, pp. 529–530). It concluded that Iran was "an area of major strategic interest to the United States" because of its strategic position with respect to the Middle East (allowing for defense in depth) and its oil resources (FRUS, 1969b, p. 530). Regarding U.S. policy, the report suggested that the United States should "keep Soviet influence and Soviet armed forces removed as far as possible from oil resources in Iran, Iraq, and the Near and Middle East" (FRUS, 1969b, p. 530). The JCS study advocated the provision of limited military aid to Iran to contribute to its internal stability and to strengthen the central government in its attempt to regain control over Azerbaijan. Less than a week after this report was received by the State Department, Secretary Byrnes approved a more proactive policy in support of the Iranian government (see further discussion below; FRUS, 1969b, pp. 533–536).[9]

Uncertainty and Time Pressure

As noted in chapter two, I expect that *presidential perceptions of high uncertainty and a lack of valid information will interact with presidential risk predispositions and affect the output of the decision process* (REF hypothesis 7). In the Truman cases, if the president perceives high uncertainty and inaccurate information but does not perceive acute time pressure, I expect to observe decisional delay and an expanded search for information (REF hypothesis 7a). If the president perceives high uncertainty and inaccurate information and also perceives acute time pressure, I expect to observe bolstering (REF hypothesis 7c).

As the evidence presented below suggests, President Truman perceived high uncertainty and acute time pressure during the initial decision period (from December of 1945 through May of 1946) and moderate uncertainty and acute time pressure during the latter decision period (from June to December of 1946). During both decision periods, the President faced two major sources of uncertainty: (1) what were Soviet intentions? and (2) what were Iranian intentions? Truman's perception of time pressure during both decision periods was largely determined by reports of events on the ground in Iran. Unfortunately, President Truman's actions during the first decision period do not support REF hypothesis 7c. Despite perceptions of high uncertainty and acute time pressure, I observed little evidence of bolstering. Finally, during the latter decision period, Truman's approval of an incremental escalation runs counter to the REF hypotheses.

The analysis of Soviet motivations and intentions became a major preoccupation for President Truman and his advisers in 1946. Prior to the Azeri uprising in November of 1945, President Truman's advisers suggested that Soviet aims were "limited to maintenance of buffer zone in Iran as protection against attack from south" (FRUS, 1969a, p. 418). The Soviets were expected to follow the pattern established in Eastern Europe: promote a friendly "popular" government in Teheran through intimidation, propaganda, and covert activity (FRUS, 1969a, pp. 418–419). George Kennan offered the analogy of Manchuria—the Soviets might attempt to dominate Azerbaijan and secure its autonomy "through orderly processes of friendly negotiation" (FRUS, 1969a, p. 424). Thus, the only U.S. initiative might be to withdraw U.S. troops from Iran as quickly as possible and hope that the Soviets would follow (see FRUS, 1969a, pp. 425–427). These estimates of Soviet intentions required immediate revision when the Azeri uprising on November 19 was protected by Soviet troops.

The initial interpretation of the events in Azerbaijan suggested that the autonomy movement had "unquestioned Soviet support" (FRUS, 1969a, p. 430). Ambassador Murray reported that the Soviets were "directly responsible for actions of Democratic Party Azerbaijan" and that Russian forces had stopped a column of Iranian troops headed for Tabriz (FRUS, 1969a, pp. 436–437). The secretary of state was reluctant to accept the reports based on Iranian information, so he instructed Murray to obtain a "first-hand report" by an "American official" (FRUS, 1969a, p. 444). This confirmation (by the assistant U.S. military attaché) was received on November 23. Just four hours later, a strong American protest was sent to Ambassador Harriman for delivery to the Soviet government (FRUS, 1969a, pp. 448–450). By November 27, Murray was able to communicate the Soviets' immediate demands: new oil concessions, air transport rights, special rights to the Caspian port of Pahlavi, and the maintenance of the "Astara-Resht-Qazvin" highway (FRUS, 1969a, p. 456). He later reported the Iranian Premier's impression that the "only thing which would satisfy Soviets would be grant of oil concession northern Iran and that any Govt which refused such grant would be branded as hostile to USSR" (FRUS, 1969b, p. 300). The issue of oil concessions was brought back to center stage and the U.S. position in the UN Security Council focused on the Soviet's attempt to coerce the Iranian government.

Despite the new evidence that led others to develop conclusions about Soviet motivations regarding Iran, President Truman was slowly developing his view of the Soviet Union as an unrepentant expansionist power. In early January (1946), the State Department had prepared a report, based on inter-rogations and captured German documents, that detailed Soviet aims in the Near East during the time of the Nazi-Soviet pact (see Kuniholm, 1980, pp. 293–294). This report suggested that strong Soviet claims on Iranian and Turkish territory contributed "to the break between the two countries" (Kuniholm, 1980, p. 294). It was also during January that Truman wrote the letter to Secretary Byrnes (discussed above) detailing his impressions of Soviet intentions regarding Turkey and Iran and indicating that he was "tired of babying the Soviets" (quoted in Kuniholm, 1980, p. 297). Truman's grow-ing distrust of the Soviets was aggravated by Stalin's speech of February 9. Stalin discussed the "capitalist encirclement" of the Soviet Union and announced a new five-year plan emphasizing "rearmament and munitions production" (Kuniholm, 1980, pp. 309–310). When asked to analyze Stalin's speech, Kennan responded with his long telegram describing Soviet moti-vations and intentions (see discussion above; FRUS, 1969c, pp. 696–709). Finally, on February 28, Secretary Byrnes spoke before the Overseas Press Club in New York. In this speech (described as "virtually an ultimatum," Jones, 1955, p. 53), Byrnes indicated the U.S. government's intention to abide by the UN charter and ensure that other great powers live up to their treaty commitments. On March 16, during another speech in New York, Byrnes suggested that "should the occasion arise, our military strength will be used to support the purposes and principles of the Charter" (Jones, 1955, p. 55). It was within this context of growing distrust that President Truman and his advisers interpreted Soviet troop movements into Azerbaijan in early March.

As briefly noted above, the initial reports from the U.S. Vice Consul at Tabriz (Rossow) argued that the Soviets were "preparing for major military operations" (FRUS, 1969b, p. 343). Great importance was attached to the fact that Soviet Army Commander, General Ivan Bagramian (a specialist in tank warfare), had "taken command of Soviet troops in Azerbaijan" (FRUS, 1969b, p. 342). The president's State Department advisers concluded that "the USSR was adding military invasion to political subversion in Iran" (FRUS, 1969b, p. 347), and also that "the United States was in no position to confront the Soviet Union in Iran" (Kuniholm, 1980, p. 322). As Secretary Byrnes prepared for his battles with Ambassador Gromyko in the UN Security Council, Kennan attempted to calm some of the administration's fears: arguing that the Soviets were not about to invade Turkey and that they had not yet decided to "forego all advantages of further cooperation with western world and to enter on path of complete defiance and armed isolation" (FRUS, 1969b, pp. 363–364). When Qavam approached Ambassador Murray to solicit U.S. approval of Iranian oil concessions to the Soviets, Byrnes indicated that "we are not in a position, in view of uncertainty of course of events in Iran, to give you definite instructions" (FRUS, 1969b, p. 375). Clearly during this period, President Truman and his advisers were highly uncertain of Soviet motivations and intentions regarding Iran. Were they dealing with an aggressive adversary bent on military expansion or a defensive (but coercive) government desiring equal rights to Iranian oil? These competing analyses of Soviet motivations were both partially supported by the available evidence.

In the latter decision period (June–December 1946), President Truman and his advisers were more certain of Soviet motivations and intentions. Once the Soviets withdrew their troops from Iran in late May, President Truman became convinced that the Soviets would follow the strategy ascribed to them in September/October of 1945. The Soviets would use intimidation, propaganda, and covert action in Azerbaijan to achieve their objectives. This perception of Soviet intentions was supported by Ambassador Allen's description of Soviet pressure on Qavam during his negotiations with Pishevari. In mid-May the Soviet ambassador told Qavam that "he was afraid Qavam's continued failure to reach agreement with Azerbaijan would result in 'iron and blood' " (FRUS, 1969b, p. 460). Throughout the summer, Qavam appeared to bend to Soviet pressure—concluding a deal with Pishevari and then including Tudeh members in his cabinet (see Lenczowski, 1968, pp. 301–303). The Shah became dissatisfied with Qavam's "passive policy" and asked for U.S. support to "counteract Soviet penetration" (FRUS, 1969b, p. 486). In early October, the Shah forced Qavam to remove the Tudeh members from his cabinet and by late November the United States was pledging moral, economic, and military support to Iran (see FRUS, 1969b, pp. 546–547). By November, the president and his advisers had concluded that the Soviets would not support the Azeri separatists and so encouraged Qavam to send troops into northern Iran. If the Soviets did react to the Iranian troop movements, the United States would "give its unqualified support to Iran" (FRUS, 1969b, p. 552). When the Azeris were routed and the Soviets did not interfere, Ambassador Allen argued that the "Soviets were finally convinced that US was not bluffing and would support any United Nations member threatened by aggression" (FRUS, 1969b,

p. 563). Truman felt vindicated—when the Soviets encountered strength, they backed down (see Truman, 1956, pp. 95–96).

The second major source of uncertainty for President Truman and his advisers was the question of Iranian intentions. Throughout the first decision period, the administration feared Iranian capitulation to Soviet demands. In early January of 1946, not only were the Soviets pressuring Premier Ebrahim Hakimi, but it also appeared that the British were "preparing make tacit deal leaving Soviets free hand in north while they consolidate British position in south" (FRUS, 1969b, p. 300). When Qavam became the Iranian premier in late January, the administration became concerned that he would make a deal with the Soviets (see Lenczowski, 1968, pp. 295–296).[10] Qavam told the U.S. ambassador that "he believed . . . Iranian difficulties with Soviets all date from oil crisis of late 1944" (FRUS, 1969b, p. 315) and indicated that he was willing to send a special mission to Moscow. Ignoring Ambassador Murray's advice, Qavam led the delegation and was personally pressured by Stalin and Molotov (Kuniholm, 1980, p. 314). George Kennan was uncertain of Qavam's ability to withstand the pressure and so was happily surprised when Qavam indicated that he had rejected the Soviet proposals and was leaving Moscow (FRUS, 1969b, p. 338). Upon returning to Teheran, Qavam was pressured by Ambassador Murray—to press Iran's case before the UN, and by Soviet Ambassador Ivan Sadchikov—to continue bilateral negotiations (FRUS, 1969b, p. 361). At this point Qavam wavered, sending contradictory instructions to Ambassador Ala and damaging Iran's case before the Security Council (see Kuniholm, 1980, p. 327). Caught between the United States and the Soviet Union, Qavam's intentions shifted based on the last ambassador he had met.[11] In early April, Qavam signed an agreement with Sadchikov that appeased the Soviets while Secretary Byrnes declared victory in the UN (based on the Soviet contention that their upcoming troop withdrawal would be unconditional) (see Kuniholm, 1980, p. 332). During this period, Iran was clearly an unreliable partner, but then again, so was the United States.

Qavam's shifting loyalties also raised questions during the second decision period. When the new U.S. ambassador, George V. Allen, arrived in Iran on May 8, it became clear that Qavam and the Shah did not see eye to eye. Qavam wished to win back Azerbaijan through "pacific penetration" while the Shah insisted on sending Iranian troops to the region (FRUS, 1969b, p. 454). In the short term, Qavam won the policy dispute: he negotiated an agreement with the Azeri separatists, founded his own political party,[12] and made concessions to the Tudeh party (see Kuniholm, 1980, pp. 348–349). While Ambassador Allen defended Qavam's policies, Rossow argued that Qavam had lost control of the situation (see FRUS, 1969b, pp. 510–511). In early October, as Qavam contemplated a more aggressive policy toward Azerbaijan, Loy Henderson argued that the Iranian premier was "following a pro-Soviet course of action" because of the lack of U.S. assurances of support (FRUS, 1969b, p. 524). As President Truman and his advisers considered the extension of moral, military, and economic support for Qavam's government, they were not certain of Qavam's intentions. Was he a patriot cleverly acting in Iran's best interest or was he a naive optimist giving in to Soviet demands?

Largely due to inflammatory reports from State Department officials in Iran, the president and his advisers perceived acute time pressure during the two decision periods. During the first decision period, urgent cables from Rossow and Murray and reports from Henderson and his NEA staff encouraged their superiors to act. In January, Rossow wrote that "unless some sort of energetic action is soon taken Azerbaijan must be written off" (FRUS, 1969b, p. 299). In early February, he reported an intensification in the rhetoric of the Pishevari regime in Azerbaijan as it called for a "Jihad" (FRUS, 1969b, p. 332). In March, Rossow called attention to the Soviet troop movements and, in a flourish meant to convey the seriousness of the situation, suggested that communications with him might be "cut at any moment" (FRUS, 1969b, p. 345). The Iranians were also contributing to the sense of growing time pressure. On March 5, Ambassador Ala reported that Qavam had officially protested the presence of Soviet troops and "would welcome and appreciate American intervention at this critical juncture" (FRUS, 1969b, p. 339). These reports certainly had an impact—triggering meetings in the State Department and the transmission of two protest notes to the Soviet Union (although they did not alter the administration's strategy of dealing with the situation through the UN Security Council, see FRUS, 1969b, pp. 346–347; Hess, 1974, p. 135). For the participants, the period of early March to early April represented the pinnacle (in terms of uncertainty and time pressure) of the Iran "crisis" (see Truman, 1956, pp. 94–96).[13] President Truman became personally involved in the decisions regarding Iran and Secretary Byrnes led the U.S. delegation to the UN himself. A "war scare" flared in the press and a *New York Times* editorial asked, "Where does the search for security end and where does expansion begin?" (quoted in Kuniholm, 1980, p. 325).

During the second decision period, reports from Ambassador Allen in Iran and Loy Henderson in Washington contributed to President Truman's perception of acute time pressure. In August, Allen reported that the situation was "gloomy but by no means desperate" (FRUS, 1969b, p. 511), Qavam's deal with Pishevari had fallen through and the Iranians were once again turning to the United States for assurances of support (FRUS, 1969b, pp. 511–512). In late September, the Ambassador had a new cause for concern—the British were inciting a revolt in southern Iran and appeared to be leaning toward a "spheres of influence" settlement (FRUS, 1969b, p. 516). When Qavam requested direct U.S. military and economic aid, Allen passed on the Iranian premier's proposal (FRUS, 1969b, pp. 519–520), but Secretary Byrnes was not yet convinced of the severity of the situation and deferred the decision regarding military aid (FRUS, 1969b, p. 521). On October 8, Loy Henderson conveyed his support for Qavam's request indicating that, "we feel that the situation is critical and that we should do everything within our power to prevent Iran from slipping into the Soviet orbit" (FRUS, 1969b, p. 524). On October 18, Henderson attempted to force a decision, arguing that: "we are faced at the present time . . . with an extremely critical situation in Iran which may require quick action on our part" and that "Iran is daily losing what remains of its independence" (FRUS, 1969b, p. 534).

Ambassador Allen was notified on November 14 that Secretary Byrnes had tentatively approved Henderson's proposals for aiding Iran (FRUS, 1969b, p. 546). Allen and Henderson had convincingly communicated the importance of U.S. aid to the policy debate between Qavam and the Shah. They had also stressed the need for a quick decision due to the upcoming Iranian elections and plans to send troops into Azerbaijan. Though the aid plan took some time to develop and implement, the announcement of concrete U.S. support buoyed the spirits of Qavam in his confrontation with the Soviets and Azeri separatists. By December 12, Allen could report that the "war is over" in Azerbaijan (FRUS, 1969b, p. 560).

Consideration of Alternatives and Final Decision

As noted in chapter two, I expect that President Truman (identified as a potential-motivated president) will tend to focus on best-case outcomes and maximum gains when considering alternatives (REF hypothesis 3). I also anticipate that President Truman is likely to behave in a risk-acceptant manner in making final decisions (REF hypothesis 5).[14] In order to evaluate these hypotheses, we must examine the manner in which alternatives were considered, and the decisions that were reached during crucial periods in the cases. For the Iranian case, two periods are worthy of careful scrutiny—December 1945–May 1946 and June–December 1946.

Regrettably, I am unable to test REF hypothesis 3 with direct evidence in this case. As one author has noted: "It is difficult to determine the exact role that Truman played in the Iranian crisis" (Gosnell, 1980, p. 302). President Truman is known to have met several times with Secretary Byrnes during the initial decision period, but there is no documentary record of the president's comments during these meetings (Truman, 1956, pp. 94–95). While Secretary Byrnes and then Under Secretary of State Acheson both note that President Truman was an informed and active participant in the policy deliberations, there is only indirect evidence of the manner in which the president considered alternatives (see Acheson, 1969; Byrnes, 1947, 1958). Unfortunately, this indirect evidence does not appear to support REF hypothesis 3 during the first decision period.

In early March (1946), Charles Bohlen opposed an aggressive U.S. protest of Soviet troop movements in Azerbaijan. His argument focused on the potential costs associated with this alternative and introduced the possibility that "the United States might wind up in a worse position than before" (Kuniholm, 1980, p. 322). Later in March, Ambassador Murray provided his analysis of a potential U.S. decision to accept Qavam's concessions to the Soviets. Murray also considered the negative consequences associated with confrontational actions: "I can see little utility in winning a resounding victory over USSR in SC meeting if it either (a) fails to result in evacuation of Iran or (b) leaves Russians smarting under humiliating defeat and determined to revenge themselves on Iran" (FRUS, 1969b, p. 374). Certainly in the following analysis, Murray was not engaging in "best-case" thinking:"In summary much as I regret possibility that Iran will be forced to pay bribe to secure what should be accorded her automatically as of right, I do not feel that proposed solution is too bad" (FRUS, 1969b, p. 375).This "best of the worst" strategy of selecting alternatives, fits more with the pattern that I observe in the Kennedy administration cases (see chapter four).

There is, however, some indirect evidence supporting REF hypothesis 3 in the latter decision period. Loy Henderson's memoranda of October 8 and 18 discussed only the positive implications of providing moral, economic, and military aid to Iran (see FRUS, 1969b, pp. 523–525, 533–536). While he elaborated extensively on the negative consequences of the current U.S. policy, he did not attempt to discuss the potential Soviet response to his aid proposal. Henderson argued that the aid plan "might strengthen the hands of this government in its efforts to preserve the independence of Iran and to prevent that country from succumbing to Soviet pressure and thus passing completely into the Soviet orbit of satellite states" (FRUS, 1969b, p. 534).There was no discussion of the negative things that "might" happen if Henderson's aid plan was approved.

In evaluating REF hypothesis 5, we must first consider whether President Truman reached a "final decision" (regarding U.S. intervention) in each decision period. Based on the evidence discussed above, I feel that the president did not reach a "final decision" during the initial period. Qavam's concessions to the Soviets allowed the United States to claim victory in the UN without having to follow through on hollow threats. The president never was forced to make the hard choices that might lead to the loss of Iran or a confrontation with the Soviets. Truman could later claim that U.S. firmness led to the Soviet withdrawal, but undoubtedly Stalin (and certainly Qavam) knew better (Truman, 1956, p. 96).Thus, REF hypothesis 5 cannot be evaluated during this period.

In the latter decision period a "final decision" was reached.The president approved Secretary Byrnes' endorsement of Henderson's proposal and the United States supplied combat arms to Iran. In my view, however, this decision is more accurately explained by REF hypothesis 6—*if there is only one alternative capable of achieving the aspiration level, that alternative is likely to be selected regardless of its level of risk.* By the fall of 1946, Henderson and Allen had become the main administration experts on Iran.They cooperated in developing and justifying Henderson's aid proposal and they did not offer any alternative policies. They suggested that U.S. inaction would lead to Soviet control of Iran and offered the only way to achieve the president's aspiration level.Their policy appeared to be successful when Qavam expressed his thanks by putting down the Azeri rebellion and later leading the political fight to repudiate the April (1946) oil agreement with the Soviets. Of course, the lack of direct evidence of President Truman's role in this period limits the strength of these findings. (A summary of the findings for this case study can be found in table 3.1.)

Table 3.1 Summary of findings for Iran 1946 case study

Aspiration level	
Immediate goal	eliminate the threat posed by the communist guerrillas and secure a noncommunist, democratic, and economically stable ally
Constraints on means	fear of potential Soviet reactions to U.S. initiatives, a concern regarding the overcommitment of U.S. economic and military capabilities, and apprehension about a potential isolationist reaction in congressional and public opinion
Commitment reinforced by	desire to demonstrate that the World War II allies would not trespass on the rights of smaller states, fear that communist success in Iran would lead to the fall of Turkey or Greece, and desire to prevent the Soviets from dominating Iran's strategic resources (particularly oil)
Uncertainty	high during December 1945 to May 1946 period—questions regarding Soviet intentions and fear that Qavam was an unreliable partner
	moderate during June to December 1946 period—convinced that the Soviets would refrain from a direct military confrontation but lingering questions regarding Qavam
Time pressure	acute during final stages of both decision periods—driven by inflammatory cables by State Department officials and by pleas from the Iranian government
Consideration of alternatives	little evidence of focus on best-case outcomes and maximum gains during December 1945 to May 1946 period—analyses by Bohlen and Murray follow "best of worst" strategy of selecting alternatives
	weak evidence of focus on best-case outcomes and maximum gains during June to December 1946 period— Henderson memoranda mainly focus on positive implications of aid package
Final decision	no final decision reached during December 1945 to May 1946 period—Qavam's concessions to Soviets defuse crisis
	weak evidence that final decision reached during June to December 1946 period was support for only alternative under consideration

Epilogue

Clearly, President Truman and his closest advisers viewed the settlement of the Iranian "crisis" as a victory for the United States (see Acheson, 1969, p. 198; Byrnes, 1947, pp. 303–304; Herrmann and Fischerkeller, 1996, p. 156 FN5; Truman, 1956, pp. 95–96). The Soviets pressed where "weakness showed" and U.S. strength pushed them back (Truman, 1956, p. 96). In December of 1946, Ambassador Allen wrote that the collapse of the Azeri separatist regime "was a major victory for UN—and for a firm policy toward USSR" (FRUS, 1969b, p. 566). The lack of Soviet intervention indicated that they were not ready for a "showdown" with the United States (FRUS, 1969b, p. 566). While the facts of the case suggest a second interpretation (focusing on Iranian appeasement), the president's interpretation is important because it influenced his behavior in Greece and Korea. The events in Iran supported Truman's developing image of the Soviet Union and further suggested that the "minds in the Kremlin worked very much as Kennan had predicted they would" (Kuniholm, 1980, p. 398). The "Cold Warriors" in Truman's administration (Acheson, Henderson, and Kennan) "cut their teeth" on Iran and secured their status as experts on Soviet motivations. The World War II alliance had come to its effective end. In the words of Walter Lippmann, the United States and the Soviet Union "had indeed reached the point where it was easier to fail than succeed" (quoted in Hess, 1974, p. 146).[15]

III.   Greece 1947–1948

Overview

The U.S. intervention in the Greek Civil War that began with the announcement of the "Truman Doctrine" on March 12, 1947 was (as Iran) a direct result of the disagreements between the United States and Soviet Union over the settlement of World War II. Unlike Iran, however, the U.S. intervention in Greece was precipitated by the collapse of the British imperial system and the Truman administration's desire to ensure global peace and prosperity (and possibly establish U.S. hegemony). While congressional and public opinion expressed fears of a willingness to pull "British chestnuts out of the fire" (Jones, 1955, p. 139), the Truman administration was developing an aggressive foreign policy of international engagement that provided for U.S. involvement in European economic and political affairs and set the foundation for the Marshall Plan and the North Atlantic Treaty Organization (NATO).

The origins of the Greek Civil War extend (at the least) to the period before World War II when "rightist" and "leftist" groups coalesced during the Metaxas dictatorship (Jones, 1989, p. 17). The devastation wrought by the Nazi occupation of Greece during the war further set the stage for conflict (Kuniholm, 1980, p. 221). Indeed, the Nazis attempted to benefit from the "personal and political rivalries" that divided the partisan groups in Greece (Jones, 1955, p. 69). As the end of the war drew near, the Greek partisans were generally divided between the left-leaning EAM (National Liberation Front, and its People's Army known as ELAS) and the rightist EDES (National Republican League). Between August of 1943 and February of 1944, the "First Round" of conflict between these groups resulted in the partisans fighting one another more often than they engaged the Germans (Kuniholm, 1980, p. 223 FN26).

Throughout World War II, Britain had held a special interest in Greece. King George II of Greece spent the war in London and a number of "royalist politicians" (led by George Papandreou) had established the Greek government in exile in Cairo and had assembled a "Greek Brigade" that fought in Italy (Jones, 1955, pp. 69–70). By August of 1944, the British coerced the EAM into joining the government in exile, thus ensuring the continuation of the Greek monarchy. Fearful of defection by the EAM or EDES, the British occupied Athens and Piraeus in order to provide security for the Greek government and to supervise the demobilization and disarmament of the partisan groups, once the Nazi troops had withdrawn. The friction between the EAM and the royalist government erupted into civil war on December 3, 1944 when Greek police fired on leftist demonstrators (Jones, 1955, p. 71). From December 3 to February 12, the "Second Round" of the Civil War was marked by brutal and bloody fighting in the streets of Athens, until British reinforcements finally forced ELAS troops to flee to the countryside. In late December, Churchill had pushed the Greek king to accept a "regency solution"; and so by February the more liberal-minded government of Nikolaos Plastiras was able to end the "Second Round" by signing the "Varkiza Agreement" with the EAM (Kuniholm, 1980, p. 225). British intervention (amounting to 75,000 troops) contributed to the defeat of the EAM and the momentary stabilization of life, at least in the major Greek cities. And yet through 1945 and 1946 the EAM remained active politically, ELAS once again became a guerrilla force, and the devastation of Greece caused by World War II and the two "rounds" of the Civil War left Greece almost entirely dependent on British economic and military aid.

Article IX of the Varkiza agreement called for a plebiscite to determine whether the public advocated a royalist or republican constitution, it also allowed for a general election of members to the constituent assembly that would draft the new constitution (Kuniholm, 1980, p. 250). Throughout 1945, rightist and leftist political parties debated both the timing and order of the plebiscite and election. Since many of the atrocities committed during the "Second Round" were publicly attributed to ELAS and the EAM, the rightists hoped for early elections to cash-in on favorable public opinion (Jones, 1955, p. 72; Kuniholm, 1980, p. 250). As one Greek government after another considered the election issue, the British enlisted the aid of the United States and France to push the Soviets to accept an early popular election. On March 31, 1946, the general election was held "under the watchful eyes of fifteen hundred American, British, French, and South African official observers" (Jones, 1955, p. 72). Buoyed by the EAM's decision to encourage left-leaning voters to abstain from the election, the Populist Party of Constantine Tsaldaris received a plurality of the votes cast and with its allies controlled 251 seats in the 354-member "revisionary parliament" (Jones, 1989, p. 17; Kuniholm, 1980, p. 353). Despite pressure from the British to form a broad coalition government, Tsaldaris could not reach an agreement with the heads of the more centrist republican parties and instead formed a populist government and announced that the plebiscite would be held on September 1 (see Alexander, 1982, pp. 190–194). The majority of Greeks (officially 68 percent)[16] voting in the plebiscite favored the return of the king, and on September 28, King George returned to Athens (Alexander, 1982, p. 216).[17]

The "Third Round" of the Greek Civil War began (according to popular consensus, see Jones, 1989, p. 18) on March 30, the eve of the general election. In reality, the attack on the village of Litokhoron simply signaled an increase in the guerrilla campaign being mounted by the Greek Communist Party (KKE). As guerrilla attacks continued to increase in the summer of 1946, the Greek government under Tsaldaris was forced to increase expenditures aimed at containing the guerrilla threat. Despite vast aid from the United Nations Relief and Rehabilitation Administration (UNRRA) and the reassuring presence of British troops, the security situation continued to deteriorate and the Greek government faced financial collapse (Jones, 1955, pp. 73–74; Kuniholm, 1980, p. 354). As the situation approached its lowest point, events in Britain caused Prime Minister Clement Atlee's government to reevaluate its role as the Greek patron.

In June of 1946, the British Cabinet had decided that economic and military aid to the Greek government must cease by March 31, 1947 (Alexander, 1982, p. 197). In September, the number of British troops in Greece was reduced to 31,000, "leaving a single division in Macedonia and a brigade in the vicinity of Athens" (Alexander, 1982, p. 214). By October, the British foreign office was actively attempting to persuade the U.S. State Department that American economic aid was necessary to salvage the situation.[18] As the winter of 1946–1947 progressed, the British domestic economy was approaching a crisis of its own. Plagued by huge budget deficits and a "calamitous" coal shortage caused by a brutal winter, Atlee's government embarked on a program to further reduce foreign financial and troop commitments (Jones, 1955, pp. 78–85; see also Jones, 1989, pp. 23–26). This British withdrawal from global commitments was hammered home to the United States on February 21, 1947 when the State Department received an aide-memoire indicating that the British would be unable to provide aid to Greece beyond March 31, 1947, and that "His Majesty's Government trust that the United States Government may find it possible to afford financial assistance to Greece on a scale sufficient to meet her minimum needs, both civil and military" (FRUS, 1971, pp. 34–35).[19]

Neither the deteriorating situation in Greece nor the British government's desire to extricate itself from its commitments to the Greek government were a surprise to Truman administration officials. The February 21 aide-memoire was a "shocker" primarily because it allowed the president and his advisers only six weeks to develop a program of American assistance (Acheson, 1969, p. 217). In fact, the United States had become increasingly involved in Greek affairs: approving an export–import bank loan to Greece in January of 1946, observing the elections in March of that year, sending an economic mission to Athens in January of 1947, and providing the head of the UN Security Council Commission investigating border incidents in Northern Greece (see Jones, 1989, pp. 26–35). As cables from Lincoln MacVeagh, the U.S. ambassador to Greece, indicate, the State Department and the president were well aware of the current situation in Greece in February of 1947 (see FRUS, 1971).

In a matter of days after the receipt of the British aide-memoire, President Truman met with his principal advisers and approved a massive plan to aid Greece and Turkey, both economically and militarily (see Acheson, 1969). After meeting with congressional leaders the president and his advisers concluded that the only way to secure quick passage of the enabling legislation was to appear before a joint session of Congress and launch a massive public information campaign (see Jones, 1955). The "Truman Doctrine" speech boldly set forth the administration's foreign policy vision, frankly stating the dire global situation and the need for U.S. action. On May 22, President Truman signed Public Law 75, which approved approximately $400 million in aid to Greece and Turkey (Kuniholm, 1980, p. 414). And yet, the massive "Truman Doctrine" aid package did not immediately change the fortunes of the Greek government. Between May of 1947 and June of 1948, President Truman would twice consider the dispatch of U.S. troops. In the late summer/early fall of 1947, as the British contemplated the withdrawal of their remaining forces in Greece, President Truman considered the deployment of U.S. ground troops. Under strong pressure from his military advisers to avoid the commitment of significant U.S. forces, Truman approved the expansion of the U.S. military advisory group in Greece and broadened their role to include operational advice to the Greek military (see Jones, 1989, pp. 79–106). Later in December–June of 1948, as the KKE proclaimed a "Free Government" in northern Greece, the president and the National Security Council (NSC) would once again consider the dispatch of U.S. troops. But continued military opposition to further escalation and the first Greek government victories supported by the effective use of U.S. operational advice and weapons (including napalm) encouraged the president to reject escalation for the moment (see Jones, 1989, pp. 137–139). Eventually the massive U.S. aid was too much for the Greek rebels (and their Balkan allies) to counter and President Truman was able to declare victory in a report to Congress in November of 1949.

Aspiration Level

As noted above, the president's "aspiration level" is expected to comprise a set of minimum level goals that the president hopes to achieve or surpass. In order to evaluate hypothesis 1 (*presidents tend to evaluate outcomes relative to an aspiration level rather than an overall value level*), we must infer the elements of President Truman's aspiration level (regarding Greece) from the documentary record. We need to find descriptions of acceptable/desirable outcomes/objectives in this case. Thus, we need to find relevant documents that address Truman's goals, desires, hopes, needs, and/or requirements in this case.

Based on the evidence presented below, I find that President Truman's immediate goal in Greece was to eliminate the threat posed by the communist guerrillas and secure a noncommunist, democratic, and economically stable ally. The means available for achieving this goal were constrained by the fear of potential Soviet reactions to U.S. initiatives, a concern regarding the overcommitment of U.S. economic and military capabilities, and apprehension about a potential isolationist reaction in congressional and public opinion. The president's commitment to achieving or surpassing his immediate goal was reinforced by his fear that communist success in Greece would lead to the fall of France, Italy, Iran, and Turkey; a desire to establish U.S. leadership of the "free world" in the wake of British retreat; and later, by a need to demonstrate the resolve of his administration and the credibility of previous U.S. commitments. This complex combination of goals and constraints formed the aspiration level that guided Truman's decision making in this case. President Truman's aspiration level was well articulated and the documentary evidence supports REF hypothesis 1.

There was almost no disagreement within the Truman administration regarding the immediate goal that should be sought in Greece. In a memorandum to President Truman that accompanied him to the White House on February 26, 1947, Secretary of State George C. Marshall stated that "the collapse of Greece would create a situation threatening to the security of the United States" (FRUS, 1971, p. 58). As early as September of 1946, Secretary of State Byrnes had communicated to his British counterpart, Foreign Secretary Bevin, that "it was essential that the Communists should not get into power in Greece. This must be avoided at all costs. He did not mind how it was done. We must keep our eye very closely on Greece" (quoted in Alexander, 1982, p. 193). One must recall the context in which Greek events took place: the contest over political influence in Eastern Europe had been won by the Soviets, and yet Truman's "get-tough" battleship diplomacy in Turkey and Iran (see section II above) had halted communist expansion (see Barnet, 1968, pp. 103–104). By 1947, President Truman had adopted the view that communist expansion must be stopped in Europe,[20] and, importantly, that it *could* be stopped by an aggressive U.S. foreign policy.[21]

The immediate administration goal in Greece was stated directly in Truman's speech to Congress on March 12. The president boldly argued: "I believe that it must be the policy of the United States to support free peoples who are resisting attempted subjugation by armed minorities or by outside pressures" (quoted in Jones, 1955, p. 272). He further stated that "Greece must have assistance if it is to become a self-supporting and self-respecting democracy" (quoted in Jones, 1955, p. 270). The economic devastation Greece suffered during World War II was cited as a justification for U.S. economic support, the oppressive pressure of "armed minorities" and outside "totalitarian regimes" was cited to justify military aid (see Jones, 1955, pp. 269–274). This immediate goal was repeated by the president throughout 1947 and 1948 in comments at press conferences and in public speeches (see Truman, 1963, 1964). Over time, as the Greek government's success against the guerrillas waxed and waned, Truman would occasionally shift emphasis from the economic to the military aspects of the aid program (see Truman, 1964, pp. 28–29). But throughout the period under examination, the president consistently emphasized his wish to secure a noncommunist, democratic, and economically stable ally.

The documentary record suggests that the goal of securing a noncommunist, democratic, and economically stable Greece was indeed President Truman's immediate goal in this case. But clearly other imperatives constrained the means available for achieving this immediate goal as well as Truman's commitment to achieving or surpassing his immediate goal. In terms of constraints on means, Truman was initially only somewhat fearful of potential Soviet reactions to U.S. initiatives. During the development of Truman's speech before Congress, George Kennan, recently chosen to be the head of the State Department's Policy Planning Staff, actively opposed any aid to Turkey and fought to limit military aid to Greece (Henderson, 1973, p. 87). Kennan argued that the belligerent tone of the president's speech "might provoke the Soviet Union to aggressive action" (Acheson, 1969, p. 221). He was particularly concerned with the portrayal of "two opposing ways of life" (Jones, 1955, p. 155). Despite Kennan's concerns, the president approved the official State Department version of the speech. But he was very careful to refrain from directly mentioning or challenging the Soviet Union (see Jones, 1955, pp. 269–274). Truman did not want to turn the Greek Civil War into a direct conflict between the Soviet Union and the United States, but he also knew that some inflammatory rhetoric was required to force the Republican Congress to act (Kuniholm, 1980, pp. 413–414).

During the later stages of U.S. intervention, when the president considered the deployment of U.S. ground troops to Greece, Truman expressed a greater concern for the potential Soviet reaction to U.S. initiatives. In the fall of 1947, the decision to provide operational advisers rather than ground troops was partially based on the belief that the limited U.S. forces available for action in Greece could not counter the adjacent communist forces that might be provoked into action (Jones, 1989, p. 99). In the spring of 1948, when Truman again considered the dispatch of U.S. ground troops, a Central Intelligence Agency (CIA) study examined the "Consequences of Certain Courses of Action with Respect to Greece" (April 5, 1948). This paper examined the potential Soviet response to the intervention alternatives under consideration by the NSC. It concluded that the deployment of U.S. troops "might alarm the USSR initially," but that "the USSR would not accept the risk of war for the sake of Greece" ("Consequences of Certain Courses of Action," April 5, 1948, p. 1). And yet, the report also suggested that partial mobilization in the United States might result in a Kremlin decision to launch a preventive war ("Consequences of Certain Courses of Action," April 5, 1948, p. 2). Since Truman's military advisers argued that partial mobilization must accompany troop deployments to Greece, the possibility of a major war with the Soviets had to be considered (see Jones, 1989, p. 155).

A second constraint on the means available for achieving Truman's immediate goal was a concern regarding the overcommitment of U.S.

economic and military capabilities.[22] The recently elected Eightieth Congress was dominated by economy-minded Republicans (Barnet, 1968, p. 113). These Republicans were engaged in an effort to reduce the government budget, particularly in foreign affairs and defense spending (Truman, 1956, p. 102). Just one week before the president's speech, the Senate voted to cut the president's budget by four and a half billion dollars (Acheson, 1969, p. 222). It was in this context that Truman proposed a $400 million dollar aid bill. In order to ensure congressional support for the aid bill, President Truman invited congressional leaders (with a few notable exceptions) to the White House on February 27 and again on March 10 (see Acheson, 1969, pp. 219–221). President Truman and his State Department advisers (Marshall and Acheson) were careful to court the favor of Senator Arthur Vandenberg, the powerful Republican Chairman of the Foreign Relations Committee. With Vandenberg as an ally, the administration was able to emphasize the bipartisan character of support for the aid proposal, even allowing a "Vandenberg amendment" to stamp the bill with the senator's imprimatur (see Acheson, 1969, pp. 223–225).

Having successfully avoided a clash with Congress over the aid program, the administration later faced a confrontation with Truman's military advisers regarding the possibility of overcommitting U.S. military resources in Greece. During both of the periods in which the president considered the deployment of U.S. ground troops, his military advisers stubbornly argued that partial mobilization must accompany troop movements to Greece. In October of 1947, the JCS reported that the United States lacked the military capability to defeat the "adjacent Soviet satellite states" should they become openly involved in the Greek Civil War (Jones, 1989, p. 99). In the spring of 1948, when the NSC formally asked the secretary of defense and the JCS to reconsider troop deployments, they replied that partial mobilization was a "necessity" (FRUS, 1974, p. 94). The intransigence of the JCS frustrated the State Department (see particularly FRUS, 1974, pp. 98–99), but the fear of overcommitment expressed by his military advisers convinced President Truman to put off the troop deployment decision.

The final constraint on the means available for achieving Truman's immediate goal was his apprehension regarding the potential for an isolationist reaction in congressional and public opinion (see Leffler, 1992, p. 145). This constraint had an impact primarily during the weeks leading up to the president's speech. In his memoirs, President Truman notes that he "could never quite forget the strong hold which isolationism had gained over our country after World War I" (1956, p. 101). Having received numerous intelligence reports suggesting the belligerent character of Soviet motivations (see "The Greek Situation," February 7, 1947, p. 1) and the deterioration in British capabilities, Truman was convinced that "without American participation there was no power capable of meeting Russia as an equal" (1956, p. 102). The president also firmly believed that " 'Fortress America' notions could only result in handing to the Russians vast areas of the globe now denied to them" (1956, p. 102). Thus, in developing the "Truman

Doctrine" speech, great attention was paid to ideological and moral issues. President Truman and his advisers were careful to avoid discussions of Greece and Turkey's "strategic value" or of U.S. interest in Near East oil resources (see Barnet, 1968, pp. 118–119; Jones, 1955, p. 162; Kuniholm, 1980, p. 413).

Indeed, the initial meeting between the president (and his advisers) and congressional leaders on February 27 set the tone for the administration's presentation of its aid request. At the meeting, General Marshall "flubbed his opening statement" (Acheson, 1969, p. 219) by following a "dry" and "cryptic" presentation that resulted in questions like "Isn't this pulling British chestnuts out of the fire?" and "How much is this going to cost?" (Jones, 1955, p. 139). In contrast, Acheson's presentation in support of his boss (full of clever metaphor and ideological rhetoric) persuaded Senator Vandenberg to tell Truman: "if you will say that to the Congress and the country, I will support you and I believe that most of its members will do the same" (quoted in Acheson, 1969, p. 219). Ironically, in order to overwhelm the isolationist stream in U.S. politics, President Truman invoked grand ideological rhetoric that extended far beyond the immediate situation. For some congressmen "the President's message sounded like a virtual declaration of war on Russia" (Shelton, March 13, 1947).[23]

In considering the factors reinforcing Truman's commitment to achieving or surpassing his immediate goal, we must first examine the president's concern that communist success in Greece would lead to the fall of France, Italy, Iran, and Turkey. This "domino thinking" was prevalent throughout the administration during this time period. A CIA report in early February of 1947 indicated that Soviet success in Greece would help them "achieve a strategic position in the Eastern Mediterranean, thereby outflanking Turkey, threatening the Suez Canal, and endangering the polities of the Near East" ("The Greek Situation," February 7, 1947, p. 1). A cable from Ambassador MacVeagh on February 11 stated that if "Greece falls to communism the whole Near East and part of North Africa as well are certain to pass under Soviet influence" (FRUS, 1971, p. 17). A report dated February 17 from Mark Ethridge, the U.S. representative to the UN Commission of Investigation in Greece, noted that the "feeling of commissioners with whom I have close contact particularly British, French, Chinese and Colombian is that if Greece goes not only Near East goes with it but also Italy and France" (FRUS, 1971, p. 24). Finally, a February 21 memo from Acheson to Marshall entitled "Crisis and Imminent Possibility of Collapse" argued that:

> The capitulation of Greece to Soviet domination through lack of adequate support from the U.S. and Great Britain might eventually result in the loss of the whole Near and Middle East and northern Africa. It would consolidate the position of Communist minorities in many other countries where their aggressive tactics are seriously hampering the development of middle-of-the-road governments. (FRUS, 1971, p. 30)

This "domino thinking" appears to have convinced President Truman of the seriousness of the Greek situation. In his memoirs Truman writes "America could not, and should not, let these free countries stand unaided. To do so would carry the clearest implications in the Middle East and in Italy, Germany, and France" (1956, p. 101). Acheson's colorful metaphor in his February 27 presentation to the congressional leadership predates the "domino" analogy but is no less explicit: "Like apples in a barrel infected by one rotten one, the corruption of Greece would infect Iran and all to the east. It would also carry infection to Africa through Asia Minor and Egypt, and to Europe through Italy and France, already threatened by the strongest Communist parties in Western Europe" (1969, p. 219; see also Marshall's comments in FRUS, 1971, p. 61). It is no wonder then, that President Truman's speech before Congress would use similar (but less explicit) language (see Jones, 1955, pp. 272–273). The president and his advisers had concluded that they were engaged in a bipolar power struggle of historic proportions,[24] between camps "divided by an unbridgeable ideological chasm" (Jones, 1955, p. 141).

Closely tied to this "domino thinking" was the second major factor reinforcing Truman's commitment to achieving or surpassing his immediate goal—a desire to establish U.S. leadership of the "free world" in the wake of British retreat (see Leffler, 1992, p. 143). The Greek "crisis" was as much a watershed in U.S.–British relations as it was in U.S.–Soviet relations. As the British Empire receded from India, Burma, Egypt, and Palestine, " 'Dunkirk' was on the lips of all" (Jones, 1955, p. 80). The British retreat was about to create a vacuum that only two states were capable of filling. In a conversation with Louis Fisher on Monday, February 24, Acheson stated bluntly that the "British are pulling out everywhere and if we don't go in the Russians will" (quoted in Isaacson and Thomas, 1986, p. 393). The "domino thinking" that was prevalent within the administration led the president and his advisers to view Greece in global as well as local terms.

A major initial concern of administration officials was whether or not the British request for U.S. aid to Greece was sincere. The State Department analysis of the British notes on Greece and Turkey considered whether the British had decided "to come to terms with the Soviet Union on a basis involving respective spheres of influence" (FRUS, 1971, p. 50). Were the British simply throwing in the towel without expecting the United States to react? A second concern was whether the United States was being asked to assume the burden of empire on Britain's behalf (see FRUS, 1971, pp. 50–51). The Truman administration did not wish to assume the responsibilities and liabilities of global involvement without receiving the benefits of such involvement. The answer to each of these questions was negative, the State Department concluded that the British request was sincere and that the United States should offer aid to Greece and Turkey (see FRUS, 1971, pp. 51–53).

Based on his own beliefs and the suggestions of his State Department advisers, President Truman concluded that it was "time to align the United

States of America clearly on the side, and the head, of the free world" (Truman, 1956, p. 102). The president "took the Greek crisis as an opportunity to announce the willingness of the United States to assume the global responsibilities of power" (Jones, 1989, p. 43). This decision was reflected in the language of the president's speech to Congress. Truman referred to the British retreat, noting that "Great Britain finds itself under the necessity of reducing or liquidating its commitments in several parts of the world, including Greece" (quoted in Jones, 1955, p. 270). He also discussed the responsibility that fell to the United States:

> The Free peoples of the world look to us for support in maintaining their freedoms. If we falter in our leadership, we may endanger the peace of the world—and we shall surely endanger the welfare of our own nation. Great responsibilities have been placed upon us by the swift movement of events. I am confident that the Congress will face these responsibilities squarely. (Quoted in Jones, 1955, p. 274)

Both the public and the Congress grasped the significance of the president's remarks, the era of U.S. isolationism was over (see Barnet, 1968, p. 122; Shelton, 1947).

The final factor reinforcing Truman's commitment to achieving or surpassing his immediate goal was a need to demonstrate the resolve of his administration and the credibility of previous U.S. commitments. Obviously, this factor was only relevant during the later stages of the U.S. intervention. After the president received word on August 1, 1947 that the British had decided to pull out their remaining troops (see FRUS, 1971, p. 268), he was forced to consider the dispatch of U.S. ground troops. The task facing the president was to convince "the enemy (as well as other nations) that America possessed the will to resist communist aggression without resorting to all-out war" (Jones, 1989, p. 80). He was in many ways constrained by the boldness of his March 12 speech to Congress. In making Greece a public demonstration of U.S. leadership and responsibility, the president had committed his administration to securing a favorable outcome. The world was watching and a "failure in Greece would lead to a dangerous weakening of resistance to communism" (quoted in Jones, 1989, p. 83). In the spring of 1948, when the deployment of U.S. troops was again being examined, the JCS argued that "withdrawal from Greece would lead to a 'substantial loss of prestige' " (quoted in Jones, 1989, p. 130). Loy Henderson stated, at the same time, that "Greece is the test tube which the peoples of the world are watching in order to ascertain whether the determination of the Western powers to resist aggression equals that of international Communism to acquire new territory and new bases for further aggression" (FRUS, 1974, p. 12). This depth of commitment did not privilege any of the escalatory options under consideration by the president, but it did remove U.S. withdrawal from serious consideration.

Uncertainty and Time Pressure

As noted above, I expect that *presidential perceptions of high uncertainty and a lack of valid information will interact with presidential risk predispositions and affect the output of the decision process* (REF hypothesis 7). In the Truman cases, if the president perceives high uncertainty and inaccurate information but does not perceive acute time pressure, I expect to observe decisional delay and an expanded search for information (REF hypothesis 7a). If the president perceives high uncertainty and inaccurate information and also perceives acute time pressure, I expect to observe bolstering (REF hypothesis 7c).

As the evidence presented below suggests, President Truman perceived only moderate uncertainty during the three decision periods under examination in this case study. He did, however, perceive acute time pressure during the initial decision period of February 21 to March 12 of 1947. During the second decision period in August–November of 1947 and the final decision period of December 1947–June 1948, initial perceptions of acute time pressure gave way to perceptions of moderate time pressure. Throughout the decision periods, Truman faced two major sources of uncertainty: (1) how would the Soviets respond to U.S. initiatives? and (2) how much aid and of what type (military or economic) was required to achieve a successful outcome in Greece? The perception of acute time pressure in February/March 1947 was fueled by cables from MacVeagh, Porter, and Ethridge, and the British aide-memoire. The perception of initially acute, but later moderate time pressure in the period of August–November was caused by reports from the field and by the British decision to withdraw their remaining forces from Greece. During the final decision period, Truman's perception of initially acute, but later moderate time pressure was caused by communist successes in Greece (particularly the creation of a "Free" rebel government). President Truman's decisions regarding Greece are only partially explained by the REF hypotheses. In March of 1947 when he perceived acute time pressure and moderate uncertainty, President Truman decided to intervene economically and militarily in Greece (as suggested by REF hypothesis 6, see discussion below). In November of 1947 when he perceived moderate time pressure and moderate uncertainty, President Truman approved an increase in U.S. military advisers in Greece and an expansion of their role to include operational advice (which appears to be an incremental strategy that runs against the predictions of either REF hypothesis 5 or 7c). Finally, in the spring of 1948 when he perceived moderate uncertainty and moderate time pressure, events on the ground in Greece began to turn around and the president was spared from making a final decision on troop deployments (preventing the evaluation of the REF hypotheses).

As discussed above, one of the first questions facing President Truman and his advisers was how the Soviets would respond to U.S. initiatives. The task of anticipating potential Soviet responses also required some motivational analysis by intelligence staffers. The sources of information on Soviet motivations and future actions were generally the CIA, the State Department, and military intelligence. Despite the usual qualifications describing the inherent difficulties of motivational analysis and prediction, the majority of intelligence reports received by the president confidently concurred that the Soviet objective was to achieve a communist Greece, but that they would not risk war with the United States to achieve their objective (see "The Greek Situation," February 7, 1947; "Consequences of Certain Courses of Action," April 5, 1948; and FRUS, 1971). In his memoirs, President Truman wrote: "Intelligence reports which I received stated that many of the insurgents had been trained, indoctrinated, armed, and equipped at various camps beyond the Greek borders. Under Soviet direction, the reports said, Greece's northern neighbors—Yugoslavia, Bulgaria, and Albania—were conducting a drive to establish a Communist Greece" (1956, p. 98). While the various intelligence services kept a close watch for changes in Soviet policy, President Truman became increasingly convinced that the United States could intervene in Greece without provoking an open Soviet reaction. Of course, during the two later decision periods the question of whether the Soviets would respond to U.S. troop deployments was a major constraint. In fact, concerns regarding the military's ability to deal with a counter-intervention by Soviet or Balkan communist forces played a major role in Truman's decision to avoid the commitment of U.S. troops (see Jones, 1989, p. 99; "Consequences of Certain Courses of Action," April 5, 1948).

The second major issue facing President Truman and his advisers was how much aid and of what type (military or economic) was required to achieve a successful outcome in Greece. Because of their limited experience in Greece, the Truman administration was initially unsure of the potential scope of the intervention enterprise. In the early weeks of 1947, cables from Ambassador MacVeagh, Paul Porter, Chief of the American Economic Mission to Greece, and Mark Ethridge had begun to shed light on the situation in Greece (see FRUS, 1971, pp. 12–29). But no one in the administration had contemplated the British withdrawal of aid on such short notice (Acheson, 1969, p. 217). On February 27, a cable was sent to Ambassador MacVeagh requesting "urgently your and Porter's comments on note concerning Greece particularly re sums mentioned and your opinion magnitude US financial aid required for all-out assistance to Greece as well as suggestions on implementation" (FRUS, 1971, p. 65). On March 3, Porter responded that "assuming US government intends to bear full burden military relief and reconstruction expenses, figures used in summary British note re Greece check approximately with our data" (FRUS, 1971, p. 65 FN1). Given the large sums under consideration, the $400 million dollars initially appropriated by Congress was a ballpark figure that allowed for aid to be shifted from economic to military areas, as needed (see "Public Law 75," May 22, 1947).

Throughout 1947, Ambassador MacVeagh and Governor Dwight P. Griswold, the chief of the American Mission for Aid to Greece (AMAG), attempted to determine the best manner in which to distribute U.S. aid. But by early August, State Department officials were already preparing to explain AMAG's failure to achieve results before the end of the year (FRUS, 1971, pp. 292–293). By September, the British decision to withdraw its troops led to the consideration of the escalation of U.S. involvement. Unsure of the situation in Greece, Major General Stephen J. Chamberlin was sent to survey the "broad strategic and operational factors of present military situation" (FRUS, 1971, p. 345 FN3). Chamberlin's report of October 20 advocated the deployment of additional U.S. advisers and the expansion of their role to include operational advice, but he stopped short of endorsing the deployment of U.S. ground troops (FRUS, 1971, pp. 375–377). Put forward as the product of an objective outside analysis, Chamberlin's recommendations were accepted by the president and the NSC (Jones, 1989, pp. 102–103).

When the issue of U.S. escalation was again raised in the Spring of 1948 the NSC embarked on a study of "The Position of the United States With Respect to Greece," considering the various economic and military aspects of the aid mission (see FRUS, 1974, pp. 2–95). The NSC 5 series (1–4) involved all of the government agencies connected to the aid program and took approximately five months to complete (January to June 1948), whereupon the situation had significantly changed in Greece, and the issue of further military escalation was no longer relevant (FRUS, 1974, p. 93).

President Truman's perception of time pressure was growing even before the receipt of the British aide-memoire. On February 7, Ambassador MacVeagh had reported a recent trend toward "specially lively guerrilla activity" (FRUS, 1971, p. 15). On February 17, Mark Ethridge reported that the "Soviets feel like Greece is ripe plum ready to fall into their hands in a few weeks" and that he felt that the "Soviets have every good reason to feel that Greece may be about to fall" (FRUS, 1971, p. 24). Finally, Paul Porter cabled that he could not "emphasize too strongly gravity of situation . . . developments here next few months could determine the future" (FRUS, 1971, p. 26). The urgency of the situation in Greece prompted Acheson to send Marshall the memorandum (originally drafted by Loy Henderson) entitled "Crisis and Imminent Possibility of Collapse in Greece." This report stated that "unless urgent and immediate support is given to Greece, it seems probable that the Greek government will be overthrown and a totalitarian regime of the extreme left will come to power" (FRUS, 1971, p. 30). Thus, the British decision to withdraw their aid to Greece and request that the United States replace them simply served to add emphasis to an already urgent situation.

In his memoirs, President Truman commented on his awareness of the urgency of the situation in Greece:

> The urgency of the situation was emphasized by dispatches from our representatives in Athens and Moscow. General Smith recorded his belief that only the presence of British troops had so far saved Greece

from being swallowed into the Soviet orbit. From Athens, Ambassador MacVeagh sent a picture of deep depression and even resignation among Greek leaders; their feeling seemed to be that only aid given at once would be of use. Time, MacVeagh urged, was of the essence. (1956, p. 100)

George Elsey later noted that, for Truman, "Time was of the essence . . . if you were going to act, you had to act fast because the time was then. It was not something you could sit around and debate for weeks or months" (1970, p. 354). Indeed, the president acted fast, giving tentative approval to the aid program on February 26 and discussing his decision with congressional leaders on February 27. The "Truman Doctrine" speech to Congress came only three weeks after the receipt of the British notes. The March 12 speech also commented on the urgency of the situation in Greece. Truman noted that "assistance is imperative if Greece is to survive as a free nation" and later that "the situation is an urgent one requiring immediate action" (Jones, 1955, pp. 269–271).

President Truman also appears to have initially perceived acute time pressure during the second decision period of August–November, 1947.[25] The president and his advisers were taken by surprise once again by their allies when they were told on July 30 that the British intended to "withdraw British troops from Greece" (FRUS, 1971, p. 268). Despite the largely "symbolic" character of the British force in Greece (see Jones, 1989, p. 81), their withdrawal prompted the Truman administration to consider the dispatch of U.S. ground troops. While the State Department attempted to persuade the British to delay the withdrawal (see FRUS, 1971, pp. 274–275), reports from U.S. personnel in Greece again suggested a need for urgent action.

On August 2, Ambassador MacVeagh cabled that he considered "this astonishingly ill-timed decision as little short of catastrophic and hope implementation may be postponed pending determination of other possible security measures equally valid with presence British troops" (FRUS, 1971, p. 276). The ambassador also reported the thoughts of a U.S. military officer in Greece, "if British troops withdrawn and not replaced with at least equal numbers of US, 'we might as well pack up and go home' " (FRUS, 1971, p. 277). By August 22, MacVeagh reported an increase in guerrilla activity and a military adviser's conclusion that "house is on fire, but few in Athens or Washington seem to realize how fast flames are spreading" (FRUS, 1971, p. 307). While in Washington, Secretary Marshall was becoming frustrated by the British government's refusal to reconsider their decision: "They are far too casual or freehanded in passing the buck of the international dilemma to US with little or no consideration for the harmful results" (FRUS, 1971, p. 313).

By September 12, (when the embassy first suggested the possibility of sending additional U.S. military advisers to Greece, see FRUS, 1971, p. 336) the diplomatic pressure on the British resulted in an offer to withdraw only 800 men with the rest of the troops remaining in Greece until at least

December 15 (FRUS, 1971, p. 337). On September 15, Governor Griswold cabled Marshall with a description of "increasing deterioration conditions" in Greece and a plan to increase the strength of the Greek army (GNA), provide operational advice to the GNA from "125 to 200" U.S. army officers, and replace the British troops in Greece with U.S. forces (FRUS, 1971, pp. 337–340). Since the British decision to leave the majority of their troops in Greece had already been made, the debate within the administration now focused on the issue of operational advice rather than the replacement of British troops. The British decision to postpone the withdrawal of their remaining troops also reduced the president's perception of time pressure. The president did not approve the dispatch of U.S. operational advisers until November 3, fully two weeks after the receipt of Major General Chamberlin's report and seven weeks after Griswold's initial proposal (see FRUS, 1971, p. 393 FN1).

The third decision period (December 1947–June 1948) also began with the president initially perceiving acute time pressure that became more moderate over time. On December 6, the State Department received a study by the Political Section of the U.S. embassy in Athens entitled "Suggestions for United States Policy in Greece." This report indicated that the "Greek situation has now reached an exceedingly delicate balance point" and that "high policy decisions should be taken in the United States with the least possible delay" (FRUS, 1971, p. 440). The report also explored an event "which would completely upset the delicate balance in Greece: to wit, the formation of a so-called 'Free Democratic Government' in rebel-held territory or even in exile" (FRUS, 1971, p. 443). On Christmas eve that event occurred, the KKE announced the creation of the "first provisional democratic government of free Greece" (quoted in FRUS, 1971, p. 462). The president again appeared to be faced with a "crisis."

The announcement of a "Free Greek" government forced the consideration of two further events: recognition of that government by Soviet satellite governments or by the Soviets themselves, and the possibility of open external aid to the "Free" government. With these concerns in mind, Loy Henderson sent a memorandum to the Acting Secretary of State Robert A. Lovett asking that the NSC complete "urgent studies" reevaluating U.S. policy regarding Greece (FRUS, 1971, p. 473). Released to NSC members on January 6, NSC 5 (entitled "The Position of the United States With Respect to Greece") expressed the Truman administration's worst fears: "Almost certainly one or more of the satellites, and possibly the USSR, will recognize this 'free' government. The objective of such recognition will probably be to facilitate open military assistance" (FRUS, 1974, p. 3). The report went on to advocate the use of U.S. troops as a final resort to save Greece, but did not explicitly state the circumstances under which U.S. troops would be deployed (FRUS, 1974, p. 5). Unsatisfied with NSC 5, President Truman's State Department and military advisers pushed for multiple revisions, eventually producing NSC 5/2, which directed the various government agencies involved in the aid program to comment on four specific military alternatives (FRUS, 1974, pp. 46–51). But by this point President Truman's perception of time pressure had waned, it had been seven weeks since the declaration of the "Free" Greek government and as yet it had not been recognized by the Soviet Union's Balkan allies. When NSC 5/4 was finally approved by the president on June 21, the situation on the ground in Greece had turned around and the decision to escalate militarily was tabled (see FRUS, 1974, pp. 93–95).

Consideration of Alternatives and Final Decision

As noted above, I expect that President Truman (identified as a potential-motivated president) will tend to focus on best-case outcomes and maximum gains when considering alternatives (REF hypothesis 3). I also anticipate that President Truman is likely to behave in a risk-acceptant manner in making final decisions (REF hypothesis 5).[26] In order to evaluate these hypotheses, we must examine the manner in which alternatives were considered, and the decisions that were reached during crucial periods in the cases. For the Greek case, three periods are worthy of careful scrutiny—February–March 1947, August–November 1947, and December 1947–June 1948.

Loy Henderson received the British aide-memoire regarding Greece on Friday, February 21 (FRUS, 1971, p. 32 FN1). Since Secretary Marshall had left Washington for a speaking arrangement, Under Secretary of State Acheson took the lead role in orchestrating the initial State Department reaction. He advised Henderson and Jack Hickerson, the director of the Office of European Affairs, to get their people together over the weekend to develop reports on the current situation in Greece, the availability of U.S. "funds and personnel," and the "significance of an independent Greece and Turkey to Western Europe" (Acheson, 1969, p. 218). That evening Acheson telephoned the president and Secretary Marshall, detailing the contents of the British notes and the initiatives Acheson had taken (Jones, 1955, p. 132). After toiling through the weekend, Henderson delivered the various policy papers to Acheson's home on Sunday evening (see FRUS, 1971, p. 41). While meeting with Henderson, Acheson commented that "under the circumstances there could be only one decision" and so the State Department officials "drank a martini or two toward the confusion of our enemies" (Acheson, 1969, p. 218).

On Monday, the official versions of the British notes were presented to Secretary Marshall by Lord Inverchapel, the British ambassador. Marshall showed the notes to President Truman during lunch and suggested that the situation "puts up the most major decision which we have been faced since the war" (FRUS, 1971, p. 45). Marshall proposed that "War, Navy, Treasury and State should give this immediate study, make recommendations to you, and that a decision in which the leaders in Congress should participate must be made within the week" (FRUS, 1971, p. 45). The president agreed and awaited the various reports that were completed on Tuesday and Wednesday (Truman, 1956, p. 100).

On Wednesday at three o'clock, President Truman met with Secretary Marshall and Under Secretary Acheson (Truman, 1956, p. 100). Acheson presented the "Report of the Committee Appointed to Study Immediate Aid to Greece and Turkey." This report included two key studies entitled "Analysis of the Proposals Contained in British Notes of February 24 Relating to Greece and Turkey (For Discussion Purposes Only)" and "Position and Recommendations of the Department of State Regarding Immediate and Substantial Aid to Greece and Turkey" (FRUS, 1971, pp. 28–55). The first report summarized the British notes and evaluated the accuracy and sincerity of the British proposals. It also detailed the consequences if the United States should "refuse to assume the type of responsibility for Greece and Turkey which the British are asking us to undertake" (FRUS, 1971, p. 51). The two major consequences of U.S. inaction were: (1) Greece and Turkey might become "Soviet puppets" allowing for "further Soviet territorial and other gains in Europe and in the Near and Middle East" (FRUS, 1971, p. 51; see discussion of "domino thinking" above); and (2) the British Government might decide to throw in the towel, joining a military alliance with the Soviet Union and setting up spheres of influence to preserve the British Empire (FRUS, 1971, p. 51). In order to avoid these disastrous consequences, the report concluded that "it would be in the interest of the United States for this Government to relieve the British Government of the major share of the financial burden which it has been bearing on behalf of Greece and Turkey" (FRUS, 1971, p. 52).

The second report detailed the State Department's specific recommendations for aid to Greece and Turkey. Regarding Greece, the recommendations were split between military and economic assistance. On the military side it suggested that, after careful consideration, the United States should provide military supplies to Greece, if required to "maintain its independence and restore domestic tranquility" (FRUS, 1971, p. 54). In terms of economic aid, the report focused on the need for an "American Administrative Organization to undertake Greek rehabilitation" (FRUS, 1971, p. 54). The report included an estimate that "if put into effect promptly and in its entirety," the proposed aid program offered "a reasonable chance of success" (FRUS, 1971, p. 54).[27] The report then detailed the diplomatic, intragovernmental, legislative, and public opinion management strategies that should be followed to secure the success of the aid program (FRUS, 1971, p. 55).

The president also had before him memoranda from Secretary Marshall and by the secretaries of state, war, and the navy. Marshall's memorandum argued that "the situation, particularly in Greece, is desperate"; that "the collapse of Greece would create a situation threatening to the security of the United States"; and that "we should take immediate steps to extend all possible aid to Greece" (FRUS, 1971, p. 58). The accompanying memorandum by the secretaries of state, war, and the navy simply rephrased the specific recommendations found in the second State Department report (FRUS, 1971, p. 59; see above).

President Truman discussed the details of this meeting at length in his memoirs. He wrote: "Under Secretary Acheson made the presentation of the study, and I listened to it with great care. The diplomatic and military experts had drawn the picture in greater detail, but essentially their conclusions were the same as those to which I had come in the weeks just passed as the messages and reports went across my desk" (1956, p. 100). Indeed, Jones writes that Truman "required no convincing" (1955, p. 138).[28] The president approved the State–War–Navy proposals and immediately set a meeting with congressional leaders for the next day (Acheson, 1969, p. 219). The issue now was "not what should be done, but how to get authorizing legislation through Congress" (Jones, 1955, p. 138). In reflecting on his decision, the president wrote:

The risks which such a course might entail were risks which a great nation had to take if it cherished freedom at all. The studies which Marshall and Acheson brought to me and which we examined together made it plain that serious risks would be involved. But the alternative would be disastrous to our security and to the security of free nations everywhere. (1956, p. 101)

Once President Truman approved the basic State Department proposals, his energies turned to convincing congressional leaders and Cabinet officials that the correct decision had been made. At the February 27 meeting with congressional leaders, Acheson's compelling presentation served to temper the doubts of those assembled, but they still wanted "to know what definite program we had for meeting the situation and what it would cost" ("J.M. Jones' Notes . . . ," February 28, 1947, p. 2). The March 10 meeting with a larger group of congressional leaders was somewhat less successful as no agreements regarding legislative support were made and Vandenberg "reiterated his insistence that the President put the crisis before Congress in its broadest setting" (Acheson, 1969, p. 222). The meeting of the Cabinet on March 7 allowed the president to speak before a much friendlier audience. He stated: "The decision is to ask Congress for 250 million and say this is only the beginning. It means U.S. going into European politics. It means greatest selling job ever facing a President. Wants opinions of Cabinet" ("Notes on Cabinet Meeting," March 7, 1947, p. 3). The Cabinet officials immediately grasped the significance of the president's decision and agreed that the time had come to "stop spread of Russian influence" ("Notes on Cabinet Meeting," March 7, 1947, p. 3). With this support from within the administration, the president decided to go ahead with his presentation to Congress and the American people.

The above discussion of President Truman's decision making during this first decision period regarding Greece provides significant indirect evidence in support of REF hypothesis 3 (*potential-motivated presidents tend to focus on best-case outcomes and maximum gains*). If we examine the various policy papers presented to the president on February 26, we can find almost no critical evaluation of the intervention alternative. While there was an extensive discussion of the dire consequences associated with refusing to accept the transfer of responsibility for Greece, there was almost no discussion of the potential negative consequences associated with taking over the military and economic needs of Greece. Indeed, the direct evidence we have of Truman's perceptions suggests that he was not bothered much by his February 26 decision. Once he decided that aid to Greece and Turkey was the only decision that could be reached, the president turned his efforts toward justifying his decision to Congress and his Cabinet.

In considering Truman's final decision to move forward with the aid program, we must first determine whether REF hypothesis 5 or 6 is more appropriate. Based on the evidence presented above, I feel that hypothesis 6 (*if there is only one alternative capable of achieving the aspiration level, that alternative is likely to be selected regardless of its level of risk*) more accurately characterizes this decision. President Truman initially only considered the two alternatives presented to him in the State Department reports—intervention or the refusal of aid. Since the dire consequences associated with refusing to step in for the British in Greece did not allow for the achievement of the president's aspiration level, the intervention option became the only alternative under serious consideration. Faced with only one way to prevent the communist domination of Greece (and beyond), the president decided to take over as Greece's patron both militarily and economically.

The second major decision period—August–November 1947—began much like the first, but concluded quite differently. On August 1, President Truman was notified of the receipt of the British government's note detailing their intention to "withdraw British troops from Greece" (FRUS, 1971, p. 268). This provoked a series of alarmist reports from Ambassador MacVeagh and Governor Griswold as they pressed for further U.S. intervention (see FRUS, 1971, pp. 276–277, 307, 336, 337–340). Griswold's September 15 report (labeled AMAG 222) proposed an aggressive new program for eliminating the guerrilla threat—increasing the strength of the GNA, providing operational advice to the GNA from U.S. army officers, and replacing the British troops in Greece with U.S. forces (FRUS, 1971, pp. 337–340). But during this decision period, two major factors privileged the limited-intervention alternative. First, on September 12 the British government offered to limit their troop withdrawals, breaking the "crisis" atmosphere (FRUS, 1971, p. 337). Second, the U.S. military actively opposed the deployment of U.S. ground troops to Greece (Jones, 1989, p. 92).

Without the time pressure of the impending British withdrawal, the administration was able to send Major General Chamberlin to Greece. His late-September mission allowed the president and his advisers to receive the input of an ostensibly objective "outside" observer. While Chamberlin did endorse Griswold's proposal to extend operational advice to the GNA, he did not see an immediate need for further U.S. escalation (FRUS, 1971, pp. 375–377). The reduction in time pressure also gave the president's military advisers the opportunity to produce critical studies of the potential

impact of the dispatch of U.S. troops. These studies emphasized the porous
nature of the Greek border and the apparent indefensibility of its frontiers
(see Jones, 1989, p. 92). They carefully weighed the advantages and disadvantages of the troop deployment alternative and determined that "the
sending of American troops was not advisable" (Jones, 1989, p. 93). On
November 3, President Truman agreed to send an "Advisory and Planning
Group" composed of less than 180 U.S. officers and enlisted men to provide
operational advice to the GNA (FRUS, 1971, p. 399). The alternative of
deploying U.S. troops was "temporarily shelved" (Jones, 1989, p. 94).

Despite the lack of direct evidence bearing on President Truman's perceptions during this decision period, we may rely on the indirect evidence
found in the reports of his State Department and military advisers. This
indirect evidence does not support REF hypothesis 3 (*potential-motivated
presidents tend to focus on best-case outcomes and maximum gains*). The careful,
critical evaluation of the alternatives under consideration provides a balanced presentation of the costs and benefits associated with the various
options. Of course, the lack of time pressure after September 12 was significant, in that it allowed President Truman's military advisers to develop their
own studies of the troop deployment option. During this decision period,
the State Department would not be the only agency producing reports for
the president.

I must also report that the REF hypotheses fail to explain President
Truman's decision to extend operational advice to the GNA. This decision
seems to be an "incremental" escalation that I would expect a *security-
motivated* president to select. A potential-motivated president is expected to
either delay the decision or engage in bolstering (REF hypotheses 7a and 7c).
I observed neither type of behavior during this decision period.

The final decision period—December 1947–June 1948—also began
somewhat like the first two, but concluded rather differently. This time it
was not a British decision that triggered administration activity, but rather
the announcement of the creation of "the first provisional democratic government of Free Greece" on December 24 (FRUS, 1971, p. 462). Once again,
State Department advocates of U.S. escalation pointed to the urgency of
the situation (see FRUS, 1971, p. 473). The speedy completion of NSC 5
("The Position of the United States With Respect to Greece") seemed to
indicate that the administration was prepared to act, but the endless revision
of this NSC document simply resulted in the troop deployment decision
being delayed indefinitely (see FRUS, 1974, pp. 3–95).

As in the second decision period, the president and his advisers identified
the triggers that would force them to act. In this case, NSC 5 pointed to a
communist-satellite or Soviet decision to recognize the "Free Greek" government and the extension of open communist military assistance as actions
that would provoke a U.S. response (FRUS, 1974, p. 3). But as the NSC contemplated the revisions of NSC 5, the anticipated triggering events did not
occur. This allowed the military opponents of intervention to once again
voice their opinions (see Jones, 1989, pp. 155–156). By the time President

Truman considered NSC 5/4 on June 21, the situation on the ground in Greece had completely turned around and the troop deployment proposal was tabled indefinitely (see FRUS, 1974, pp. 93–95).

Once again, despite the lack of direct evidence bearing on President Truman's perceptions during this decision period, we may rely on the indirect evidence found in the reports of his State Department and military advisers. This indirect evidence does not support REF hypothesis 3 (*potential-motivated presidents tend to focus on best-case outcomes and maximum gains*). As in the second decision period, the careful and balanced evaluation of the troop deployment alternative runs against the expectations of this hypothesis. Indeed, the extended deliberations involved in the drafting of NSC 5 and its revisions (1–4) explicitly attempted to include the evaluations of all of the relevant government agencies (FRUS, 1974, pp. 46–51).

The decision to table indefinitely the troop deployment alternative *may* be viewed as *somewhat* supportive of REF hypothesis 7a. As President Truman's perception of uncertainty and time pressure waned across this decision period, he became less and less inclined to select one of the troop deployment alternatives. Unfortunately, the lack of a final decision during this period, precludes the evaluation of either hypothesis 5 or 6. (A summary of the findings for this case study can be found in table 3.2.)

Epilogue

President Truman's speech on March 12, 1947 included chilling rhetoric that was meant to mobilize the budget-minded Eightieth Congress. The president noted that the time had come when "nearly every nation must choose between alternative ways of life" (Jones, 1955, p. 272). He then carefully stated the Truman Doctrine—"I believe it must be the policy of the United States to support free peoples who are resisting attempted subjugation by armed minorities or outside pressure" (Jones, 1955, p. 272). The significance of the president's speech was clearly understood by those involved in its drafting. Joseph Jones giddily writes of this period:

> It was a time when men thought not in terms of what could be done but of what should be done, when only the timid idea was banished and all others welcomed, a time of courage, of bold decision, of generous response. It was a time when American democracy worked with unexampled efficiency and inspiration to produce national agreement. It was a great time to be alive. (Jones, 1955, p. 259)

Despite the global rhetoric of the president's speech, Howard Jones argues that the Truman Doctrine "was part of a global strategy capable of handling most foreign policy problems by *carefully controlled response*" (1989, p. 235, emphasis added). Thus, Greece was eventually used to justify Vietnam because its "lessons" were "grossly distorted" by later administrations (Jones, 1989, p. 235). On the other side, Isaacson and Thomas (1986) and Kuniholm

Table 3.2 Summary of findings for Greece 1947–1948 case study

Aspiration level	
Immediate goal	eliminate the threat posed by the communist guerrillas and secure a noncommunist, democratic, and economically stable ally
Constraints on means	fear of potential Soviet reactions to U.S. initiatives, a concern regarding the overcommitment of U.S. economic and military capabilities, and apprehension about a potential isolationist reaction in congressional and public opinion
Commitment reinforced by	fear that communist success in Greece would lead to the fall of France, Italy, Iran, and Turkey; a desire to establish U.S. leadership of the "free world" in the wake of British retreat; and by a need to demonstrate the resolve of Truman administration and the credibility of previous U.S. commitments
Uncertainty	moderate during all three decision periods—consensus view that Soviets would not risk war to achieve objectives, but questions regarding Soviet response to U.S. troop deployments and potential scope of military and economic involvement
Time pressure	acute during February to March 1947 period—urgent reports from State Department officials and timing of British aide-memoire
	moderate during August to November 1947 period—initial panic at threat of British troop withdrawal subsides in September when British agree to leave majority of troops in Greece until December
	moderate during December 1947 to June 1948 period—creation of "Free Greek" government stimulates NSC 5 series, but lack of outside recognition allows for deliberation
Consideration of alternatives	moderate evidence of focus on best-case outcomes and maximum gains during February to March 1947 period—almost no critical evaluation of intervention alternative found in policy papers presented to president committed to this course of action
	little evidence of focus on best-case outcomes and maximum gains during August to November 1947 period—Chamberlin mission and military studies produce balanced analyses of advantages and disadvantages of troop deployment
	little evidence of focus on best-case outcomes and maximum gains during December 1947 to June 1948 period—NSC 5 series leads to balanced analysis of advantages and disadvantages of troop deployment
Final decision	strong evidence that final decision reached during February to March 1947 period was support for only alternative capable of achieving aspiration level
	little evidence of delay or bolstering during August to November 1947 period—decision to extend operational advice to GNA appears to be risk-averse incrementalism
	weak evidence of delay during December 1947 to June 1948 period—NSC 5 series allowed to run its course, but events in Greece preclude the need for a final decision

(1980) hold President Truman and his advisers responsible for contributing to the climate of confrontation that marked the early Cold War. For much of the U.S. public and many congressmen, the Truman Doctrine speech was taken as fact and served as a guide to future policy.[29] Indeed, despite the claims that U.S. intervention in Greece was "carefully controlled," Isaacson and Thomas point out that U.S. actions "eerily foreshadowed Vietnam" (1986, p. 401).[30] And of course, the perception that emerged from Iran (that the Soviets would back down when faced with U.S. resolve, see above) received further confirmation and undoubtedly contributed to Truman's decision to intervene in Korea.

IV.　Korea 1950

Overview

The murky origins of the U.S. commitment to Korea may be traced to 1943 and Roosevelt's meetings with Chiang Kaishek and Winston Churchill at the "Cairo conference." During this conference, Chiang encouraged Roosevelt to consider the settlement of the war in Asia, particularly the disposition of Manchuria and Formosa. Roosevelt and Chiang agreed that these two areas should be returned to China, and also promised in the "Cairo Declaration" that "in due course Korea shall become free and independent" (quoted in Pelz, 1983, p. 98). This policy for the disposition of Korea was privately endorsed by Stalin in Teheran in 1943 and again at Yalta in 1945 (Pelz, 1983, pp. 98–99; Truman, 1956, p. 316). The allies would oversee a trusteeship for Korea, a peripheral area in the war that was still under Japanese occupation. In fact, Korea was so peripheral in Roosevelt's mind that he developed this policy with little consultation and almost no consideration of its practicality or chances for success (Pelz, 1983, p. 99).

After Roosevelt died in April of 1945, President Truman attempted to continue his policy of "trusteeship" for Korea. But, when the Japanese suddenly surrendered on August 9, there was no preexisting agreement between the Americans and the Soviets regarding zones of occupation in Korea. State Department planners suggested to Truman that U.S. troops should at least share in the occupation of Korea (Pelz, 1983, pp. 104–105). And so, the 38th parallel was selected as a convenient line of demarcation between the U.S. and Soviet occupation zones (Truman, 1956, p. 317). As 1945 wore on, the United States and the Soviet Union entered into negotiations over Korea and in January of 1946, a "Joint Commission" of Soviet and U.S. military commanders was established to negotiate the implementation of the "trusteeship" plan (Pelz, 1983, pp. 107–109; Truman, 1956, pp. 319–320). As negotiations continued through 1946 and 1947, the "trusteeship" policy was revealed to be a complete failure. The Soviet and American negotiators could not agree on which Korean political parties were worthy of recognition and almost every Korean political party opposed "trusteeship," preferring immediate independence.

In 1947, the Truman administration moved from the "trusteeship" policy for all of Korea to a policy of military and economic support for South Korea (Pelz, 1983, p. 110). As U.S. interests in Western Europe and the Mediterranean were threatened and as the U.S. Congress pushed for demobilization and budget cuts, Truman and his advisers decided to put Korea on the UN agenda and begin to plan for the withdrawal of U.S. troops from the region.[31] A "United Nations Temporary Commission on Korea" convened in January of 1948 and was denied access to the Soviet zone of occupation (Truman, 1956, p. 327). In May, the UN Commission supervised elections in the South for representatives to a National Assembly (Pelz, 1983, p. 111). On July 20, Syngman Rhee became the first president of the "Republic of Korea" (ROK) and on August 15, the U.S. military occupation of Korea was ended as control was transferred to Rhee's government (Truman, 1956, pp. 327–328). This new "Republic" was countered on September 9—when the "Democratic People's Republic of Korea" (DPRK) was created in the North.

After the withdrawal of Soviet troops from the DPRK in December of 1948, the Truman administration began to seriously consider the withdrawal of American troops from the ROK. In the minds of Truman's military advisers (who were "preoccupied" with preparations for a general war), Korea held little strategic value (George and Smoke, 1974, pp. 145–146; Stueck, 1981, p. 155). It was believed that this small contingent of U.S. troops might be better employed in Japan in the event of a global war. Truman's decision to withdraw U.S. troops by June of 1949 was taken despite State Department intelligence estimates that suggested that "US troop withdrawal would probably result in a collapse of the U.S.-supported Republic of Korea, an event which would seriously diminish US prestige and adversely affect US security interests in the Far East" ("Consequences of US Troop Withdrawal," February 28, 1949, p. 1). By 1950, only 500 U.S. troops were in the ROK as part of a "Korean Military Advisory Group (KMAG)" (George and Smoke, 1974, p. 145). In his famous National Press Club speech on January 12, 1950, Secretary of State Acheson excluded the ROK from the U.S. "defense perimeter" in Asia (Paige, 1968, p. 67). And on May 5, 1950 Senator Tom Connally indicated that Korea might be abandoned to the communists (Paige, 1968, p. 68). Thus, by June of 1950 it appeared that the Truman administration was moving from a policy of reduced support for the ROK to tacit withdrawal.

At approximately 4:00 a.m. (local time) on Sunday June 25, the first battles in what would become the "Korean War" began on the Ongjin peninsula.[32] As North Korean troops pressed the attack along the 38th parallel, officials in Washington were taken completely by surprise. President Truman was on his way to Independence to spend a weekend with his wife and daughter, Secretary of Defense Louis A. Johnson and Chairman of the JCS General Omar Bradley were just returning from a trip to the "Far East," and Secretary of State Acheson was at his farm in Sandy Spring, Maryland (see Cumings, 1990; Paige, 1968).

The first news of the fighting to reach a government official in Washington came from the United Press when a "Mr. David Gonzales" requested "confirmation of a dispatch that had just been filed by Seoul correspondent Jack James" (Paige, 1968, p. 88). The official contacted, W. Bradley Connors, public affairs officer of the State Department's Bureau of Far Eastern Affairs, in turn called Dean Rusk, then serving as assistant secretary of state for Far Eastern Affairs. Rusk asked Connors to contact the U.S. ambassador in Seoul, John J. Muccio, and then departed for the State Department (accompanied by Secretary of the Army Frank Pace Jr. who was, coincidentally, attending the same dinner party, FRUS, 1976, pp. 126–127). By the time Rusk and Pace reached the State Department, a telegram had been received from Ambassador Muccio relating that the North Korean attack appeared to constitute an "all out offensive against [the] ROK" (FRUS, 1976, p. 126). As numerous State Department officials joined Rusk and Pace, Secretary Acheson was notified and Ambassador Muccio's telegram was forwarded to President Truman, the Army Department, and U.S. embassies around the world. At 11:20 p.m., Secretary Acheson reached President Truman by phone and received approval to request a meeting of the UN Security Council for Sunday, June 25 (Washington was 13 hours behind Korean time). State Department officials worked throughout the night preparing the formal request for the Security Council meeting; "a resolution to be introduced by the United States Acting Representative, Ernest Gross; and . . . a statement to be made by Mr. Gross" (FRUS, 1976, p. 127).

During the six-day period from Sunday, June 25 through Friday, June 30, President Truman would approve: an initial limited military intervention to protect the evacuation of U.S. dependents (see "Teleconference," June 25, 1950), a further intervention allowing the use of U.S. naval and air forces below the 38th parallel (see "Teleconference with MacArthur," June 26, 1950), a subsequent escalation allowing Air Force operations north of the 38th parallel (see JCS to CINCFE MacArthur June 29, 1950), and finally full-scale involvement of U.S. ground troops to prevent the fall of South Korea (see JCS to CINCFE MacArthur, June 30, 1950). During this busy week, Truman consulted with his primary advisers in five major meetings. He also met twice with congressional leaders to encourage their support for his policies and held one press conference on June 29 to defend his decisions publicly (see Paige, 1968). After making the final decision to commit U.S. ground troops to the battle, President Truman left Washington for a "weekend cruise in Chesapeake Bay with his daughter Margaret," ending his "most strenuous week in office thus far" (Paige, 1968, p. 269).

Aspiration Level

As noted above, the president's "aspiration level" is expected to comprise a set of minimum level goals that the president hopes to achieve or surpass. In order to evaluate hypothesis 1 (*presidents tend to evaluate outcomes relative to an aspiration level rather than an overall value level*), we must infer the elements of President Truman's aspiration level (regarding Korea) from the documentary record. We need to find descriptions of acceptable/desirable outcomes/ objectives in this case. Thus, we need to find relevant documents that address Truman's goals, desires, hopes, needs, and/or requirements in this case.

Based on the evidence presented below, I believe that President Truman's immediate goal in Korea was to thwart the North Korean invasion and return to the *status quo ante* at the 38th parallel. The means available for achieving this goal were constrained by the fear of potential Soviet reactions to U.S. initiatives and a concern regarding the overcommitment of U.S. military capabilities. The president's commitment to achieving or surpassing his immediate goal was reinforced by his desire to demonstrate resolve and the credibility of U.S. commitments both to the Soviets and to U.S. allies; by his fear that communist success in South Korea would lead to the fall of Indochina, Formosa, and possibly Japan; by his fear of negative reactions from Republicans in Congress who were already criticizing the administration for "losing" China; and by his desire to show that the UN could be an effective instrument for combating territorial aggression. This complex combination of goals and constraints formed the aspiration level that guided Truman's decision making in this case. President Truman's aspiration level was well articulated and the documentary evidence supports REF hypothesis 1.

In elaborating on the conclusions presented above, it may be useful to first consider how the apparent abandonment of South Korea in 1949 and early 1950 can be reconciled with Truman's decisions during the final week of June. President Truman's decision to commit U.S. ground troops to the defense of South Korea should not simply be viewed as a complete reversal of the foreign policy of his administration, but rather as a significant alteration in the context in which Korea policy was made. Despite Acheson's speech excluding South Korea from the U.S. "defense perimeter" (Paige, 1968, p. 67), President Truman and his advisers had not "written-off" their South Korean allies. As George and Smoke have noted, "the 'strategic' significance of South Korea was assessed exclusively with reference to the contingency of another *general* war" (1974, p. 146, emphasis in original). In much of the military planning prior to June of 1950, the general assumption was that the invasion of South Korea would come as the result of a Soviet decision to initiate World War III. In this context, South Korea would have little strategic value and would not be a core theater of concern for U.S. military planners. Indeed, during the Blair House meetings between President Truman and his advisers (on Sunday, June 25 and Monday, June 26), the president considered the possibility that the North Korean attack was a "strategic feint" meant to draw U.S. forces away from other areas (see "Memorandum of Conversation," June 25, 1950; "Memorandum of Conversation," June 26, 1950). Also, in a conversation with George Elsey (June 26, 1950), the president pointed to Iran on a globe and indicated that,

"Here is where they [the Soviets] will start trouble if we aren't careful." The full U.S. commitment to the defense of South Korea (represented by Truman's decisions on June 30) was not approved until the administration was relatively confident that the North Korean invasion was not the first move of World War III. As George and Smoke (1974; see also Stueck, 1981, p. 155) note, dealing with Korea as a localized conflict forced the administration to consider the "value" of Korea in a different context. This new context required new thinking regarding U.S. goals in the region. Thus Korea, viewed as a "limited" conflict perceived to be a "test" of U.S. resolve, was a much better candidate for U.S. military intervention.

In a teleconference between Army Chief of Staff General J. Lawton Collins and General Douglas MacArthur's Chief of Intelligence Major General C. A. Willoughby on the morning of June 25, Major General Willoughby concluded that North Korean troops were "engaged in an all-out offensive to subjugate South Korea" (FRUS, 1976, p. 136). From Sunday, June 25 to Friday, June 30, President Truman would consider the depth of the U.S. commitment to its South Korean allies. During the Blair House conferences on Sunday and Monday, President Truman and his advisers settled on his administration's immediate goal—stopping the North Korean invasion and returning to the *status quo ante* at the 38th parallel. This goal was publicly stated in the UNSC resolution drafted in the State Department during the early morning hours of June 25 and approved by the Security Council that evening (with the Soviet ambassador absent). The resolution called for "the immediate cessation of hostilities" and called upon "the authorities of North Korea to withdraw forthwith their armed forces to the thirty-eighth parallel" (FRUS, 1976, p. 155).

At the initial Blair House meeting on Sunday June 25, General Bradley suggested that "we must draw the line somewhere" and President Truman "stated he agreed on that" ("Memorandum of Conversation," June 25, 1950, p. 2).[33] But at this first meeting, uncertainty regarding Soviet intentions inclined the president to favor a measured response to the situation. While he was at least minimally committed to the goal stated in the UNSC resolution, Truman had not yet decided on the means that would be employed to achieve this goal. At this meeting, he approved the provision of ammunition and equipment to ROK forces and U.S. air and naval cover for the safe evacuation of U.S. dependents ("Memorandum of Conversation," June 25, 1950, pp. 4–5; "Teleconference," June 25, 1950). The minutes of the second Blair House meeting (on June 26, 1950) also show Truman's commitment to his immediate goal. Despite the fact that he authorized U.S. air and naval forces to come to the aid of ROK troops, the president was careful to make sure "that no action should be taken north of the 38th parallel" ("Memoranda of Conversation," June 26, 1950, p. 2). At this stage in the conflict, Truman and his advisers were clearly focusing on saving South Korea, while avoiding provocative actions against the DPRK.

At a meeting with congressional leaders on Tuesday, June 27, Truman was asked if "the United States was now committed to defend South Korea from invasion" and the president responded in the affirmative ("Notes on Meeting in Cabinet Room," June 27, 1950, p. 3). Finally, the president issued a press statement on June 27 to reiterate his administration's immediate goal. In this statement he cited the June 25 UNSC resolution and indicated his administration's intention to "render every assistance to the United Nations in the execution of this resolution" (FRUS, 1976, p. 202). The key debates that would continue during the NSC meetings on June 28 and 29 would focus on how far the administration was willing to go to prevent the fall of the ROK.

There were two major constraints on the means available for achieving Truman's immediate goal: the fear of potential Soviet reactions to U.S. initiatives and a concern regarding the overcommitment of U.S. military capabilities. The North Korean invasion was immediately interpreted as a Soviet initiative (see Kirk to Acheson, June 25, 1950). The key question for President Truman and his advisers was whether this was a strategic "feint" (as discussed above) or a limited probe of U.S. resolve. If the North Korean invasion was the prologue to World War III, U.S. intervention could prove disastrous. Conversely, if the North Korean invasion was a Soviet test of U.S. resolve, U.S. intervention would not bring massive Soviet or Chinese retaliation. So long as Soviet motivations were unknown, President Truman was reluctant to make decisions that were not immediately necessary (see "Memorandum of Conversation," June 25, 1950, p. 4). At each of the key meetings during the week of June 25–30, the escalation of U.S. intervention was carefully measured to avoid triggering an aggressive Soviet response.

At the first Blair House meeting, the prevailing view of Truman's advisers was that the Soviets were not yet ready for war. The Air Force Chief of Staff, General Hoyt Vandenberg, was the lone dissenter. He cautioned that "he would not base our action on the assumption that the Russians would not fight" ("Memorandum of Conversation," June 25, 1950, p. 3). This comment led to an exchange with President Truman regarding Russian air strength in the Far East. Vandenberg was supported by Secretary of the Air Force Thomas E. Finletter, who argued that U.S. forces "in the Far East were sufficient if the Russians *do not come in*" ("Memorandum of Conversation," June 25, 1950, p. 4, emphasis added). Based on Vandenberg's concerns, Truman directed the Air Force to "prepare plans to wipe out all Soviet air bases in the Far East" ("Memorandum of Conversation," June 25, 1950, p. 5).

At the second Blair House meeting, President Truman and his advisers remained unsure of Soviet motivations. While the situation on the ground in Korea was deteriorating, the president was still concerned with limiting U.S. involvement. Although he approved U.S. air and naval attacks on North Korean troops, he was careful to emphasize that "no action should be taken north of the 38th parallel" ("Memorandum of Conversation," June 26, 1950, p. 2). During this meeting, Truman also attempted to neutralize the issue of Formosa by approving the deployment of the U.S. 7th fleet between the island and communist China, and by instructing Chiang Kaishek to end attacks against the mainland (FRUS, 1976, p. 198; "Memorandum of

Conversation," June 26, 1950, p. 2). The president did not want the Generalissimo to use this opportunity to drag the United States into a confrontation with China.

As estimates of Soviet intentions filtered into the White House on Tuesday and Wednesday, and after the fall of Seoul to North Korean troops, President Truman began to consider further U.S. military intervention. On June 27, Alan G. Kirk, the U.S. ambassador to the Soviet Union, cabled the State Department that "we believe US, on basis calculated risk, may with some degree assurance estimate that Soviets will not engage in war with US if we take firm stand and effective action to assist ROK immediately to halt and throw back North Korean aggression" (FRUS, 1976, p. 199). On June 28, the CIA estimated that the Soviets were not yet ready for war and "that the USSR will seek to localize the Korean conflict" (CIA, June 28, 1950, p. 1). At the NSC meeting that afternoon, General Vandenberg pushed the president to allow air and naval operations north of the 38th parallel, but the president hesitated. Instead Truman directed the NSC to "resurvey all policies affecting the entire perimeter of the USSR," to prepare plans for "the courses of action to be followed in the event that Soviet forces enter Korean hostilities," and to give "special attention . . . to obtaining intelligence concerning clear evidence of Soviet participation in Korean hostilities" ("Memorandum for the President," June 29, 1950, pp. 3–4).

At the second NSC meeting on June 29, Defense Secretary Johnson read a proposed directive for General MacArthur. This directive would allow U.S. air and naval operations north of the 38th parallel and the deployment of U.S. army service units to "insure the retention of a port and air base in the general area [of] Pusan-Chinhae" (FRUS, 1976, p. 240). The directive also informed MacArthur that if Soviet forces entered the Korean hostilities U.S. troops were to "defend themselves," "take no action on the spot to aggravate the situation," and "should report the situation to Washington" (FRUS, 1976, p. 217). Once again, President Truman expressed his concern regarding the potential escalation of the conflict. He stated: "I do not want any implication in the letter that we are going to war with Russia at this time. We must be damn careful. We must not say that we are anticipating a war with the Soviet Union. We want to take any steps we have to push the North Koreans behind the line but I don't want to get us overcommitted to a whole lot of other things that could mean war" ("Draft" n.d., pp. 1–2; "Memorandum for the President," June 30, 1950, p. 1). Clearly, the evidence presented above suggests that President Truman was concerned with potential Soviet reactions to U.S. initiatives.

The other major constraint on the means available for achieving Truman's immediate goal was a concern regarding the overcommitment of U.S. military capabilities. As early as the second Blair House meeting on Monday June 26, President Truman and his advisers had begun to address the issue of troop mobilization. General Bradley argued that "if we commit our ground forces in Korea we cannot at the same time carry out our other commitments without mobilization" ("Memorandum of Conversation,"

June 26, 1950, p. 7), but suggested that the president did not need to make that decision immediately. At the first NSC meeting on Wednesday, the president announced that "he didn't intend to back out unless there should develop a military situation which we had to meet elsewhere" ("Memorandum of Conversation," June 28, 1950, p. 2), and authorized "a review of our military capabilities in order to indicate the extent of our freedom of choice" ("Memorandum for the President," June 29, 1950, p. 4). Finally, at the second NSC meeting on Thursday, Truman expressed his desire to avoid becoming "so deeply committed in Korea that we could not take care of other situations which might develop" ("Memorandum for the President," June 30, 1950, p. 1).

This fear of overcommitment was due to the rapid demobilization of the U.S. military that Truman had overseen from 1946 to 1949. As David McLellan notes, "any relationship between America's foreign policy goals and its military strategy was purely coincidental" during this period (quoted in Pelz, 1983, p. 113). Indeed, as U.S. foreign policy commitments grew from 1945 to 1947, U.S. military forces shrunk from 12 million to 1.6 million men and the defense budget went from 81.6 billion to 13.1 billion dollars (Foot, 1985, p. 41). On the eve of the war, the "Army had only ten trained divisions, each of which was under strength by a third" and MacArthur's Far East Command was "well below half of its authorized strength" (Pelz, 1983, p. 118). Despite the fact that Truman could blame some of this budget cutting on Republicans in Congress and on public opposition to tax increases, he could not ignore the fact that the United States was ill-prepared for global war and certainly lacked the in-theater capabilities to manage a full-scale intervention in Korea. If U.S. troops became bogged down in Korea, increased defense budgets and troop mobilizations would be required to substantiate global commitments of the United States.

In considering the factors reinforcing Truman's commitment to achieving or surpassing his immediate goal, we must first examine the president's desire to demonstrate resolve and the credibility of U.S. commitments both to the Soviets and to its allies. As noted above, the North Korean invasion was immediately perceived to be a Soviet initiative. Early reports also suggested that it was a probe of U.S. resolve. The initial cables from the U.S. embassy in Moscow estimated that the North Korean attack was a "clear-cut challenge which in our considered opinion US should answer firmly and swiftly as it constitutes direct threat our leadership of free world against Soviet Communist imperialism" (Kirk to Acheson, June 25, 1950, p. 1). The embassy still believed that the Soviets were not prepared to launch a full-scale war and suggested that "determined countermeasures will deter the Soviets" (FRUS, 1976, p. 169). Further correspondence between the State Department and Ambassador Kirk indicate the desire to avoid engaging Soviet prestige, thus allowing Moscow to stay out of the conflict without losing face (see FRUS, 1976, pp. 169–170, 176–177, 199, 204, 212, 229–230, 253–254). This perception of the North Korean attack as a Soviet probe, was also suggested by an intelligence estimate dated June 25. This report argued that Korea "offers a test on ground militarily most favorable to the Soviet Union of the resolution of the US in its announced policy of 'total diplomacy' " and that the loss of South Korea would deal a "severe blow" to U.S. prestige and encourage other Southeast Asian peoples to "get on the bandwagon" (FRUS, 1976, p. 150). Finally, the CIA on June 28 estimated that by "choosing Korea as the area of attack, the USSR was able to challenge the US specifically and test the firmness of US resistance to Communist expansion" (CIA, June 28, 1950, p. 1). There is clear evidence that these beliefs were eventually accepted by President Truman and his advisers.

On Monday June 26, President Truman told George Elsey that, "Korea is the Greece of the Far East. If we are tough enough now, if we stand up to them like we did in Greece three years ago, they won't take any next steps. But if we just stand by, they'll move into Iran and they'll take over the whole Middle East. There's no telling what they'll do, if we don't put up a fight now" ("President Truman's Conversations," June 26, 1950).[34] This "domino thinking" was also evident in Truman's comments to the congressional leaders on Tuesday: "If we let Korea go down, the Soviet will keep right on going and swallow up one piece of Asia after another. We had to take a stand some time or else let all Asia go by the board" ("Persons Present," June 27, 1950, p. 4). While some uncertainty remained regarding whether the Chinese might intervene in Korea (see "Persons Present," June 30, 1950, p. 6), by Friday the president had accepted the view that the North Korean attack was a test of U.S. resolve and that Soviet troops would probably not become involved in the conflict.

President Truman's decision to intervene in Korea was also intended to demonstrate resolve to U.S. allies. The June 25 State Department intelligence estimate (discussed above) noted that the "capacity of a small Soviet satellite to engage in a military adventure challenging, as many Europeans will see it, the might and will of the US, can only lead to serious questioning of that might and will" (FRUS, 1976, p. 154). In his memoirs, Truman wrote "in Europe, the Middle East, and elsewhere the confidence of peoples in countries adjacent to [the] Soviet Union would be very adversely affected, in our judgment, if we failed to take action" (1956, p. 339). As cables flowed into the State Department from U.S. embassies in Europe, it became clear that allied governments were "watching to see what the United States will do" (FRUS, 1976, pp. 174–175). It also became clear that several European governments were encouraging the United States to act (see FRUS, 1976, pp. 174–175, 185, 193–195). After the president's statement on Tuesday June 27, the allied response was immediate and supportive. At the first NSC meeting on Wednesday, Truman was relieved to hear Averell Harriman report that "prior to the President's announcement, the Europeans were gravely concerned that the United States would not meet the challenge in Korea. After the announcement, however, . . . they felt great relief since they believed disaster would be certain otherwise" ("Memorandum for the President," June 29, 1950, p. 2).

The second major factor reinforcing Truman's commitment to achieve or surpass his immediate goal was his fear that communist success in South

Korea would lead to the fall of Indochina, Formosa, and possibly Japan. Beyond the ideological elements of the "domino theory" discussed above, President Truman and his advisers (particularly the JCS) were also concerned that Korea might be used as a military base to subvert U.S. and allied positions in other parts of Asia. At the first Blair House meeting, Chief of Naval Operations (CNO) Admiral Forrest P. Sherman argued that "Korea is a strategic threat to Japan," in favoring U.S. intervention ("Memorandum of Conversation," June 25, 1950, p. 3). Beyond Japan, if the North Korean attack indicated a new communist campaign in Asia, the obvious next targets might be Formosa or Indochina. At the second Blair House meeting on Monday, Formosa and Indochina were major topics of discussion and President Truman approved the deployment of the 7th fleet between China and Formosa and increased U.S. aid and involvement in Indochina ("Memorandum of Conversation," June 26, 1950, p. 3). He also approved "an increase in the United States military forces in the Philippines and an acceleration of aid to the Philippines" ("Memorandum of Conversation," June 26, 1950, pp. 2–3).

The third major factor reinforcing Truman's commitment to achieve or surpass his immediate goal was his fear of negative reactions from Republicans in Congress, who were already criticizing the administration for "losing" China. Truman was careful to avoid discussing domestic political considerations during the Blair House and NSC meetings, but as a wily politician, he could not have been unaware of the domestic political ramifications that would follow from the loss of Korea to the communists. Recall that 1950 was the year of the Klaus Fuchs confession, the arrest of Julius Rosenberg, the perjury verdict for Alger Hiss, and the rise of Senator Joseph R. McCarthy (see Foot, 1985; Pelz, 1983). Prior to the president's statement on June 27, debate in the House and Senate was quite rancorous over Korea. One senator noted that, "It is fairly clear that what happened in China and what is now happening in Korea were brought about deliberately by the advisers of the President at Yalta and by the advisers of the State Department since then" (quoted in Pelz, 1983, p. 129). Even after the president's statement had received bipartisan support, Robert Taft (a leading Republican presidential hopeful) blamed the Korea "crisis" on the "bungling and inconsistent foreign policy of the administration" (quoted in Pelz, 1983, p. 129). Unfortunately for Truman, his refusal to ask Congress to approve his Korean intervention would later haunt him when the tide turned after the Chinese invasion in the fall.

The final major factor reinforcing Truman's commitment to achieve or surpass his immediate goal was his desire to show that the UN could be an effective instrument for combating territorial aggression. The initial decision to bring the North Korean invasion to the attention of the UN may have been influenced by the composition of the State Department group that dealt with the problem on the night of June 24 (see Paige, 1968, p. 284); but regardless of its origins, this decision was clearly seized upon by the president in justifying U.S. intervention. At the first Blair House meeting, General

Bradley cynically noted that the United States should "act under the guise of aid to the United Nations" ("Memorandum of Conversation," June 25, 1950, p. 2). But President Truman was somewhat more idealistic, stressing that "we are working entirely for the United Nations" ("Memorandum of Conversation," June 25, 1950, p. 5) and later that "we must do everything we can for the Korean situation—for the United Nations" ("Memorandum of Conversation," June 26, 1950, p. 7). Indeed, at the Tuesday meeting with congressional leaders, Truman chided Acheson for briefing the congressmen without discussing the role of the UNSC ("Persons Present," June 27, 1950, pp. 3–4). Truman agreed with Senator Connally that "if the United Nations cannot bring the crisis in Korea to an end, then we might just as well wash up the United Nations and forget it"; and assured the congressmen that "he was going to make absolutely certain that everything we did in Korea would be in support of, and in conformity with, the decision by the Security Council of the United Nations" ("Persons Present," June 27, 1950, p. 7). Later in the week, the president would make his famous off-the-cuff remark, agreeing with a reporter that the U.S. intervention was a "police action under the United Nations" (Truman, June 29, 1950, p. 2). Whether the United States was acting for the UN or simply manipulating the institution as a tool of U.S. foreign policy, the prestige of the UN was now tied to the success of the U.S. effort to thwart the North Korean invasion.

Uncertainty and Time Pressure

As noted above, I expect that *presidential perceptions of high uncertainty and a lack of valid information will interact with presidential risk predispositions and affect the output of the decision process* (REF hypothesis 7). In the Truman cases, if the president perceives high uncertainty and inaccurate information but does not perceive acute time pressure, I expect to observe decisional delay and an expanded search for information (REF hypothesis 7a). If the president perceives high uncertainty and inaccurate information and also perceives acute time pressure, I expect to observe bolstering (REF hypothesis 7c).

As the evidence presented below suggests, President Truman perceived high uncertainty early in the week of June 25–30 and moderate uncertainty at the end of the week. Conversely, the president perceived moderate time pressure early in the week and acute time pressure by Friday morning. During this week, Truman faced two major sources of uncertainty: (1) what were Soviet intentions? and (2) how much U.S. assistance was needed by the South Koreans? The perception of time pressure was determined by events on the ground in Korea. Once Seoul fell and MacArthur concluded that the situation was desperate, President Truman and his advisers had reached the acute stage of the "crisis." As suggested by REF hypothesis 7a, when President Truman perceived high uncertainty but moderate time pressure, he delayed making a final decision regarding U.S. intervention in order to gather more accurate information (while also approving some increases in U.S. military assistance). But by the end of the week, when Truman perceived acute time pressure combined with a *reduction* in uncertainty, he decided on full-scale U.S. intervention (as suggested by REF hypothesis 6, see discussion below).

As noted above, the North Korean invasion appears to have caught the Truman administration completely off-guard. The surprise and swiftness of the North Korean assault created a "crisis" atmosphere in Washington that was punctuated by high initial uncertainty. The obvious first question for the president and his advisers was how to interpret these events. Was this an act of aggression by the DPRK against the ROK? Or was this the first salvo of World War III? An inaccurate interpretation of events could result in the loss of South Korea or a U.S. defeat in a Soviet trap. Thus, estimating Soviet intentions became the crucial task for analysts in the Departments of State and Defense, and the CIA.

The initial reports that reached the White House suggested that earlier intelligence estimates *were accurate*—the Soviets were not ready to risk full-scale war with the West (see Kirk to Acheson, June 25, 1950). With this assumption in mind, the July 25 State Department estimate suggested that the North Korean invasion was a Soviet probe of U.S. resolve (FRUS, 1976, p. 150). At the first Blair House meeting, President Truman expressed uncertainty regarding the accuracy of these estimates. He appeared to be particularly concerned with General Vandenberg's caution that Soviet intentions should not be assumed ("Memorandum of Conversation," June 25, 1950, p. 3). The decisions reached at this meeting reflect the high level of perceived uncertainty. Truman ordered General MacArthur to send "a survey group to Korea," instructed the Air Force to "prepare plans to wipe out all Soviet air bases in the Far East," and directed the State and Defense Departments to make a "careful calculation . . . of the next probable place in which Soviet action might take place" ("Memorandum of Conversation," June 25, 1950, pp. 4–5). At the close of this meeting, Truman "again emphasized the importance of making the survey of next possible moves by the Soviet Union" ("Memorandum of Conversation," June 25, 1950, p. 5). The president had made only the "necessary decisions" in the face of high uncertainty.

On Monday, the president was coming to accept the notion that the North Korean attack was a Soviet challenge, but remained worried about potential communist moves against Formosa and Iran (see "President Truman's Conversations," June 26, 1950). In the early morning hours, Acheson had sent a circular telegram to U.S. embassies and consulates asking them to "maintain utmost vigilance" for evidence of further Soviet moves (FRUS, 1976, p. 166). At the Blair House meeting that night, part of the conversation focused on the State and Defense Department estimates of where the next Soviet move might come: State favored Formosa while MacArthur had suggested Iran ("Memorandum of Conversation," June 26, 1950, p. 5).

At the meeting with congressional leaders on Tuesday, President Truman noted that he "still hoped there would be no Soviet involvement in the attack but their possible next moves were being studied" ("Notes on meeting in Cabinet Room," June 27, 1950, p. 1). That afternoon, another cable from Ambassador Kirk asserted that "we estimate Soviets not yet ready to embark on World War III" and that the United States "may with some degree assurance estimate that Soviets will not engage in war with US if we take firm stand and effective action to assist ROK immediately to halt and throw back North Korean aggression" (FRUS, 1976, p. 199). On Wednesday, the CIA estimate of Soviet intentions supported this view—arguing that "the USSR will seek to localize the Korean conflict" (CIA, June 28, 1950, p. 1). But at the NSC meeting that night, Truman again expressed uncertainty, directing the NSC to "resurvey all policies affecting the entire perimeter of the USSR," prepare "recommendations as to the courses of action to be followed in the event that Soviet forces enter Korean hostilities," and pay special attention to intelligence "concerning Soviet activities in the vicinity of Yugoslavia and Northern Iran" ("Memorandum for the President," June 29, 1950, pp. 3–4). The president was not yet convinced.

One of the main reasons for Truman's concern was the fact that the Soviets had not responded to U.S. diplomatic approaches. As the NSC meeting opened on Thursday, Truman was very reluctant to approve instructions to MacArthur that allowed the possibility of combat between U.S. and Soviet troops ("Draft" n.d., pp. 1–4). In the middle of this discussion, Acheson reminded Truman about the telegram received that afternoon from Ambassador Kirk. Kirk had finally met with Gromyko and the Soviet response was "interpreted as a clear statement that the Russians were not going to put their armed forces in *as* their own forces" ("Draft" n.d., p. 4, emphasis in original). Acheson was now "convinced" that the "Russians do not intend to enter directly into the Korean dispute" ("Draft" n.d., p. 5). This piece of evidence impressed Truman to the extent that he authorized U.S. air and naval action north of the 38th parallel ("Memorandum for the President," June 30, 1950, pp. 2–3). The president was now convinced that the initial intelligence estimates were accurate (although some uncertainty remained as to Chinese intentions, but this possibility was remarkably viewed as less of a concern, see "Draft" n.d., p. 5). The high level of uncertainty regarding Soviet intentions that Truman perceived at the beginning of the week had been replaced by a strongly held belief that the Soviets would not intervene in response to U.S. military actions.

The second major source of uncertainty for President Truman was the extent of intervention that would be required to save the ROK. Given his fear of Soviet escalation and concern regarding overcommitment, Truman did not want to use more resources than necessary to achieve his immediate goal. But in the early stages of the conflict, there was a high level of uncertainty as to what level of commitment would be needed. The initial hope was that the South Koreans could repulse the attack with only material assistance from the U.S. military. Unfortunately, the lackluster U.S. aid program for the ROK had left it ill-prepared for the North Korean assault (Pelz, 1983, p. 118). The State Department's own intelligence estimates detailed the extent of the DPRK's superiority (see "Consequences of US

Troop Withdrawal," February 28, 1949, p. 1; "Current Capabilities," June 19, 1950, p. 1). Indeed, Truman had not sent planes and tanks to the ROK because his administration feared that Rhee would use offensive weapons for an invasion of the north (see Cumings, 1990, pp. 598–599).

At the Blair House meeting on Sunday, the JCS favored the use of U.S. air and naval assets in the region. Secretary Pace later suggested that "the original decision to go in was made on the basis of the belief that this could be handled by air and naval forces" (Pace, January 1972, p. 71). While Secretary Finletter disputed Pace's assertion (see Finletter, 1972, pp. 33–34), the minutes of the meeting certainly reveal guarded optimism in that direction on the part of General Vandenberg and Admiral Sherman. In fact, General Bradley, Secretary Pace, and Secretary Johnson all indicated their opposition to putting ground troops in Korea, preferring to rely on air and naval operations ("Memorandum of Conversation," June 25, 1950, pp. 2, 4).

At the Blair House meeting on Monday, President Truman discovered that U.S. pilots had taken their orders too literally and were "avoiding combat where the direct carrying-out of their mission was not involved" ("Memorandum of Conversation," June 26, 1950, p. 1). Thus, the president ordered U.S. air and naval forces to give the ROK troops support south of the 38th parallel ("Memorandum of Conversation," June 26, 1950, p. 2). Later in the evening, General Collins commented on the seriousness of the military situation and noted that it "was impossible to say how much our air can do" ("Memorandum of Conversation," June 26, 1950, p. 6). This comment led to the first real consideration of supplying U.S. ground troops, but the discussion was limited to the effect of this action on other U.S. commitments ("Memorandum of Conversation," June 26, 1950, p. 7).

On Wednesday, the CIA reported that Seoul had fallen but that the morale of ROK troops had been buoyed by the news of U.S. support (CIA "Korean Situation," June 28, 1950, p. 1). This report encouraged renewed hope that further intervention would not be needed. Despite this glimmer of hope, General Vandenberg told the NSC that evening that "we could not get the full value of our air support unless we could attack especially the north Korean bases and fuel supplies" ("Memorandum of Conversation," June 28, 1950, p. 3). Truman put off the decision to authorize operations north of the parallel until Thursday.

On Thursday morning the CIA report was much more bleak. The U.S. military aid that had reached ROK forces did not stabilize the situation and U.S. air and naval operations had not produced significant results (CIA "Korean Situation," June 29, 1950, p. 1). At the NSC meeting Thursday night, Truman authorized air and naval operations north of the 38th parallel and the deployment of limited ground forces ("Memorandum for the President," June 30, 1950, pp. 2–3). Before this latest escalation could have an effect, the Pentagon received MacArthur's report on his reconnaissance mission to Korea. In his report, MacArthur confidently stated that the "only assurance for the holding of the present line, and the ability to regain later the lost ground, is through the introduction of US ground combat forces into the Korean battle area" (FRUS, 1976, p. 249). The president accepted MacArthur's estimate and approved the dispatch of U.S. troops on Friday morning (Truman, 1956, pp. 343–344).

The above discussion also sheds light on the buildup of time pressure from June 25–30. From Saturday to Friday, the progress of events in Korea dictated the pace of decision making in the White House. As the North Korean troops advanced deeper into the ROK, President Truman was forced to make new decisions before the effects of his previous decisions could be determined. Early in the week, the president and his advisers frequently commented on time as a factor in decision making. When the president was notified of the invasion on Saturday night, Acheson encouraged him to remain in Independence while the State and Defense Departments gathered information and developed alternatives (Acheson, 1969, p. 404). On Sunday, Acheson cabled Ambassador Muccio that his "greatest concern" was "whether Korean army can pull things together for brief period required for US decision and action or help" (FRUS, 1976, p. 162). Muccio replied that after their initially heavy losses the ROK army had regrouped and the situation seemed to have "stabilized" (FRUS, 1976, p. 166). Thus, at the first Blair House meeting, Secretary Finletter cautioned the president "that only the necessary decisions be made that night" and Truman noted that he "would wait for further action until the UN order is flouted" ("Memorandum of Conversation," June 25, 1950, pp. 4, 5).

On Monday night, the CIA produced a gloomy memorandum detailing the situation in Korea. The collapse of Seoul was "imminent" and it was "problematical whether cohesive southern Korean resistance will continue beyond next 24 hours" (CIA "Korean Situation," June 26, 1950, pp. 1–2). But since the increased air and naval operations approved at the second Blair House meeting had not yet been launched, the president refrained from making any new decisions on Tuesday. By Wednesday, the situation in Korea had become more clear. The CIA reported that both Kimpo airfield and Seoul had fallen but that Korean morale had improved after the announcement of U.S. support. This report suggested that once U.S. air operations were executed with "maximum effort" the tide might turn (CIA "Korean Situation," June 28, 1950, p. 1). It was at the NSC meeting on Wednesday that General Vandenberg suggested attacking North Korean bases, whereupon the president stated that "we may have to do it but he didn't want to decide that now" ("Memorandum of Conversation," June 28, 1950, p. 3).

As noted above, President Truman's perception of acute time pressure and reduced uncertainty crystallized on Thursday. The CIA report on the military situation gave ROK forces "a slightly less than 50-50 chance of holding the present defense line" (CIA "Korean Situation," June 29, 1950). On Friday, MacArthur's report on the situation called for an immediate decision. It stated, "Unless provision is made for the full utilization of the Army–Navy–Air team in this shattered area our mission will at best be needlessly costly in life, money and prestige. At worse, it might even be doomed to failure" (FRUS, 1976, p. 250). The urgency of MacArthur's request was amplified during a teleconference between Washington and Tokyo. MacArthur told his military superiors that "time is of the essence and a clear cut decision without delay is imperative" (FRUS, 1976, p. 251). Secretary Pace left the teleconference to telephone the president at 5:00 in the morning. The president approved the dispatch of one regimental combat team and immediately assembled his advisers to discuss further troop commitments (Acheson, 1969, p. 412). For Truman, the time of decision was at hand and could not be avoided.

Consideration of Alternatives and Final Decision

As noted previously, I expect that President Truman (identified as a potential-motivated president) will tend to focus on best-case outcomes and maximum gains when considering alternatives (REF hypothesis 3). I also anticipate that President Truman is likely to behave in a risk-acceptant manner in making final decisions (REF hypothesis 5).[35] In order to evaluate these hypotheses, we must examine the manner in which alternatives were considered, and the decisions that were reached during crucial periods in the cases. For the Korean case, only one period is worthy of careful scrutiny— June 24–30.

Upon his arrival at Washington's National Airport on the night of June 25, President Truman expressed his initial response to the North Korean attack—"By God, I'm going to let them have it" (Webb to Snyder, April 25, 1975, p. 2). While Secretary Johnson immediately offered his support for the president's comment, Under Secretary of State James E. Webb cautioned Truman to refrain from reaching any conclusions before hearing the recommendations discussed at the Departments of State and Defense conference that morning (Webb to Snyder, April 25, 1975, p. 2). Later that evening at the first Blair House meeting, President Truman had "before him" a packet of papers that included: "White 3" Ambassador Muccio's initial cable describing the North Korean attack, the "text of the resolution adopted by the United Nations Security Council Sunday afternoon," telegram "1726" detailing the views of the U.S. Embassy in Moscow, and a memorandum drafted by the State Department (possibly by Acheson alone, see Paige, 1968, p. 127) entitled "Points Requiring Presidential Decision" ("Blair House Meeting," June 25, 1950). The State Department cables from Korea and Moscow helped frame the situation for the president in the manner suggested above. The State Department memorandum was the sole policy paper under consideration at this meeting.

The State Department memorandum served as Acheson's notes for his presentation opening the Blair House discussions. This paper included five specific recommendations for U.S. action with accompanying discussion sections ("Points Requiring Presidential Decision" n.d.). The five recommendations included: instructing MacArthur to supply needed arms and equipment to the ROK forces, giving MacArthur wide discretion in using air and naval assets to support the evacuation of U.S. personnel, initiating consideration of what U.S. military action under UN auspices would be appropriate, interposing the U.S. 7th fleet between Formosa and Communist China, and executing military aid programs to Indochina, Burma, and Thailand ("Points Requiring Presidential Decision," n.d., pp. 1–6). It is interesting to note that the State Department paper generally focused on the benefits that would result from prompt U.S. action, but neglected to consider the chances for failure or potential negative consequences that might result from these initiatives.

The initial response to Acheson's presentation was General Bradley's assertion that "we must draw the line somewhere," which was immediately endorsed by the president ("Memorandum of Conversation," June 25, 1950, p. 2). Bradley noted the positive impact that U.S. air action would have on ROK morale even if "they were unable to spot the North Korean Tanks" ("Memorandum of Conversation," June 25, 1950, p. 2). In reference to U.S. naval action, Bradley noted "it would probably not be necessary for them to shoot but that they might frighten off the North Korean amphibious forces" ("Memorandum of Conversation," June 25, 1950, p. 2). The only negative comment offered by Bradley was his concern regarding the deployment of U.S. ground units ("Memorandum of Conversation," June 25, 1950, p. 2). Admiral Sherman seconded Bradley's views, and further suggested that the "present situation in Korea offers a valuable opportunity for us to act" ("Memorandum of Conversation," June 25, 1950, p. 3). General Vandenberg offered the only voice of caution regarding air action, indicating that the United States could handle the North Korean air force but might face trouble if the Russian air force intervened ("Memorandum of Conversation," June 25, 1950, p. 3). This uncertainty regarding Russian intentions (discussed above) was also highlighted by Secretary Finletter when he advised that "only the necessary decisions be made that night" and that the United States should only take "calculated risks" in attempting to "keep the peace" ("Memorandum of Conversation," June 25, 1950, p. 4). Given the uncertainty regarding Soviet intentions, Truman agreed to only the first three of Acheson's five recommendations. The president expressed a willingness to go further in supporting the ROK, but the lack of time pressure allowed him to delay the other decisions and gather more information about the situation ("Memorandum of Conversation," June 25, 1950, p. 5).

As events deteriorated on Monday, June 26, Secretary Acheson reformulated his five recommendations into a draft statement for the president (Acheson, 1969, p. 407; Paige, 1968, p. 161). General Vandenberg opened the Blair House meeting that night with a report that the first North Korean fighter had been shot down by U.S. pilots, to which the president responded that "he hoped it was not the last" ("Memorandum of Conversation," June 26, 1950, p. 1). Acheson then presented four recommendations (two of which had been presented at the Sunday meeting): instructing U.S. air and naval forces to "offer the fullest possible support" to the ROK south of the 38th parallel, interposing the U.S. 7th fleet between Formosa and Communist

China, providing military aid and sending a military mission to Indochina, and strengthening U.S. forces and increasing military aid to the Philippines (Acheson, 1969, pp. 407–408). The president approved each of Acheson's suggestions with little debate. His main concern was that U.S. planes should not cross the 38th parallel, at one point adding "not yet" ("Memorandum of Conversation," June 26, 1950, p. 2). Secretary Johnson also liked Acheson's proposals, stating that "if we hold the line as indicated that that was alright" ("Memorandum of Conversation," June 26, 1950, p. 3). There is very little evidence of any consideration of the chances for failure or the potential costs of the actions proposed by Acheson.

After discussing Acheson's draft statement and plans for submitting the second Security Council resolution to the UN, the president and his advisers returned to a discussion of what might happen next in Korea. When General Collins cautioned the group that the military situation in Korea "was bad" and that it "was impossible to say how much our air can do," Acheson replied that "it was important for us to do something even if the effort were not successful" ("Memorandum of Conversation," June 26, 1950, p. 6). Secretary Johnson seconded Acheson's views and asked the Joint Chiefs if they had any objections to "the course of action which had been outlined," there "was no objection" ("Memorandum of Conversation," June 26, 1950, p. 6). The president then briefly raised the possibility of troop mobilization, but was advised that "it would be preferable to wait a few days" ("Memorandum of Conversation," June 26, 1950, p. 7). Secretary Johnson seems to have spoken for the president and his advisers when he said that "he hoped these steps already authorized will settle the Korean question" ("Memorandum of Conversation," June 26, 1950, p. 7). At approximately 10:17 p.m. (EDT), Truman's instructions were sent to MacArthur (Paige, 1968, pp. 180–181).

The NSC meeting on Wednesday was scheduled for its regular weekly time and produced little in the way of new initiatives (see Paige, 1968, p. 221). There were no policy papers under consideration and so the discussion mainly focused on bringing those assembled up to date on events in Korea and on potential future U.S. moves. The major product of this meeting was a recognition that the United States was now firmly committed to aid the ROK and that this commitment might require deeper U.S. involvement. Acheson stated "we may find ourselves in trouble in Korea" and thus, "what has been done may make it imperative to accept full-out war" ("Memorandum for the President," June 29, 1950, p. 1). Truman agreed with Acheson, indicating that "we should not back out of Korea unless a military situation elsewhere demanded such action" ("Memorandum for the President," June 29, 1950, p. 1). As a result of this discussion, the Defense Department was directed to review U.S. military capabilities to indicate Truman's "freedom of choice" ("Memorandum for the President," June 29, 1950, p. 4).

Toward the end of the NSC meeting, Secretary Finletter and General Vandenberg introduced the issue of U.S. air attacks north of the 38th parallel.

The meeting minutes indicate that the president did not want to consider this action without "further consideration" ("Memorandum of Conversation," June 28, 1950, p. 3). This discussion marked the first real debate between the president and his military advisers regarding the effectiveness of current U.S. actions. It was only after General Vandenberg expressed his concerns that Acheson asked, for the first time, for an estimate of "the possibilities of our air against North Korean armor" ("Memorandum of Conversation," June 28, 1950, p. 3). Vandenberg replied that both weather and terrain were limiting the effectiveness of U.S. air attacks and that even when a North Korean tank or airplane was destroyed, "another would come in from the Northern bases" ("Memorandum for the President," June 29, 1950, p. 3). As disturbing as this information was, it did not move Truman to action. The president was not yet ready to deal with problems of implementation.

As events deteriorated further in Korea and as MacArthur returned to Tokyo from his survey mission, Secretary Johnson asked the president to call another meeting of the NSC (Paige, 1968, p. 240). The basic document under consideration at this meeting was a draft directive from the JCS to MacArthur. Secretary Johnson presented the draft directive at the outset of the meeting and the discussion focused on its details. The directive sought to eliminate the "principal impediments to the effective implementation of the military mission in Korea" (Paige, 1968, p. 247; see also Smith, 1951, p. 86). The draft directive broadened MacArthur's instructions to allow operations north of the 38th parallel, authorized the deployment of U.S. service units (particularly those dealing with communication and transportation), authorized the deployment of U.S. ground troops to retain a port and airbase near Pusan, and included rules of engagement in the event that Soviet forces intervened in the conflict (JCS to CINCFE MacArthur, June 29, 1950; Paige, 1968, p. 247).

The only real debate over the proposed directive focused on the instructions for MacArthur in the event that the Soviets intervened. The president interrupted Secretary Johnson's presentation to state: "I do not want any implication in the letter that we are going to war with Russia at this time" ("Draft" n.d., p. 1). The president's fear of overcommitment subsided when he was assured that MacArthur's instructions would not be released publicly and the "document would remain top secret" ("Draft" n.d., p. 4). He was also relieved to hear of the Soviet response to Ambassador Kirk and the State Department's interpretation of this exchange (see discussion above, "Draft" n.d., pp. 4–5). The rest of the meeting focused on clarifying the instructions regarding operations north of the 38th parallel and discussing the merits of deploying ground troops.

There was surprisingly little discussion (and almost no disagreement) regarding the escalatory elements of the draft directive. Secretaries Johnson and Pace, the main proponents of these new military initiatives, were only weakly challenged by the president. He was mainly concerned with giving MacArthur too much authority and directed his comments toward limiting the scope of the instructions. Truman "said that he just wanted to destroy air bases, gasoline supplies, ammunition dumps and places like that north of the 38th parallel" ("Draft" n.d., p. 2). The president also appears to have discussed limiting MacArthur's use of ground troops:

> He said that he only wanted to restore order to the 38th parallel; he did not want to do anything north of it except to "keep the North Koreans from killing the people we are trying to save. You can give the Commander-in-Chief (MacArthur) all the authority he needs to do that but he is not to go north of the 38th degree parallel." ("Draft" n.d., p. 2)

Secretary Acheson amplified the president's concerns, indicating that U.S. planes should be ordered to stay well clear of Manchuria and Russia (Paige, 1968, p. 247). Acheson also supported the deployment of U.S. ground troops, but cautioned that "the present proposal . . . is quite different from an unlimited commitment to supply all of the ground forces required in South Korea" ("Memorandum for the President," June 30, 1950, p. 1). Once again, there is very little evidence of any consideration of the chances for failure or the potential costs of the proposed military actions.

In contrast to the well-documented discussions from June 24 to 29, the events of Friday June 30 are somewhat murky. First, MacArthur's telegram regarding the dire situation in Korea was not received by the Pentagon until 1:31 a.m., fully 16 hours after MacArthur was reported to have drafted it (Paige, 1968, pp. 239–240).[36] Second, the Friday morning meeting between President Truman and his advisers—where he agreed to commit two U.S. divisions to Korea—is the only meeting for which there are no declassified minutes (and possibly no minutes at all). And yet despite these problems, we may construct a somewhat detailed account of the events leading up to Truman's final decision.

During the early morning teleconference, Secretary Pace called the president to relay MacArthur's request for an immediate decision regarding the deployment of one regimental combat team to Korea (Paige, 1968, p. 256; Smith, 1951, p. 88). The president immediately approved MacArthur's request, but delayed a final decision on the two-division commitment until he could meet again with his advisers (Paige, 1968, p. 256). At 7:00 a.m., Truman was briefed on the military situation in the ROK and then called Secretaries Pace, Johnson, and Acheson to discuss MacArthur's request (Smith, 1951, p. 88). Truman's Defense Department advisers drafted a simple directive to MacArthur and then met with Truman, Acheson, and Harriman to make a final decision (Paige, 1968, p. 257; Smith, 1951, p. 88).

At this 30-minute meeting, there was complete unanimity regarding MacArthur's recommendation. Acheson later stated that "this was a necessary step to be taken, and it was one that you had to do" ("Princeton Seminars," February 13–14, 1954: Track 2, p. 8). Secretary Pace would later note that this decision "was a much more fundamental decision than the original one although it was largely overlooked at the time" (1972, p. 74).

For Pace, "at that point you can't really call it a decision" (1972, p. 75). For Truman, the meeting was largely about whether or not to accept two divisions of Chinese nationalist troops that had been offered by Chiang Kaishek (1956, p. 343). Fortunately for the president, all of his advisers opposed this move and he decided to decline this offer (Paige, 1968, pp. 258–259). At 1:22 p.m., the word was sent out to General MacArthur and the United States was "then fully committed in Korea" (Acheson, 1969, p. 413).

The above discussion of President Truman's decision making during the Korea "crisis" provides a great deal of evidence in support of REF hypothesis 3 (*potential-motivated presidents tend to focus on best-case outcomes and maximum gains*). The extensive quantity of direct Truman statements from the meetings held from June 25 to 30 allows for the rigorous evaluation of this hypothesis. Clearly, President Truman and his advisers continually ignored the relative costs of the recommendations that were being considered. The president appears to have had great faith in his advisers, and so he refrained from asking pointed questions and challenging their assumptions and estimates. The president appears to have been particularly confident in the advice of his military commanders—recall that questions regarding the potential effectiveness of U.S. air operations did not emerge until the *Wednesday* NSC meeting. Indeed, when Truman agreed to MacArthur's recommendations on Friday, there appears to have been no discussion of whether two divisions was the extent or just the beginning of U.S. intervention. There is also some nondirect evidence bearing on the evaluation of hypothesis 3. The few policy papers delivered to the president during this crucial week, generally ignored considerations of costs and benefits and chances of success or failure. In fact, I am struck by the lack of well staffed-out policy analysis in the White House, particularly in contrast to the Kennedy administration (see chapter four).[37]

In considering Truman's final decision to commit U.S. ground troops, we must first determine whether REF hypothesis 5 or 6 is more appropriate. Based on the evidence presented above, I feel that hypothesis 6 (*if there is only one alternative capable of achieving the aspiration level, that alternative is likely to be selected regardless of its level of risk*) more accurately characterizes this decision. If we look at the Korea case as a single decision, we clearly see that the military intervention option was really the only alternative under consideration. At no time did the president or his advisers consider pulling out of Korea or accepting a diplomatic solution to the "crisis." Indeed, even if we view this case as a sequence of decisions (see Paige, 1968, pp. 278–279), there is no point where we observe the consideration of distinct alternatives. At the meetings during the week of June 24–30, not one of Truman's advisers challenged the overall representation of the problem facing them. And although the JCS were at times concerned regarding the chances for success of the various military options, they did not offer viable alternative options. The policy proposals presented to President Truman throughout this crucial week all represented steps along the same path, with almost no suggestion of alternative goals or alternative means for achieving the president's aspiration level. Essentially, the president was presented with a series of single options (or sets of options) that were viewed as the only options capable of achieving the aspiration level. Upon his arrival at Washington's National Airport on Sunday, June 25, the president had stated "By God, I'm going to let them have it" (Webb to Snyder, April 25, 1975, p. 2), and by Friday, June 30, he had. (A summary of the findings for this case study can be found in table 3.3.)[38]

Epilogue

For Harry Truman, Korea was a challenge that had to be met. "The Reds were probing for weaknesses in our armor; we had to meet their thrust without getting embroiled in a worldwide war" (Truman, 1956, p. 337). For others, the decisions reached in the final week of June 1950 were just, but

Table 3.3   Summary of findings for Korea 1950 case study

Aspiration level	
Immediate goal	thwart the North Korean invasion and return to the *status quo ante* at the 38th parallel
Constraints on means	fear of potential Soviet reactions to U.S. initiatives and a concern regarding the overcommitment of U.S. military capabilities
Commitment reinforced by	desire to demonstrate resolve and the credibility of U.S. commitments both to the Soviets and to U.S. allies; fear that communist success in South Korea would lead to the fall of Indochina, Formosa, and possibly Japan; fear of negative reactions from Republicans in Congress who were already criticizing the administration for "losing" China; and desire to show that the United Nations could be an effective instrument for combating territorial aggression
Uncertainty	high uncertainty early during the week of June 25–30 that moderated as the administration became convinced that the invasion was a Soviet probe, but lingering concern over the extent of intervention that would be required to save the ROK
Time pressure	moderate time pressure early in the week quickly turned acute as the fall of Seoul appeared imminent, U.S. air operations had only a limited impact, and MacArthur stressed the need for a final decision
Consideration of alternatives	strong evidence of focus on best-case outcomes and maximum gains during week of June 25–30—almost no consideration of the relative costs of the limited options under consideration during meetings with the president
Final decision	strong evidence that final decision reached during week of June 25–30 was support for only alternative capable of achieving aspiration level—no consideration of diplomatic or nonmilitary alternatives

Truman's inability to deter the North Koreans is criticized (see Paige, 1968, pp. 347–352). More recently, scholars have focused on the longer-term implications of the Korean War. Bernstein (1977, p. 34) argues that the conflict contributed to the militarization of the United States and set the precedent for other large-scale U.S. military interventions "without a Congressional declaration of war." Finally, scholars like Bruce Cumings have examined the War from the Korean perspective, emphasizing its effects on the Korean people and questioning the accuracy of traditional interpretations of U.S. decision making (1990). Unfortunately, this would not be the last U.S. experience in this type of conflict. For Kennedy's problems in Southeast Asia lay just around the corner.

V. Conclusions

The Truman administration cases—Iran, Greece, and Korea—provide empirical support for several of the hypotheses that compose my REF. Unfortunately, as table 3.4 reveals, the Iran and Greece cases also provide evidence that runs against a number of the hypotheses. Clearly, hypotheses 1 and 1a (relating to the president's aspiration level) receive the most support across the cases. In each instance, President Truman perceived and articulated a complex combination of goals and constraints. I found extensive direct and indirect evidence of the aspiration level guiding the president's decision making. President Truman consistently evaluated options relative

Table 3.4   Degree of support for REF hypotheses across cases and decision periods

	Iran		Greece		Korea	
Decision period	1[a]	2[b]	1[c]	2[d]	3[e]	1[f]
Hypotheses						
1	S	M	S	S	S	S
1a	S	M	S	S	S	S
3	A	W	M	A	A	S
5	NA	NA	NA	A	NA	NA
6	NA	W	S	NA	NA	S
7a	NA	NA	NA	NA	W	S
7c	A	A	NA	A	NA	NA

Key: S = strong, M = moderate, W = weak, A = evidence runs against hypothesis, NA = hypothesis not applicable.

[a] December 1945–May 1946
[b] June–December 1946
[c] February 21–March 12, 1947
[d] August–November 1947
[e] December–June 1948
[f] June 24–June 30, 1950

to his aspiration level rather than some overall value level. Based on these case studies, I feel that hypotheses 1 and 1a are indeed "plausible" and that this part of the REF is on target.

REF hypothesis 3 (relating to how potential-motivated presidents are expected to process information) is only partially supported by the results discussed above. While I found strong direct and indirect support for this hypothesis in the Korean case, three of the five decision periods for Iran and Greece produced indirect evidence that runs *against* the hypothesis. I am encouraged by the fact that in Korea (the case with the most direct evidence of President Truman's decision making process), I found ample evidence of a focus on best-case analysis. I am also somewhat heartened by the weak support for this hypothesis in the first decision period regarding Iran and the moderate support for this hypothesis in the first decision period regarding Greece. But I cannot ignore the evidence for the remaining decision periods.[39] In chapter five, I explore a number of potential explanations for these negative results and suggest revising the REF in this area—both to deal with evidentiary problems and to consider other ways in which individual risk predispositions might affect information processing.

REF hypothesis 5 (*potential-motivated presidents are likely to behave in a risk-acceptant manner*) cannot be adequately evaluated through these case studies. Results for this hypothesis were only obtained during one decision period, and the evidence from that period ran against the hypothesis. Indeed, REF hypothesis 6 (*if there is only one alternative capable of achieving the aspiration level, that alternative is likely to be selected regardless of its level of risk*) turned out to be the more relevant hypothesis for the Truman cases. This hypothesis received strong support in the Greece and Korea cases, and was weakly supported by the Iran case. These results suggest that potential-motivated presidents may be less likely to develop a range of alternatives when time pressure is acute (see discussion in chapter five). This appears to be another area where the REF requires substantial revision.

The REF hypotheses that deal with uncertainty, information accuracy, and time pressure—7a&c—received mixed support. In the two instances where President Truman perceived moderate or high uncertainty and little time pressure, he delayed making a significant decision. The strongest support for hypothesis 7a is found in the Korean case where Truman delayed making a decision until he was convinced that the Soviets would not intervene in response to U.S. military actions, that U.S. troops were required to turn the tide of the battle, and that an immediate decision was required. Hypothesis 7c, on the other hand, is not well supported. In fact, the evidence from three of the six decision periods under examination runs against this hypothesis. The Iran and Greece cases provide evidence that, when faced with perceptions of high uncertainty and acute time pressure, President Truman was more likely to engage in incrementalism rather than bolstering. This result is obviously disturbing. Clearly, this hypothesis needs to be reworked.

Overall, I feel that my REF (in its current form) only partially explains President Truman's risk behavior in these cases. While I am obviously encouraged by the results for the Korea case, I am also discouraged by the negative results obtained in the Iran and Greece cases. In chapter five, I consider possible explanations for the negative results obtained in the Iran and Greece cases and suggest substantial revision of REF hypotheses 3, 5, and 7c. In the next chapter, I evaluate the REF in three case studies from the Kennedy administration—Laos, Vietnam, and the Congo.

CHAPTER FOUR

Kennedy Case Studies

I. Introduction and Overview

In Laos, Vietnam, and the Congo, President John Fitzgerald Kennedy dealt with the legacy of President Dwight David Eisenhower and his Secretary of State John Foster Dulles. In each of these cases, previous U.S. commitments forced the new president to consider his response to "Communist aggression" early in his term. Particularly in Laos and Vietnam, Kennedy and his advisers were confronted with deteriorating situations that required immediate attention. Over time, President Kennedy considered various levels of military intervention by U.S. forces in these regions. Kennedy's decision making during these cases is well documented, providing an excellent opportunity for evaluating the hypotheses that compose the Risk Explanation Framework (REF).

The Laos, Vietnam, and Congo case studies all follow the same structure. First, an overview narrative of the case provides important contextual information. Then, the various elements of the REF are evaluated through discussions relating to the president's aspiration level, perceptions of uncertainty and time pressure, consideration of alternatives, and final decision. A concluding section of this chapter considers the implications for theory of the results obtained. Throughout each case study an attempt is made to remind the reader of the relevant elements of the REF that are being evaluated in each section. I strive to marshal a "critical mass" of data supporting my observations and conclusions, but I recognize and point out areas where the documentary evidence is thin and certain hypotheses cannot be evaluated in a rigorous manner.

II. Laos 1961

Overview

On July 20, 1958 the International Control Commission for Laos (which had been created as part of the 1954 Geneva agreements regarding Indochina) adjourned following the first successful election in an independent Laotian state. Prince Souvanna Phouma formed a government of "national union," which included members of the Neo Lao Hak Xat (NLHX, the political arm of the Pathet Lao). These events angered members of the Eisenhower administration, which had been providing military and economic aid to Laos to prevent a Pathet Lao victory (George et al., 1971, pp. 38–39; Hilsman, 1967, pp. 118–119; Sorensen, 1965, pp. 639–640). The Eisenhower administration decided to withhold the regular U.S. aid payment to the Laotian government, causing a parliamentary crisis that led to the removal of Souvanna Phouma and his replacement by Phoui Sananikone (George et al., 1971, pp. 38–39; Hilsman, 1967, p. 118). Sananikone favored neutrality in the Cold War (as had Souvanna Phouma), but he desired a "pro-Western" neutrality that allowed no NLHX participation in government and wished to prevent the North Vietnamese from using trails in northeastern Laos (Hilsman, 1967, pp. 119–120).

At the end of 1959, Sananikone made a serious mistake when he attempted to consolidate his hold on power by removing a Central Intelligence Agency (CIA) supported group of ministers. On December 31, 1959 General Phoumi Nosavan removed the Sananikone government from power in a bloodless coup and reluctantly called for new elections to be held in April of 1960 (Hilsman, 1967, pp. 121–122; Schlesinger, 1965, p. 326). These elections (which were clearly rigged, see Hilsman, 1967, p. 122) allowed Phoumi to form a pro-Western, anticommunist government. This hard-line policy resulted in another coup, engineered by paratroop Captain Kong Le in August of 1960, which provided an opportunity for the return of Souvanna Phouma, negotiations with General Phoumi, and headaches in the Eisenhower administration (see George et al., 1971, pp. 39–40; Hilsman, 1967, pp. 123–125; Schlesinger, 1965, pp. 326–327). As Phoumi negotiated in bad faith and prepared to launch another coup, Souvanna Phouma accepted a Soviet offer to airlift military equipment from Hanoi to Vientiane (the Laotian capital) (Hilsman, 1967, p. 125). The Soviet airlift came too late to alter events on the ground and Phoumi took Vientiane on December 16. Kong Le's forces fled north to join the Pathet Lao and Souvanna Phouma fled to Cambodia (George et al., 1971, pp. 40–41). On January 20, as John Fitzgerald Kennedy was inaugurated in Washington, Soviet aid flowed to the Pathet Lao and Kong Le troops and General Phoumi's forces prepared for civil war.

President-elect Kennedy had met with President Eisenhower on January 19. During this meeting, Eisenhower appraised Kennedy of the situation in Laos. He noted that "any proposal which would include communists in the government would end up with the communists in control of the government" and called Laos the "cork in the bottle" of Southeast Asia (FRUS, 1994a, p. 19). The situation was viewed very seriously by the outgoing administration, and Kennedy left the meeting with the impression that Eisenhower felt military intervention was "preferable to a communist success in Laos" (FRUS, 1994a, p. 20). Laos would become the first "crisis" faced by the new administration.

Over the next five months President Kennedy would seriously consider U.S. military intervention in Laos on two separate occasions. In late March, after a series of Pathet Lao victories, the president used a "tacit" ultimatum (see George et al., 1971, p. 58) and small-scale troop movements to coerce the Soviets into agreeing with a British proposal favoring a diplomatic solution in Laos. In late April/early May, as the Pathet Lao continued to expand and consolidate their control over parts of Laos, Kennedy rejected an immediate large-scale intervention, but allowed contingency planning to continue in the State and Defense Departments. When a cease-fire was declared in Laos on May 3, President Kennedy and his advisers enjoyed their first success since the disaster of the Bay of Pigs. The tumultuous events in Laos, Cuba, and the Congo during this period provided a baptism by fire for the new president and his closest advisers.[1]

Aspiration Level

As noted in chapter two, the president's "aspiration level" is expected to comprise a set of minimum level goals that the president hopes to achieve or surpass. In order to evaluate hypothesis 1 (*presidents tend to evaluate out-comes relative to an aspiration level rather than an overall value level*), we must infer the elements of President Kennedy's aspiration level (regarding Laos) from the documentary record. As noted in figure 2.2, we need to find descriptions of acceptable/desirable outcomes/objectives in this case. Thus, we need to find relevant documents that address Kennedy's goals, desires, hopes, needs, and/or requirements in this case.

Based on the evidence presented below, I believe that President Kennedy's immediate goal in Laos was to create a "truly" neutral state that would align itself with neither superpower. The means available for achiev-ing this goal were constrained by the fear of potential communist reactions to U.S. initiatives, the potential for a negative domestic reaction should the United States send troops to Laos, and the fear of overextending the U.S. military posture globally. The president's commitment to achieving or surpassing his immediate goal was reinforced by his fear that communist success in Laos would lead to the fall of South Vietnam and Thailand, his concern regarding the need to demonstrate resolve and the credibility of U.S. commitments to the Southeast Asia Treaty Organization (SEATO) allies, and by his fear of a negative reaction from Republicans in Congress who might castigate him in the press for negotiating with communists. This complex combination of goals and constraints formed the aspiration level that guided Kennedy's decision making. President Kennedy's aspiration level was well articulated and the documentary evidence supports REF hypothesis 1.

In order to understand President Kennedy's aspiration level, it is useful to first consider the goals of the Eisenhower administration in Laos. Roger Hilsman groups the policy alternatives in Laos according to the personalities that represented them (1967, pp. 105–106). And so, Prince Souvanna

Phouma represented true neutrality, Phoui Sananikone represented pro-Western neutrality, and Phoumi Nosavan represented pro-Western anticommunism. The Eisenhower administration never accepted Souvanna Phouma's brand of neutrality. In fact, while Souvanna sought to form a government of national union, J. Graham Parsons, the U.S. ambassador to Laos, "struggled for sixteen months to prevent a coalition" (quoted in Hilsman, 1967, p. 111). From 1958 to 1961 the Eisenhower administration vacillated between supporting Sananikone's pro-Western neutrality and Phoumi's militant anticommunism. Within the administration, the State Department favored Sananikone, while the Defense Department and CIA supported General Phoumi (see Hilsman, 1967, pp. 118–121). Souvanna Phouma could not garner U.S. support because he wanted to form a coalition with the communists, a stance that was unacceptable to Eisenhower and Dulles (see FRUS, 1994a, pp. 19–25).[2]

Having attended the meeting with President Eisenhower on January 19, Kennedy was clearly aware of the previous administration's views. Eisenhower had stated that SEATO intervention was preferable to accepting a coalition with the communists (see FRUS, 1994a, pp. 19–20), but the Kennedy administration was not prepared to blithely accept the policies of the previous administration. Over the inaugural weekend, an "Inter-Agency Task Force on Laos" prepared its first report. In its report, the Task Force noted that: "There is also an advantage to the United States through the fact of the new Administration, in that there will appear to many critics of our past policies a potentiality for a new approach" (FRUS, 1994a, p. 30). From late January to early March, the Kennedy administration struggled with the development of its own policies regarding Laos.

During the two-month period in which President Kennedy developed his aspiration level regarding Laos, debate within the administration was quite heated. Doves like Senator Mike Mansfield encouraged the new president to advocate strict neutrality in Laos. Mansfield wrote to the president, "There are risks in such a policy but the risks in our present policies seem even greater for they create the illusion of an indigenous Laotian barrier to a communist advance when, in fact, there is none" (Mansfield to Kennedy, January 21, 1961, p. 1). Hawks like Kenneth P. Landon supported the continuation of support for General Phoumi. He wrote to Walt Rostow, then the deputy special assistant for national security affairs, "Neutrals are like manure, useful if spread very thin but a nuisance in a heap" (Landon to Rostow, February 7, 1961, p. 7). By early March, President Kennedy was ready to sit down with his advisers and commit to a new policy on Laos. Admiral Harry D. Felt, Commander-in-Chief, Pacific, was recalled for consultation and a reassessment of the administration's Laos policy was initiated. Rostow wrote to Kennedy, "In short, our initial dispositions with respect to Laos, both diplomatically and militarily, have not succeeded; and we enter a new phase" (Rostow to Kennedy, March 9, 1961, p. 2).

At a crucial White House meeting on March 9, President Kennedy and his top advisers reevaluated U.S. goals in Laos. In discussing a planned

14-nation conference, Kennedy "remarked that it looked like all were in favor of Souvanna except us, and perhaps Thailand and South Vietnam, and this did not look like a very good lineup" (FRUS, 1994a, p. 76). The point was made that "the *neutral Laos* that we were seeking was different than the one we are working for now. The Laos we are fighting for now should be anti-Communist, but neutral—in other words, keep the Laotian government from strong Communist influence. Before, we sought a pro-Western 'neutral' Laos" (FRUS, 1994a, p. 78, emphasis in original). Kennedy then observed, "Well, look at Vietnam. What kind of a government are we going to get? Couldn't we settle now for a non-Communist Laos?" (FRUS, 1994a, p. 78). President Kennedy was slowly coming to accept the goal of a neutral Laos where Souvanna Phouma could once again play a role in the government. On March 12, Secretary Rusk sent a "Top Secret" cable to Phnom Penh asking Souvanna to return to Laos (see FRUS, 1994a, pp. 89–90). All that remained was to express the administration's new policy publicly.

On March 10, U.S. Ambassador to the Soviet Union Llewellyn E. Thompson sent a cable from Moscow indicating that his impression was that "for first time Khrushchev fully convinced that we are genuinely seeking neutral status and that he is much intrigued by possibly settling this problem" (Thompson to Rusk, March 10, 1961, p. 1). Unfortunately for the Kennedy administration, this newfound understanding with Khrushchev did not result in Pathet Lao restraint. As the situation continued to deteriorate on the ground in Laos and as the administration seriously considered significant military intervention for the first time, President Kennedy held a press conference to publicly reiterate his administration's objectives in Laos (and present a "tacit" ultimatum [George et al., 1971, p. 58] to the Soviets, see discussion below). Kennedy stated "we strongly and unreservedly support the goal of a neutral and independent Laos, tied to no outside power or group of powers, threatening no one, and free from any domination . . . and if in the past there has been any possible ground for misunderstanding of our support for a truly neutral Laos, there should be none now" (Kennedy Press Statement, March 23, 1961, p. 1; see also Kennedy "Presidential Statements on Laos" n.d.).

The documentary record suggests that the goal of a "truly" neutral Laos was indeed President Kennedy's immediate goal in this case. But clearly other imperatives constrained the means available for achieving or surpassing the immediate goal, as well as Kennedy's ability to accept a settlement that fell short of his immediate goal. In terms of constraints on means, Kennedy carefully considered potential Chinese and Soviet responses to U.S. military intervention and was particularly concerned with the assertion by the Joint Chiefs of Staff (JCS) that nuclear weapons might need to be employed if Chinese troops invaded Laos (see FRUS, 1994a, pp. 59–61, 162–164; Kennedy, "Notes" n.d., p. 4; Sorensen, 1965, pp. 644–645). He was also concerned with potential threats to the lives of U.S. troops and the possibility of overextending the U.S. military posture globally (see Schlesinger, 1965, pp. 338–339; Sorensen, 1965, p. 645). In terms of factors reinforcing Kennedy's commitment to achieving or surpassing his immediate goal, Kennedy and his advisers were concerned with SEATO perceptions of U.S. weakness and lack of resolve and particularly with the implications that the loss of Laos would hold for future events in Vietnam and Thailand (see FRUS, 1994a, pp. 72–79, 105–107, 142–144; Rusk, "Oral History," December 2, 1969, p. 7). Domestically, the president feared congressional Republicans castigating him in the press for negotiating with communists, but also was concerned with the potential for negative public opinion should the United States send troops to Laos (see Hilsman, 1967, p. 134; Kennedy, "Notes" n.d., pp. 2,6; Schlesinger, 1965, pp. 338–339).

Uncertainty and Time Pressure

As noted in chapter two, I expect that *presidential perceptions of high uncertainty and a lack of valid information will interact with presidential risk predispositions and affect the output of the decision process* (REF hypothesis 7). In the Kennedy cases, if the president perceives high uncertainty and inaccurate information but does not perceive acute time pressure, I expect to observe decisional delay and an expanded search for information (REF hypothesis 7a). If the president perceives high uncertainty and inaccurate information and also perceives acute time pressure, I expect to observe incrementalism (REF hypothesis 7b).

As the evidence presented below suggests, President Kennedy's perceptions of uncertainty and time pressure waxed and waned during the various stages of the Laos "crisis." During the period from April to March of 1961, President Kennedy perceived persistent uncertainty and increasing time pressure. The decisions that emerged during this period were marked by incrementalism as Kennedy slowly increased the pressure on Moscow without fully committing U.S. troops. This pattern of incrementalism in the face of uncertainty and time pressure provides support for REF hypothesis 7b. By late April, Kennedy perceived acute time pressure combined with a *reduction* in uncertainty. He then may have finally decided against U.S. intervention in Laos, following a risk-averse course (as suggested by REF hypothesis 4, see discussion below).

Perceptions of uncertainty and time pressure had significant impacts on President Kennedy's decision making during the Laos "crisis." Initially, the situation in Laos was believed to be "deteriorating progressively" and the Inter-Agency Task Force on Laos suggested that "time appears to be against us if we do not increase our support of RLG [Royal Lao Government] forces" (FRUS, 1994a, p. 28). Despite these gloomy impressions, President Kennedy put off the first serious consideration of significant U.S. intervention until mid-March. In early February, General Phoumi had launched an offensive against Pathet Lao and Kong Le troops on the Plaines des Jarres (PDJ). It was hoped that the success of this offensive would halt the deterioration in Laos and turn the tide in favor of Phoumi's forces. Unfortunately for

Kennedy, by late February General Phoumi's forces were "stuck" (FRUS, 1994a, p. 62) and by early March the communists had launched a "probing offensive" (FRUS, 1994a, p. 71) that had routed Phoumi's troops. In a meeting on March 3, Kennedy decided to recall Admiral Felt for consultations and on March 9 Rostow wrote to Kennedy "we enter a new phase" (Rostow to Kennedy, March 9, 1961, p. 2) following the failure of the administration's military and political initiatives.

During the key White House meetings of March 9, 20, and 21, Kennedy's perception of growing time pressure forced the first serious consideration of significant U.S. military intervention. Schlesinger notes that Kennedy feared an "immediate communist takeover" and could not "accept any visible humiliation over Laos" (1965, p. 332). But perceptions of uncertainty persisted, particularly after the March 20 meeting where the JCS shook Kennedy by advocating large-scale intervention and the possible use of nuclear weapons or no U.S. intervention at all (see FRUS, 1994a, pp. 35–36; Hilsman, 1967, pp. 127–129; Schlesinger, 1965, pp. 332–333). Despite the deteriorating situation on the ground in Laos, Kennedy was again reminded that "the diplomatic road was not finally blocked" (Schlesinger, 1965, p. 332). Kennedy decided that the situation was serious enough to merit some form of action, but not yet critical (see Hilsman, 1967, pp. 130–131). He decided on a "two stringed" (FRUS, 1994a, p. 95) approach combining negotiation and action, this policy resulted in the March 23 news conference including the "tacit" ultimatum to the Soviets.

The crisis character of events in Laos broke briefly in early April when the Soviets responded favorably to diplomatic initiatives proposed by the British government. But as the month progressed, the Soviets and British could not agree on the terms for a cease-fire and the Pathet Lao/Kong Le troops continued to expand their position on the ground. On April 13 Rostow sent a memo to Kennedy detailing Soviet intentions: "the Communist tactic in Laos is to delay on the cease-fire while the situation crumbles politically and militarily" (FRUS, 1994a, p. 126). Communist troops were in a position to threaten Paksane and Takhek and Rostow noted that the "collapse of these two towns would cut Laos in half isolating Vientiane and Luang Prabang from the south" (FRUS, 1994a, p. 126). The administration was distracted from events in Laos from April 17 to 19 as they dealt with the Bay of Pigs debacle, but on April 26 the State Department received an urgent telegram (from the U.S. Ambassador to Laos Winthrop Brown) that could not be ignored. Brown noted that the town of Muong Sai had fallen and he did not see how "we can afford to let enemy continue his forward movement toward key centers of Laos beyond a certain point" (FRUS, 1994a, p. 139). Following the receipt of Brown's telegram, Acting Secretary of State Chester Bowles sent a memorandum to President Kennedy entitled "Deteriorating Situation and Need for Critical Decisions." Bowles noted that the United States now had "a choice between two difficult and unpleasant alternatives": military intervention or a government that would eventually "convert Laos into a Communist puppet" (FRUS, 1994a, pp. 140–141).

In an afternoon meeting on April 26, President Kennedy and his advisers concluded that a large-scale "conflict would be unjustified, even if the loss of Laos must be accepted" (FRUS, 1994a, p. 143). The president withheld from making a final decision because "the possibility of a strong American response" was "the only card left to be played in pressing for a cease-fire" (FRUS, 1994a, p. 143). From April 26 until May 2, President Kennedy and his advisers met five times to consider military intervention in Laos. Before a final decision could be reached a cease-fire was declared and the situation stabilized.[3] There is evidence that suggests that President Kennedy's perception of uncertainty was altered by several new pieces of information during this time period. In separate meetings on April 22, 25, and 27, Kennedy met with President Eisenhower, Governor Nelson Rockefeller, and a group of bipartisan legislative leaders. Kennedy's handwritten notes from each of these meetings indicate that he could find no support for U.S. military intervention in Laos (Kennedy, "Notes" n.d.). It was also during this period that the JCS were asked to provide their views on where U.S. intervention in Laos would lead. The resulting mix of conflicting opinions (see FRUS, 1994a, pp. 169–170) disturbed Kennedy, particularly further information regarding the defensibility of the Laotian terrain and the acknowledgment by the JCS that nuclear bombings of China, North Vietnam, and the Soviet Union were a real possibility (see Sorensen, 1965, pp. 644–645).

Consideration of Alternatives and Final Decision

As noted in chapter two, I expect that President Kennedy (identified as a security-motivated president) will tend to focus on worst-case outcomes and maximum losses when considering alternatives (REF hypothesis 2). I also anticipate that President Kennedy is likely to behave in a risk-averse manner in making final decisions (REF hypothesis 4).[4] In order to evaluate these hypotheses, we must examine the manner in which alternatives were considered, and the decisions that were reached during crucial periods in the cases. For the Laos "crisis," two periods are worthy of careful scrutiny— March 9–April 1 and April 26–May 3.

During the initial meeting of March 9, President Kennedy considered a plan to increase military and covert assistance to the Lao Armed Forces (FAL) so that they might recapture the PDJ. Kennedy expressed a number of concerns regarding the opposition of France and Britain, the political goals of the United States in Laos, the strength of communist forces in Laos, and the weakness of the Phoumi-led FAL (see FRUS, 1994a, pp. 72–79). The president tentatively approved the plan, but put its implementation on hold while diplomatic efforts continued (see FRUS, 1994a, pp. 80, 86–88). As the Soviet airlift proceeded and as Phoumi's forces were routed on the ground, the president met again with his advisers on March 20 and 21 to consider further actions.[5] In these "off the record" meetings, Walt Rostow advocated the movement of U.S. forces into Thailand so that they might be pre-positioned to intervene in the Mekong Valley (see FRUS, 1994a, pp. 94–95).[6] The JCS opposed Rostow's limited commitment, instead arguing for a large-scale intervention of "60,000 troops with air cover, and even the use of nuclear weapons, or else no intervention" (FRUS, 1994a, p. 94).

Given the lack of documentary evidence regarding Kennedy's concerns during this period, it is difficult to evaluate REF hypothesis 2. By examining the accounts provided by Schlesinger (1965) and Hilsman (1967), we may find suggestive evidence of Kennedy's concerns, but we must be careful to not overstate our conclusions. Each of these accounts portrays a reluctant Kennedy dissatisfied with the advice of his military advisers. Schlesinger comments on the indecisive character of the two meetings and argues that the president's "objective remained a political settlement" (1965, p. 333). Hilsman notes that the political solution favored by Kennedy "offered a possible way around this black-and-white choice with the additional advantage that it did not close out the other alternatives" (1967, p. 130). While Kennedy opposed the full-scale intervention suggested by the JCS, he was also reluctant to consider the "do nothing" option. As noted above, mounting time pressure suggested the need for some form of action on the part of the United States.

During the March 21 meeting, Kennedy agreed to a combination of diplomatic and military moves (see FRUS, 1994a, pp. 95–96). His March 23 press conference would clarify U.S. objectives and provide the Soviets with a "tacit" ultimatum with vague references to a potential future U.S. "response" (Kennedy Press Statement, March 23, 1961). In terms of diplomatic initiatives, the British presented an aide-memoire to the Soviets calling for a cease-fire and a new Geneva conference on Laos. Kennedy also approved the preliminary steps "necessary to the movement of American troops into the Mekong Valley of Thailand" (George et al., 1971, p. 58). These steps included the movement of U.S. marines and helicopters into Udorn, Thailand; the movement of the 7th fleet into the South China Sea; the alerting of a combat force on Okinawa; and the departure of 2,000 marines from a movie set in Japan (Schlesinger, 1965, pp. 333–334). Kennedy's "carrot and stick" tactics were acknowledged in a Pravda "Observer" (a pseudonym believed to indicate the official Soviet view) article on March 27 (Pravda Observer Article, March 27, 1961), and on April 1, the Soviets responded positively to the British proposal (see FRUS, 1994a, pp. 110–111).

While diplomatic wrangling continued in early April, the Kennedy administration began to develop policy options in the event that these initiatives failed to achieve a cease-fire in Laos. As noted above, Pathet Lao/Kong Le troops continued their advance—threatening Luang Prabang, Vientiane, and the Mekong Valley. When Muong Sai fell and Ambassador Brown sent his frantic cable on April 26 (FRUS, 1994a, pp. 139–140), President Kennedy was once again faced with an occasion to decide whether to intervene militarily in Laos. The period from April 26 to May 2 was the high point of the Laos "crisis" for President Kennedy and his advisers. The various policy papers and meeting transcripts for this period provide a rich documentary resource for the evaluation of the REF hypotheses.

The initial White House meeting on April 26 was characterized by gloomy fatalism. Chester Bowles was acting as secretary of state while Dean Rusk was in Ankara, Turkey at a Central Treaty Organization (CENTO) conference. Bowles's two memoranda of April 26 set the tone for the meeting. His first memorandum described the "intolerable" military situation in Laos and noted that the upcoming Geneva conference might become "little more than a Communist victory celebration" (FRUS, 1994a, p. 141). It was this memo that presented the president with two "difficult and unpleasant alternatives": military intervention or support for a Souvanna Phouma government that would eventually "convert Laos into a Communist puppet" (FRUS, 1994a, p. 141). In a second memo, Bowles fleshed out his arguments further. He noted a recent broadcast from Peking demanding U.S. withdrawal in exchange for a cease-fire and suggested that China had emerged as "the major force which we must contend in Southeast Asia" (Bowles to Kennedy, April 26, 1961, p. 1). Bowles expressed his belief that U.S. military intervention in the Mekong Valley would "face the near certainty of a massive Chinese Communist move into the area"; and that the recent broadcasts from Peking "underscore this probability" (Bowles to Kennedy, April 26, 1961, p. 2). He also criticized Pentagon plans that advocated the use of nuclear weapons in response to this contingency, and argued that "it would be a serious mistake for the United States to send troops into Laos, except in the unlikely event that some kind of UN force could be organized, as in Korea" (Bowles to Kennedy, April 26, 1961, p. 4). Bowles finished by considering the domestic response to the loss of Laos, concluding that:

> The Prudent course of action is to cut our *immediate* losses, proceed to secure the best possible agreement in regard to Laos . . . , prepare a strong military position in Thailand and Vietnam and then proceed to secure the essential moral and material support for the greater [global] contest. . . . This will appear, I am afraid, as a conservative proposal at a time when many people are hungry for action. Nevertheless, I deeply believe that a military move in Laos involving the major built-in risks to which I refer would be a serious mistake. (Bowles to Kennedy, April 26, 1961, pp. 8–9, emphasis in original)

Special Assistant to the President for National Security Affairs McGeorge Bundy's notes of the April 26 meeting indicate that the Peking broadcasts were "particularly in mind" for the president (FRUS, 1994a, pp. 142–143). Several of Kennedy's advisers disagreed with Bowles's opinions regarding the probability of an aggressive Chinese response, but they agreed with the president that "on balance it seemed wise to avoid a test if possible" (FRUS, 1994a, p. 143). The president "explicitly refused to decide against intervention at this time" in order to keep his options open, but did approve further diplomatic initiatives (FRUS, 1994a, p. 143). He also encouraged Secretary of Defense Robert S. McNamara to begin contingency planning, should the need arise to "place substantial U.S. forces in South Vietnam and Thailand" (FRUS, 1994a, p. 144).

The fact that the president explicitly refused to decide against intervention at the April 26 meeting allowed those who favored the intervention alternative to regroup and develop a better argument in support of their views. On April 27 at a "long and confused" (Schlesinger, 1965, p. 337) National Security Council (NSC) meeting, Rostow persisted in advocating the task force's plan for a limited intervention while the JCS maintained that an all-or-nothing intervention was required. Rostow later noted that this was the "worst meeting he's ever attended in all his government service. Everyone had a different idea and the military was completely at odds" (Newhouse n.d., p. 25). In the afternoon, Kennedy met with congressional leaders who opposed the intervention to varying degrees (FRUS, 1994a, p. 147). The president assured the congressmen that no decision had been reached and left for a speech in New York. While in New York, he "paid an unannounced visit to MacArthur, who advised him against intervention" (Newhouse n.d., p. 27).

When Rusk returned from Ankara on April 29, a major meeting of Kennedy's advisers was held at the State Department. During this meeting, Robert Kennedy played the role of his brother—probing for clarity and attempting to discern a consensus opinion (FRUS, 1994a, pp. 150–154). As factions developed among the participants, three alternative positions emerged. The Laos Task force (Rostow) and the State Department (Rusk) favored limited intervention to prevent the fall of Laos and demonstrate U.S. resolve to its SEATO allies; the Defense Department (McNamara) and the JCS developed an all-or-nothing position favoring full-scale intervention and a commitment to "go the distance" (with some dissent from Air Force Chief of Staff Curtis LeMay who suggested that air power alone could solve the problem); the final minority position advocated by Bowles favored the acceptance of the loss of Laos and a renewed commitment to make a stand in Vietnam and Thailand (FRUS, 1994a, pp. 150–154). This contentious morning meeting at the State Department turned into another contentious meeting of the NSC. Kennedy again refused to commit to a final course of action and additional meetings were planned for May 1 and 2 (see FRUS, 1994a, pp. 154–156).

In order to clarify the positions that developed over the weekend, Rusk sent Kennedy a memorandum describing two alternative policy tracks. Track 1 noted that Kong Le had recently called for a cease-fire—the success of which would lead down the "ICC-14-nation conference route" (FRUS, 1994a, p. 159). Track 2 planned for the failure of the cease-fire negotiations and continued Pathet Lao victories. This track advocated UN pressure on the Soviet Union and the implementation of SEATO Plan 5—a limited intervention of U.S. and SEATO troops (FRUS, 1994a, pp. 160–162). In an interesting "comment" Rusk discussed the potential goals of the U.S. should the cease-fire succeed. In describing U.S. objectives in a Geneva conference on Laos, Rusk noted, "Our actions and the realities of Laos will all anticipate a 'mixed-up-Laos.' The more we can fracture it the better. It will be best for the time being for Laos to become a loose federation or confederation of somewhat autonomous strong men" (FRUS, 1994a, p. 161).

The last chance for the proponents of intervention came at the May 1 NSC meeting. McNamara proposed that SEATO troops (mostly U.S.) move into the panhandle of Laos. The opposition to this proposal focused on the possible negative outcomes associated with such a move. McNamara's notes read as follows:

2. Allen Dulles said we must anticipate a Chinese response if we move into the panhandle.
4. Chet B[owles]: are likely to face full-scale war with the Chinese in 4 to 5 yrs; should have neutrals with us (India, Burma, etc.); Laos, inclu[ding] the panhandle, is not the place to start.
6. Maxwell Taylor: opposed to US troops in Laos.
   Risk in view of:
   a. Potential PL [Pathet Lao] moves during our action endanger and outflank US & Thai troops
   b. Chicom jet bomber moves
   c. Chicom fighter attacks on B-26's

What are the chances of improving our political position by military action & what are the chances of weakening it—
   a. unlikely to avoid a communist-dominated gov't.
   b unlikely to avoid a uncontrolled Laos-SVN border.
   c. May lose support of Britain, Fr. & Western world.
   d. May not have support of US—note attitude of Cong. lders
   e. Run risk of
      a) temporary military reversals
      b) long debilitating war (FRUS, 1994a, p. 163)

Dissatisfied with the presentation by the JCS, Lyndon Johnson is believed to have requested that they file their views in memoranda for the president (see FRUS, 1994a, pp. 164, 166–170). Kennedy again made no final decision, but did acknowledge that he was prepared "under certain conditions to deploy U.S. forces to Thailand" (FRUS, 1994a, p. 164).

As the cease-fire negotiations were approaching success in Laos, Kennedy and his advisers met for a final time on May 2 to discuss the JCS memoranda. In a summary memorandum, McNamara and Deputy Secretary of Defense Roswell Gilpatric described an intervention and nonintervention "course."[7] In supporting the intervention course, McNamara and Gilpatric attempted to list the "Pros and Cons of the Two Courses" (FRUS, 1994a, p. 168). Their argument was, however, limited to a comparison of the "Negative Aspects of the Non-Intervention Course" and the "Risks and

Disadvantages of the Intervention Course" (FRUS, 1994a, p. 168). Indeed, their advocacy of the intervention course entirely avoids a comparison of "Pros." This document suggests a focus on choosing the "least bad" alternative, rather than the "best" alternative (providing indirect support for REF hypothesis 2, see discussion below). In light of the "rapidly developing situation" in Laos, Kennedy again avoided making a final decision, instead asking the secretaries of the Departments of State and Defense to develop a "joint recommendation on U.S. action with respect to Laos" (FRUS, 1994a, p. 171). On May 3, a cease-fire was declared in Laos and on May 16, the Geneva conference opened (Newhouse n.d., p. 2).

The above discussion of Kennedy's consideration of the alternatives during the Laos "crisis" provides some evidence in support of REF hypothesis 2 (*security-motivated presidents tend to focus on worst-case outcomes and maximum losses*). Unfortunately, the limited amount of direct Kennedy statements from the meetings on March 20, 21, April 27, 29, and May 2 constrains the rigorous evaluation of this hypothesis. Clearly, during the March 9, April 26, and May 1 meetings, Kennedy focused almost exclusively on the relative costs associated with the various alternatives. From reading the documentary record during this period, I am struck with the impression of a reluctant president making choices between "difficult and unpleasant alternatives" (FRUS, 1994a, pp. 140–141). There is also some nondirect evidence that may bear on the evaluation of hypothesis 2. Many of the policy papers forwarded to the president during this period follow the pattern of focusing on costs to the exclusion of benefits. The most striking example of this is the Defense Department memorandum penned by McNamara and Gilpatric. Even when an explicit attempt was made to focus on "Pros" as well as "Cons," McNamara and Gilpatric could only discuss "negative aspects," "risks," and "disadvantages" (FRUS, 1994a, pp. 166–169). Of course, I would rather not characterize Kennedy's own manner of information processing by relying on nondirect sources, so these results can only be viewed as suggestive.

In evaluating REF hypothesis 4 (*security-motivated presidents are likely to behave in a risk-averse manner*) in this case, we must determine whether Kennedy behaved in a risk-averse, risk-seeking, or risk-neutral manner. Despite the fact that Kennedy avoided making a final decision in this case, I feel that we may characterize the course that Kennedy followed—marked by decisional delay and incrementalism—as suggestive of risk-aversion. Kennedy certainly had decided that the all-out intervention advocated by the JCS was too risky. The JCS plan could result in an immediate defeat, a long and drawn out conflict, or even nuclear war. Kennedy clearly perceived that the worst-case outcome of a U.S.–Soviet/Chinese War was possible, and recognized that his advisers were unsure of Soviet and Chinese intentions, potential domestic U.S. reaction, and potential British and French reactions (recall the discussion of "riskiness" in chapter two). Had the "crisis" continued, Kennedy may have put troops in Thailand and South Vietnam, but there is little documentary evidence supporting Rostow's assertion that Kennedy would have deployed troops to Laos to save the Mekong Valley (see Rostow, 1964, pp. 77–78). As it was, Kennedy's tactics of delay and incrementalism allowed future options to remain open, letting events on the ground in Laos dictate when new decisions and possibly new commitments would need to be made. (A summary of the findings for this case study can be found in table 4.1.)

Epilogue

Hilsman describes the Kennedy administration's record in Laos as a "victory-of sorts" (1967, p. 154). Despite the failure of the Geneva conference to bring peace to the region, Laos had been kept from the communists. For Schlesinger, Kennedy's "diplomacy under pressure . . . was marked by restraint of manner, toughness of intention and care to leave the adversary a way of escape without loss of face" (1965, p. 340). For both former advisers, Laos was viewed as a "dress rehearsal" for Kennedy's greatest triumph—the Cuban missile crisis (Hilsman, 1967, p. 155; Schlesinger, 1965, p. 340). Of course, an alternative view argues that "Kennedy left Laos somewhat better off than he found it, not because he was unwilling to intervene but because he had concluded that intervention would demand too high a price" (Walton, 1972, p. 32). Laos also may be viewed as the dress rehearsal for Vietnam. The Laos "crisis" sparked Kennedy's interest in counterinsurgency tactics, and the decision to "neutralize" Laos contributed to the decision to "make a stand" in South Vietnam.

III.   Vietnam 1961

Overview

The Geneva agreements of 1954 divided Vietnam at the 17th parallel. Shortly after the conclusion of these accords, Emperor Bao Dai appointed Ngo Dinh Diem as premier of the "Republic of Vietnam" (South Vietnam). Roger Hilsman described Diem as "an extraordinarily devout Catholic," a "celibate," and a "patriot" (1967, p. 416; neglecting to mention that Diem also served the Japanese during World War II, see Bassett and Pelz, 1989, p. 226). Through political and military maneuvering Diem consolidated his power, and in 1955 he unseated Bao Dai to become president and Chief of State (Hilsman, 1967, p. 417). In 1956, with the approval of the Eisenhower administration, Diem refused to permit the elections called for in the Geneva accords. In response to Diem's increasingly dictatorial ways, the southern Vietminh increased its guerrilla offensive during the period from 1957 to 1959 (Bassett and Pelz, 1989, p. 226). Dissatisfaction with Diem was not limited to the Vietminh, as members of his own military initiated a coup in November of 1960 that almost toppled Diem's regime (Hilsman, 1967, p. 418). By the time of Kennedy's inauguration in January of 1961, repressive measures by Diem were eroding his regime's bases of support and the

Table 4.1 Summary of findings for Laos 1961 case study

Aspiration level	
Immediate goal	Create a "truly" neutral state that would align itself with neither superpower
Constraints on means	Fear of potential communist reactions to U.S. initiatives, the potential for a negative domestic reaction should the United States send troops to Laos, and the fear of overextending the United States military posture globally
Commitment reinforced by	Fear that communist success in Laos would lead to the fall of South Vietnam and Thailand, concern regarding the need to demonstrate resolve and the credibility of U.S. commitments to the SEATO allies, and fear of a negative reaction from Republicans in Congress who might castigate Kennedy in the press for negotiating with communists
Uncertainty	High uncertainty during March 9–April 1 period—questions about Phoumi's reliability and Soviet intentions, Kennedy shaken when JCS advocate large scale intervention and possible use of nuclear weapons
	Moderate uncertainty during April 26–May 3 period—meetings with Eisenhower, Rockefeller, and bipartisan legislative leaders suggest no domestic support for large scale intervention; individual JCS reports shed light on inherent difficulty of intervention alternative and potential for escalation
Time pressure	Moderate time pressure during March 9–April 1 period—communist "probing offensive" suggested situation was deteriorating but not yet perilous
	Acute time pressure during April 26–May 3 period—fall of Muong Sai, Ambassador Brown's telegram and Bowles's memorandum all suggest "loss" of Laos may be imminent
Consideration of alternatives	Weak evidence of focus on worst-case outcomes and maximum losses during March 9–April 1 period—Kennedy expresses concerns about potential negative consequences of intervention alternative and dissatisfaction with advice from JCS, but meeting on March 21 was "off the record"
	Moderate evidence of focus on worst-case outcomes and maximum losses during March 9–April 1 period—Kennedy choosing between two "difficult and unpleasant alternatives" and focused on potential for Chinese response; McNamara/Gilpatric memorandum focuses on "negative aspects," "risks," and "disadvantages"
Final decision	Strong evidence of incrementalism during March 9–April 1 period—Kennedy approves minor troop movements, British aide-memoire, and holds "tacit ultimatum" press conference
	Weak evidence of risk averse decision during April 26–May 3 period—Kennedy remains reluctant to support intervention alternative in May 2 meeting, but May 3 cease-fire precludes need for final decision

Vietminh were attempting to take advantage of this window of opportunity by stepping up guerrilla activity.

For Eisenhower and Dulles, Vietnam was a Cold War battleground and Diem was viewed as a bulwark against communism. U.S. military and economic assistance to South Vietnam followed immediately in the wake of the Geneva accords. Through treaties and public assurances, the Eisenhower administration "had pledged in 1954 and again in 1957 to help resist any aggression or subversion threatening the political independence of the Republic of Vietnam" (Sorensen, 1965, p. 651). As part of the U.S. commitment to South Vietnam, a U.S. "Military Assistance Advisory Group" (MAAG) attempted to train and equip a 150,000-man South Vietnamese army (Hilsman, 1967, p. 417). Despite the significance of the U.S. military commitment to South Vietnam, the Eisenhower administration was careful to keep the MAAG within the size restrictions of the Geneva accords (Kattenburg, 1982, pp. 108–109).[8] Although the situation in South Vietnam was deteriorating in late 1960, Laos was in more dire straits. Thus, Laos was the focus of attention when Eisenhower briefed the new administration on January 19; Vietnam was virtually ignored during the transition (FRUS, 1994a, pp. 19–20).

During 1961, President Kennedy and his advisers would make major decisions regarding U.S. support for South Vietnam on at least five occasions. In late January/early February, Kennedy approved a counterinsurgency plan for Vietnam (for details of the plan see FRUS, 1988, pp. 1–12). This early decision was sparked by a report from General Edward Lansdale that "shocked President Kennedy when he saw it" (Hilsman, 1967, p. 419). After reading Lansdale's report, Kennedy reportedly asked Rostow "This is the worst one we've got, isn't it?" (Rostow, 1964, p. 44). On April 20, the president directed Roswell Gilpatric to head a "Presidential Task Force on Vietnam" that would develop a "program of action to prevent Communist domination of South Viet-Nam" (FRUS, 1988, p. 74). On May 11, the Task Force Report was approved, resulting in increased U.S. military and economic aid (see FRUS, 1988, pp. 132–134).

After Vice President Johnson's visit to Vietnam in mid-May and Dr. Eugene Staley's "Special Financial Group" mission to Vietnam in late June, President Kennedy and his advisers faced a third major decision period. Aside from considering the recommendation's of Dr. Staley's team, Kennedy was faced with a request by President Diem for a 100,000-man increase in the South Vietnamese army (FRUS, 1988, p. 185). It was at this point (in late July) that Kennedy first considered sending a military mission to South Vietnam, but based on advice from Rostow and General Maxwell D. Taylor, Kennedy postponed the mission until further planning could be conducted in Washington (FRUS, 1988, pp. 256–257). Kennedy also postponed a final decision on Diem's request, but did approve a 30,000 man increase in the South Vietnamese army (see FRUS, 1988, p. 264).

The fourth major decision period occurred in September and October as Viet Cong activity increased significantly and a massive flood of the

Mekong river valley provided a potential excuse for U.S. military intervention (see FRUS, 1988, pp. 335–336). In an October 11 meeting, Kennedy considered a State Department paper entitled "Concept for Intervention in Vietnam" (see FRUS, 1988, pp. 340–342). At this meeting, Kennedy approved a small increase in U.S. military aid to South Vietnam, but withheld further consideration of the alternatives under consideration. Kennedy decided that it was now time to send a military mission to South Vietnam and asked General Taylor to be its leader (FRUS, 1988, pp. 343–344).

The final major decision period covered November 1 through November 15 as Kennedy and his advisers considered the recommendations of the "Taylor Report." It was during this period that the president seriously contemplated, for the first time, the deployment of U.S. troops to South Vietnam in numbers that exceeded the limits set by the Geneva accords. During this period, the Taylor report would be transformed into a joint State–Defense Department proposal that would be evaluated against alternatives presented by Walt Rostow and Averell Harriman. At 9:00 p.m. on November 15, instructions were sent to Ambassador Frederick Nolting outlining plans for a "sharply increased joint effort to avoid a further deterioration in the situation in South Viet-Nam and eventually contain and eliminate the threats to its independence" (Rusk to Nolting, November 15, 1961, p. 1). Despite this strong language, Kennedy refused to approve the deployment of substantial numbers of U.S. ground troops and refused to formally commit his administration to the defense of South Vietnam (see FRUS, 1988, pp. 607–610). And yet he did approve substantial increases in military and economic aid that increased the U.S. role in the defense of Diem's regime.

Aspiration Level

As noted above, the president's "aspiration level" is expected to comprise a set of minimum level goals that the president hopes to achieve or surpass. In order to evaluate hypothesis 1 (*presidents tend to evaluate outcomes relative to an aspiration level rather than an overall value level*), we must infer the elements of President Kennedy's aspiration level (regarding Vietnam) from the documentary record. We need to find descriptions of acceptable/desirable outcomes/objectives in this case. Thus, we need to find relevant documents that address Kennedy's goals, desires, hopes, needs, and/or requirements in this case.

Based on the evidence presented below, I believe that President Kennedy's immediate goal in Vietnam was to preserve the independence of the non-communist South under Diem's regime. The means available for achieving this goal were constrained by the fear of a negative reaction from Democrats in Congress and the fear of potential communist reactions to U.S. initiatives. The president's commitment to achieving or surpassing his immediate goal was reinforced by his fear that communist success in South Vietnam would lead to the fall of Southeast Asia, his concern regarding the need to demonstrate resolve and the credibility of U.S. commitments to the SEATO allies, and by his fear of a negative reaction from Republicans in Congress who would criticize the administration for "losing" Vietnam. Once again, a complex combination of goals and constraints formed the aspiration level that guided Kennedy's decision making. President Kennedy's aspiration level was well articulated and the documentary evidence supports REF hypothesis 1.

As in the Laos case, it is useful here to first consider the goals of the Eisenhower administration and the impact they had on the formation of Kennedy's aspiration level. As noted above, the Eisenhower administration had publicly pledged to assist the South in resisting "aggression or subversion threatening the political independence of the Republic of Vietnam" (Sorensen, 1965, p. 651). From 1954 to 1960, U.S. military and economic aid supported Diem's drive to consolidate power in the South. The U.S. MAAG provided military equipment and instruction to a 150,000-man army structured "to meet conventional war as the Americans had known it in Korea" (Hilsman, 1967, p. 417). As Diem's authoritarian method of governing became more and more unpopular, U.S. aid "increased . . . to compensate for the political weaknesses of the Diem regime" (Sorensen, 1965, p. 651). By January of 1961, the Defense Department, State Department, and CIA were all involved in the enterprise in Vietnam.

As noted previously, there is a somewhat heated debate over the extent to which Eisenhower's policies in Vietnam constrained the Kennedy administration. Kennedy's admirers argue that the U.S. commitment to Vietnam had been established by Eisenhower, Kennedy simply adapted tactics to the deteriorating situation on the ground. Sorensen writes, "whether or not it would have been wiser to draw it in a more stable and defensible area in the first place, this nation's commitment in January, 1961—although it had assumed far larger proportions then when it was made nearly seven years earlier—was not one that President Kennedy felt he could abandon without undesirable consequences throughout Asia and the world" (1965, p. 651). Hilsman follows this line further, "President Kennedy grumbled occasionally about the United States being 'overcommitted' in Vietnam and Southeast Asia, but he could not go back on the commitments already made" (1967, p. 420; see also Hess, 1993, p. 69). While I feel that these statements accurately characterize the perceptions of the president and his key advisers, I do not accept the logic that they imply. As shown in the Laos case, the new administration possessed the "potentiality for a new approach" (FRUS, 1994a, p. 30) to the region. I agree with Kattenburg's contention that in 1961 "honorable disengagement had appeared possible" (1982, p. 113), but I also acknowledge that Kennedy and his advisers *perceived* that they were constrained by the previous administration's policies. I would argue that Kennedy's rejection of Eisenhower's policy in Laos, heightened his commitment to Eisenhower's policy in Vietnam. Rostow notes that Kennedy "did not as far as the external record shows, [at] any moment think of applying a Laos solution or the one he finally adopted to Viet Nam" (Rostow, 1964, p. 76).

President Kennedy's views on Vietnam were initially influenced by an early trip to the region in 1951. In 1954 a young Senator Kennedy spoke in opposition to U.S. intervention in Vietnam in the wake of the French defeat (see Walton, 1972, pp. 162–163). But by 1956, Kennedy the "Cold Warrior" called Vietnam "the cornerstone of the Free world in Southeast Asia, the keystone to the arch, the finger in the dike, . . . a proving ground of democracy in Asia, . . . [and] a test of American responsibility and determination" (quoted in Bassett and Pelz, 1989, p. 226). While Kennedy seldom mentioned Vietnam in his public statements during 1961, on two occasions he indicated the depth of his administration's commitment. In an August 2 statement, Kennedy noted "that the United States is determined that the Republic of Viet-Nam shall not be lost to the Communists for lack of any support which the United States Government can render" (Kennedy, 1962, p. 545). And again on October 26 in a letter to President Diem, Kennedy declared "that the United States is determined to help Viet-Nam preserve its independence, protect its people against Communist assassins, and build a better life through economic growth" (Kennedy, 1962, p. 681).

Internally there was much less debate within the Kennedy administration over the goals for Vietnam than there was over the goals for Laos. As early as April of 1961, the "Presidential Task Force on Vietnam" (led by Roswell Gilpatric) had suggested a program goal "to counter the Communist influence and pressure upon the development and maintenance of a strong, free South Vietnam" (FRUS, 1988, p. 74). In a May 19 NSC meeting, Kennedy accepted the task force's recommendations. The first point in the "National Security Action Memorandum" (NSAM) approved at this meeting noted, "The U.S. objective and concept of operations stated in the report are approved: to prevent Communist domination of South Vietnam; to create in that country a viable and increasingly democratic society, and to initiate, on an accelerated basis, a series of mutually supporting actions of a military, political, economic, psychological and covert character designed to achieve this objective" (FRUS, 1988, pp. 132–133). General Taylor notes that his instructions from President Kennedy on October 13 were "drawn in strict consistence with the statement of policy set forth in the May NSAM which it, in effect, reaffirmed . . . I was not asked to review the objectives of this policy but the means being pursued for their attainment . . . The question was how to change a losing game and begin to win, not how to call it off" (1972, p. 226).

Gary Hess comments on the extent to which the acceptance of this immediate goal constrained the alternatives presented to President Kennedy. Hess notes,

> Kennedy never altered his fundamental thinking . . . about the problems facing the United States in Vietnam. That consistency was reinforced by the way in which problems were presented to him.

Assuming that U.S. interests necessitated support of the South Vietnamese government, policymakers submitted choices in terms of determining the appropriate levels of increased U.S. support. Only rarely did officials question the basic U.S.-South Vietnamese connection, and, when they did, they had to move cautiously to avoid losing influence. (1993, p. 69)

We should be careful, however, to avoid overstating the cohesiveness of the Kennedy administration's thinking on Vietnam. Clearly, policy advocates emerged (particularly Chester Bowles, Averell Harriman, J. K. Galbraith, and Mike Mansfield) that questioned the basic objective of U.S. policy. And indeed, much of the debate in November of 1961 focused on the extent to which Kennedy was willing to fully commit himself to the achievement of this objective.

The evidence suggests that Kennedy's immediate goal remained consistent through the period from May to November of 1961. In his instructions to General Taylor, Kennedy wrote "I would like your views on the courses of action which our Government might take at this juncture to avoid a further deterioration in the situation in South Vietnam and eventually to contain and eliminate the threat to its independence" (quoted in Taylor, 1972, p. 225). This language was repeated in a telegram to Ambassador Nolting on October 12 (FRUS, 1988, p. 360). In a November 14 memorandum, Rostow wrote "It is universally agreed that the objective of the proposed exercise in Viet-Nam is to induce the Communists to cease infiltration, return to the Geneva Accord, while assisting South Viet-Nam in reducing the force of some 16,000 guerrillas now operating in the country" (FRUS, 1988, p. 601). Finally, in a letter dated November 16, the day after his fateful decisions, Kennedy suggested to Khrushchev that he "as the head of a government which was a signatory to the Geneva Accords, should use all the influence that you possess and endeavor to bring the DRV to the strict observance of these accords" (FRUS, 1988, p. 638). Kennedy's consistent immediate goal in Vietnam focused on securing an independent South under the control of a strong Diemist regime.

The documentary record suggests that the goal of preserving the independence of the noncommunist South under Diem's regime was indeed President Kennedy's immediate goal in this case. But clearly other imperatives constrained the means available for achieving this immediate goal as well as Kennedy's commitment to achieving or surpassing his immediate goal. In terms of constraints on means, Kennedy was wary of the potential reactions of congressional Democrats should he agree to the deployment of U.S. ground forces to Vietnam. On November 2, Kennedy received a lengthy memorandum from Senator Mike Mansfield arguing against intervention by U.S. troops. Mansfield feared that intervention in Vietnam "could become a quicksand for us" (FRUS, 1988, p. 467). During one of the crucial November meetings when Kennedy considered the Taylor recommendations, the president noted that, "We have a congressional prob. Sen. Russell & others are opposed . . . Troops are a last resort. Should be SEATO forces. Will create a tough domestic problem" (FRUS, 1988, p. 577). Finally, during the crucial November 15 NSC meeting, Kennedy "compared the obscurity of the issues in Viet Nam to the clarity of the positions in Berlin, the contrast of which could even make leading Democrats wary of proposed activities in the Far East" (FRUS, 1988, p. 608). At the end of the meeting, Kennedy "again expressed apprehension on support of the proposed action by the Congress as well as by the American people" and noted that his "impression was that even the Democratic side of Congress was not fully convinced" (FRUS, 1988, p. 610).

A second constraint on the means available to the president was his fear of potential Soviet and Chinese communist reactions to U.S. initiatives. In the White House meeting on November 11, President Kennedy asked whether the introduction of U.S. troops would "mean a war with China" (FRUS, 1988, p. 578). As in the Laos case, Kennedy was preoccupied with a concern over the potential escalation of the current conflict. Kennedy tried to impress his concerns upon Walt Rostow, asking him to reread Special National Intelligence Estimate (SNIE) 10-4-61 entitled "Probable Communist Reactions to Certain U.S. Actions in South Viet-Nam." In a November 12 memorandum Rostow took exception to the SNIE's conclusions, arguing that the Chinese communists would not intervene in support of North Vietnam "except as a suicidal act" (FRUS, 1988, p. 579). But Kennedy remained concerned with this possibility and opened the November 15 NSC meeting with a discussion of Chinese communist assets in the region. During this meeting, Director of Central Intelligence Allen Dulles "cautioned that it should not be assumed that Chinese setbacks as well as the ideological rift were such that the Soviets and Chinese would not be able nor willing to engage jointly any nation which threatened Communist interests" (FRUS, 1988, p. 607).

In terms of factors reinforcing his commitment to achieving or surpassing his immediate goal, Kennedy was worried that communist success in South Vietnam would lead to the fall of all Southeast Asia (see Hilsman, 1967, pp. 423–424; Schlesinger, 1965, p. 542). In discussing the importance of Vietnam to the Kennedy administration, Secretary Rusk noted that "the geographic position of South Vietnam and its relation to Laos, Cambodia, Thailand, and the resources, the population, all led us to take Vietnam very seriously very early in our Administration" (Rusk, December 9, 1969, p. 45). President Kennedy discussed the "domino theory" in a September 9, 1963 interview, "I believe it . . . China is so large, looms so high just beyond the frontiers, that if South Vietnam went, it would not only give an improved geographic position for a guerrilla assault on Malaya, but would also give the impression that the wave of the future in southeast Asia was China and the Communists" (quoted in George et al., 1971, p. 47). Indeed, after the debacle in Laos, Vietnam took on even more importance.

A second, related factor reinforcing his commitment to achieving or surpassing his immediate goal was Kennedy's desire to demonstrate the credibility of U.S. commitments, particularly to his SEATO allies. Hilsman suggested that Kennedy could not gracefully back out of the Eisenhower administration's commitments: "he could not refuse to give more of the same kind of assistance without disrupting the whole balance of power and fabric of the security structure of the region, where so many countries had based their policy on continued American involvement" (1967, p. 420; see also Hess, 1993, pp. 68–71). In fact, the basic State–Defense proposal presented to the president on November 11 argued that "the loss of South Viet-Nam to Communism would not only destroy SEATO but would undermine the credibility of American commitments elsewhere" (Johnson to Bundy, November 11, 1961, p. 1).

A final factor reinforcing his commitment to achieving or surpassing his immediate goal was Kennedy's fear of anticommunist congressional Republicans. After the failure of the Bay of Pigs and the muddle of Laos, Kennedy was beginning to face charges that he was soft on communism. In particular, the Republicans had "criticized him for canceling air strikes during the Bay of Pigs operation; for talking 'big' and then backing 'down when the chips were down' in Laos; for agreeing to negotiate on Berlin; and for failing to respond to the construction of the Berlin Wall in August" (Bassett and Pelz, 1989, p. 237). Indeed, Senator Barry Goldwater could be found on the cover of *Time* magazine in the summer of 1961 chiding Kennedy's softness (Bassett and Pelz, 1989, p. 237). Once again, the State–Defense proposal of November 11 tapped into the president's concerns, noting that the "loss of South Viet-Nam would stimulate bitter domestic controversies in the United States and would be seized upon by extreme elements to divide the country and harass the Administration" (Johnson to Bundy, November 11, 1961, p. 1).

Uncertainty and Time Pressure

As noted above, I expect that *presidential perceptions of high uncertainty and a lack of valid information will interact with presidential risk predispositions and affect the output of the decision process* (REF hypothesis 7). In the Kennedy cases, if the president perceives high uncertainty and inaccurate information but does not perceive acute time pressure, I expect to observe decisional delay and an expanded search for information (REF hypothesis 7a). If the president perceives high uncertainty and inaccurate information and also perceives acute time pressure, I expect to observe incrementalism (REF hypothesis 7b).

As the evidence presented below suggests, President Kennedy's perception of high uncertainty persisted across the five major decision periods in 1961. During this time period, Kennedy sent three major missions to the region and created two separate task forces for dealing with the most important Vietnam policy issues. From April to November of 1961, Kennedy's perception of time pressure became increasingly acute as the rainy season ended and the Viet Cong launched their major offensive in the South. In the fall of 1961, Kennedy was faced with pressure from the South Vietnamese as well as from his key advisers. Finally, in November of 1961 Kennedy felt that he had to come to some decision. As suggested by REF hypothesis 7a, when President Kennedy perceived high uncertainty but little (or moderate) time pressure, he delayed making a final decision regarding U.S. intervention in order to gather more accurate information (while also approving some increases in U.S. military and economic aid). In late October and early November, when Kennedy perceived acute time pressure and persistent uncertainty, he engaged in incrementalism as suggested by REF hypothesis 7b, approving the majority of the State–Defense recommendations but refusing to deploy U.S. troops and formally commit his administration to the defense of South Vietnam.

Perceptions of uncertainty and time pressure had significant impacts on President Kennedy's decision making regarding Vietnam in 1961. Despite the president's 1951 visit to Southeast Asia, neither he nor his top advisers possessed an intimate knowledge of the region. Robert McNamara lamented that "we faced a complex and growing crisis in Southeast Asia with sparse knowledge, scant experience, and simplistic assumptions . . . When it came to Vietnam, we found ourselves setting policy for a region that was terra incognita . . . Worse, our government lacked experts for us to consult to compensate for our ignorance" (McNamara, 1995, pp. 29–32). Since the transition meeting with Eisenhower had not focused on Vietnam, Kennedy was initially surprised by the report he received from General Edward Lansdale in late January (see FRUS, 1988, pp. 13–19; Hilsman, 1967, p. 417). Rostow's notes from this meeting state that Lansdale's report "for the first time, gave him [Kennedy] a sense of the danger and urgency of the problem in Vietnam" (FRUS, 1988, p. 16). Kennedy was impressed with Lansdale's knowledge of Vietnam and his experience fighting guerrillas in the Philippines (see Schlesinger, 1965, p. 540). Thus, Lansdale became one of Kennedy's chief confidants regarding Vietnam policy.

The major presidential initiative that resulted from this January 28 meeting was a desire to identify individuals personally responsible for the four "crisis" areas of Vietnam, Congo, Laos, and Cuba (FRUS, 1988, p. 19). Kennedy stated that "we must change our course in these areas and we must be better off in three months than we are now" (FRUS, 1988, p. 19). A number of interdepartmental "Task Forces" were created to take responsibility for these "crises." The Presidential Task Force on Vietnam was created on April 20. Led by Roswell Gilpatric, the task force included representatives from the Defense Department, State Department, White House, U.S. Information Agency, and CIA. This group was asked to develop a plan to prevent the "Communist Domination of South Vietnam" over the course of the next *week* (FRUS, 1988, p. 74).

Theodore Sorensen (along with McGeorge Bundy) encouraged Kennedy to approve "only the basic concept of an all-out internal security effort to save Vietnam" (FRUS, 1988, p. 84). Highlighting the glaring questions that the task force report raised, Sorensen asked the president to postpone his decision until after Vice President Johnson's mid-May trip to Southeast Asia. Sorensen argued that "we need a more *realistic* look" (FRUS, 1988, p. 84, emphasis in original). At the May 11 NSC meeting that produced NSAM 52, Kennedy approved the basic concept of operations and an expansion in the size and scope of the MAAG. But the president only approved contingency planning regarding increases in the South Vietnamese army and the possible commitment of U.S. forces to Vietnam. Finally, the president approved the continuation of the Vietnam Task Force under a new director, Sterling J. Cottrell (see FRUS, 1988, p. 133).

Vice President Johnson's report on his trip to Vietnam advised caution to President Kennedy. Johnson argued that the "situation in Viet Nam is more stable than is indicated by newspaper and other reports reaching Washington in recent weeks . . . we must keep our perspective . . . we must not react in panic and in consequence, perhaps, do precisely that which will worsen the situation" (FRUS, 1988, pp. 152–153). Johnson's interpretation of the situation in South Vietnam contrasted sharply with the impressions of the Vietnam Task Force. The task force report had stated that "Viet-Nam is nearing the decisive phase in its battle for survival" and that "the situation is critical, but not hopeless" (FRUS, 1988, pp. 94–95). President Kennedy appears to have accepted Johnson's view. In taking a deliberate and measured approach to the problems in South Vietnam, Kennedy sent the Special Financial Group Mission to Vietnam (led by Eugene Staley) from June 17 to July 15, in order to hammer out "a financial plan on which to base United States-Vietnamese joint efforts" (FRUS, 1988, p. 179).[9] The length of this trip delayed further decisions on Vietnam policy until late July.

In late July, President Kennedy and his advisers faced another set of decisions regarding the recommendations of the Staley Group's report, and a June 9 request by President Diem for another increase in the South Vietnamese army. At this time, General Taylor began promoting "the need for a rational analysis of the need for military forces in Laos and Thailand, as well as in Vietnam" (FRUS, 1988, p. 243). Taylor advocated "Southeast Asia" planning rather than simply Vietnam planning, expressing the "need" for a "tightly knit Southeast Asia Task Force" (FRUS, 1988, p. 244). In discussing this new task force's interim report, Kennedy suggested that the group's planning might benefit from a visit by Taylor to Vietnam, but refrained from approving any major new initiatives in the region (FRUS, 1988, p. 255). In a July 29 memorandum, Rostow and Taylor suggested that it was "premature to send a mission" at that time, but that "on the other hand the rainy season will soon be over; and our ducks should then be in a row" (FRUS, 1988, p. 257).

Throughout the summer of 1961 the pressure of time did not weigh heavily on President Kennedy because the rainy season in the region prevented the initiation of large-scale military operations. In mid-August the president was warned that the Viet Cong would "most likely continue concentrate efforts coming months," and that he could expect a "high number incidents most sectors with possible increase end of rainy season November" (FRUS, 1988, p. 274). Unfortunately for Kennedy, the Viet Cong did not wait until November. In a September 5 attack, the Viet Cong employed modern weapons, and "for first time, wore khaki uniforms into battle" (FRUS, 1988, p. 292). As September wore on, the number of communist attacks in the South "was triple the average of previous months" (Bassett and Pelz, 1989, p. 234; Rust, 1985, p. 40). Based on the stepped-up communist offensive and the outcome of the Laotian situation, President Diem requested a "bilateral defense treaty" with the United States (FRUS, 1988, p. 316). In a memorandum on October 5, Rostow noted "We must move quite radically to avoid perhaps slow but total defeat" (quoted in Rust, 1985, p. 40). To complicate matters further, Ambassador Nolting reported on October 11 that a catastrophic flood was devastating the populated regions of the Mekong river valley (FRUS, 1988, p. 335).

On October 11, the Vietnam Task Force delivered a paper to the president entitled "Concept for Intervention in Viet-Nam." In an afternoon meeting on that same day, Kennedy approved only a small increase in military aid to the South Vietnamese. He decided that the time had come for the Taylor mission (FRUS, 1988, p. 343). The day before the Taylor mission arrived in Vietnam, the body of kidnapped Colonel Hoang Thuy Nam was found in a river in Saigon (FRUS, 1988, p. 393). This event reinforced the perception that the situation was deteriorating. Rostow notes that when the Taylor mission arrived in Saigon "none of us felt that it could hold more than three months unless something radical was done" (Rostow, 1964, p. 84). Of course, Taylor faced the delicate task of convincing the president that the situation was serious, *but not hopeless* (see FRUS, 1988, p. 478). Finally, the Taylor mission had the unintended consequence of convincing the Vietnamese that a major new U.S. initiative was on the horizon (see FRUS, 1988, p. 542).

Prior to the first key meeting on November 11, the president prepared for his advisers a list of eight questions regarding the State–Defense proposal that had adopted many of the recommendations of Taylor's report. The president particularly expressed reluctance regarding the potential deployment of U.S. forces (see FRUS, 1988, p. 576). His memorandum to Rostow on November 12 also indicates that Kennedy was unsure of the potential reaction of communist China to the proposed U.S. military initiatives (FRUS, 1988, pp. 578–579). Another memorandum on November 14 indicates that, even on the eve of his critical November 15 decisions, Kennedy had a number of significant questions for his advisers (FRUS, 1988, pp. 693–604). Finally, the notes of the key November 15 NSC meeting indicate that Kennedy continued to perceive high uncertainty. He worried about Chinese communist intervention, negative congressional and domestic opinion, and the chances for success of the proposed alternatives (see FRUS, 1988, pp. 607–610).

Consideration of Alternatives and Final Decision

As noted earlier, I expect that President Kennedy (identified as a security-motivated president) will tend to focus on worst-case outcomes and maximum losses when considering alternatives (REF hypothesis 2). I also anticipate that President Kennedy is likely to behave in a risk-averse manner in making final decisions (REF hypothesis 4).[10] In order to evaluate these hypotheses, we must examine the manner in which alternatives were considered, and the decisions that were reached during crucial periods in the cases. For the Vietnam case, two periods are worthy of careful scrutiny—October 5–11 and November 3–15.

In response to the events of September and early October, Kennedy's advisers developed plans to deploy U.S. and SEATO troops to South Vietnam. During the short decision period from October 5 to 11, two alternative policy papers circulated within the administration. Chester Bowles was dissatisfied with the state of Washington planning regarding Vietnam, he proposed an "alternative political approach" that might save Kennedy from "having to choose between diplomatic humiliation or a major military operation" (FRUS, 1988, p. 322, emphasis in original). Bowles had previously acted as the "conservative voice of reason" in the Laos "crisis." In his October 5 memorandum, Bowles proposed that a "Laos solution" could be applied to all of Southeast Asia. At worst, the communists would continue their operations in South Vietnam and the United States would have a much clearer mandate for intervening. Bowles wrote "in view of the ugly nature of the alternatives, I believe that this risk [disruption of U.S. relations with its SEATO allies] should be run, since the likely course of events under present circumstances may lead them and us into a setback with the gravest world-wide implications" (FRUS, 1988, p. 324). Once again, Bowles was offering Kennedy a political alternative that left his military options open, but in October of 1961 Bowles no longer held much influence. By October of 1961, "political alternatives" smacked of Laos, and Laos smacked of failure.

The "military" alternative to the Bowles proposal suggested "an effort to arrest and hopefully to reverse the deteriorating situation" in South Vietnam (FRUS, 1988, p. 340). The "Concept for Intervention in Viet-Nam" was developed by the Vietnam Task Force. This paper advocated the deployment of 22,800 SEATO forces to halt communist infiltration into South Vietnam in order to free the South Vietnamese army to fight elsewhere. These troops would also "help in logistics, communications, airlift, and combat air support" ("Concept for Intervention" n.d., p. 1). Under the heading of "Anticipated Later Phases," the report acknowledged that "supplemental military action must be envisaged" and that the "ultimate force requirements cannot be estimated with any precision" (apparently the JCS guessed three divisions, "Concept for Intervention" n.d., p. 3). The report also included a section of seven "cons" and seven "pros." The "cons" focused on the limited aims of the intervention plan, the fact that the United States would have broken the Geneva accords, the risk of anticolonial sentiment, and the fact that a change in communist tactics might limit the utility of a stationary force. The "pros" focused on the potential boost to Vietnamese morale, the ability to extract political concessions from Diem, the fact that SEATO troops might act as a bargaining chip in negotiations with the communists, and the fact that "if we go into South Viet-Nam now with SEATO, the costs would be much less than if we wait and go in later, or lose South Viet-Nam" ("Concept for Intervention" n.d., pp. 5–6). The paper concluded with a supplemental note indicating the "wider military implications" of the intervention plan. This note pointed out that in the later stages of the intervention, the chances of massive Chinese communist or Soviet intervention "might well become substantial" ("Concept for Intervention" n.d., Supplemental Note 2).

At the White House meeting on October 11, the "Concept for Intervention in Viet-Nam" paper was the only proposal considered by the president. There is no documentary record of the president's comments during this meeting, but there is a record of the decisions that he reached (see FRUS, 1988, pp. 343–344). Apparently, Kennedy was not yet convinced of the necessity for military intervention, he instead decided to send Taylor, Rostow, and Lansdale (among others) to South Vietnam to evaluate the feasibility of three alternatives (FRUS, 1988, p. 343). The first alternative was the "Concept for Intervention" discussed that morning, the second alternative involved the deployment of fewer troops simply to establish a U.S. "presence," while the third alternative involved simply providing more of the same type of military and economic assistance that had already been approved (FRUS, 1988, p. 344; see also Rust, 1985, p. 42). The president did approve one element of the "Concept for Intervention" during the October 11 meeting. He allowed the deployment of a "Jungle Jim" squadron (which included 12 aircraft and 110 men) to South Vietnam. This squadron would augment the MAAG, allowing for the training of Vietnamese airmen ("Concept for Intervention" n.d., Supplemental Note 1; see also FRUS, 1988, p. 343).

Given the lack of documentary evidence regarding Kennedy's concerns during this period, it is difficult to evaluate REF hypothesis 2. As in the early period of the Laos case, we find only suggestive (nondirect) evidence of Kennedy's information processing. Both the Bowles and the task force proposals discuss the possibility of the worst-case scenario occurring—that is, Chinese communist or Soviet intervention—but we have no direct evidence indicating the role that this information played in Kennedy's decision process. In fact, the balanced presentation of "pros" and "cons" in the task force report provides evidence that seems to contradict REF hypothesis 2, but again we have no direct evidence showing that Kennedy paid attention to both "pros" and "cons." In evaluating REF hypothesis 4, I would simply argue that no final decision was made. The REF hypotheses that are more relevant to this decision period, are clearly those relating to uncertainty and time pressure (as discussed above).

After President Kennedy received General Taylor's report on November 3, a new round of debate engulfed his administration. Taylor's report immediately faced a challenge in the form of a "political alternative" advocated by J. K. Galbraith, the U.S. ambassador to India. Later in the process, Taylor's report was transformed by Rusk and McNamara into a joint State–Defense proposal. During the crucial period of November 11–15, Averell Harriman submitted a revised "political alternative" based on Bowles's October 5 memorandum. Finally, Walt Rostow proposed a military deployment plan based on SEATO Plan 5 Plus.

The recommendations included in the Taylor Mission report were of three types: demands for political, governmental, and administrative reforms by the Diem government; increases in material and technical aid for the development of a counterguerrilla program; and the deployment of an 8,000-man U.S. military task force to bolster Vietnamese morale, aid in flood relief, conduct combat operations for self-defense, provide an emergency reserve, and act as an advance party if SEATO or CINCPAC (Commander in Chief, Pacific) military plans were invoked (see FRUS, 1988, pp. 477–532; Hilsman, 1967, p. 422). Upon receiving Taylor's report, the president indicated that he was "instinctively against [the] introduction of US forces" (FRUS, 1988, p. 532). He asked his advisers to prepare for a NSC meeting, where they would consider "the quality of the proposed program," as well as the "implications and meaning of the program if implemented" (FRUS, 1988, p. 533). The policy debate that ensued, focused on the potential deployment of U.S. troops and the depth of the new commitment to Diem's regime.

Galbraith's memorandum of November 3 was the initial "political alternative" to the Taylor proposal. Galbraith's arguments echoed those presented by Bowles on October 5. He noted that "our long-run objective should be the creation of an independent, economically viable and politically neutral state, rather than a limping American satellite" (FRUS, 1988, p. 474). In that light, Galbraith recommended: a get-tough policy with Diem; a UN resolution "confirming the independence of the Republic of Vietnam" and "calling for the immediate dispatch of United Nations observer groups to Vietnam"; and a "prompt agreement at Geneva on a neutral Laos" (FRUS, 1988, p. 475). Galbraith concluded by noting that "the program recommended here avoids the high risk and limited promise alternative of armed intervention" (FRUS, 1988, p. 476). While the president was instinctively opposed to military intervention, he was also acutely aware of the problems of a "Laos solution" for Vietnam. And so, the Galbraith memorandum did not convince the president to change his approach to Vietnam policy.

The Taylor report was initially considered by Kennedy's top advisers at a November 4 State Department meeting. General Taylor outlined his report and responded to direct questions. As the meeting progressed, Kennedy's advisers focused on the issue of U.S. troop deployments. McNamara (Rusk did not attend this meeting) argued that the 8,000-man force would not "convince anyone of our resolve" (FRUS, 1988, p. 533). He felt that the upcoming NSC meeting should focus on three questions: "What is US objective in South Vietnam? How far do we want to go? [and] How far do we want to state it publicly?" (FRUS, 1988, p. 533). Under Secretary of State U. Alexis Johnson shared McNamara's view that the flood relief deployment was not the best use of U.S. troops, but then asked, "Can we save South Viet-Nam with steps short of putting in US forces?" (FRUS, 1988, p. 533). At that point Rostow and JCS Chairman General Lyman L. Lemnitzer supported McNamara. Lemnitzer stated that the United States "must commit the number of troops required for success," while Rostow noted that "Hanoi and Peking have basic weaknesses which lessen the risk to US action" (FRUS, 1988, p. 534). Taylor protested that the president wanted recommendations to "bolster the GVN to win their *own war*" (FRUS, 1988, p. 534, emphasis added), defending the quality of his proposals. But despite Taylor's dissent McNamara, Johnson, and Rostow agreed that a new proposal needed to be developed.

The NSC meeting to consider General Taylor's proposals was postponed twice (on November 7 and 8) so that Secretaries Rusk and McNamara could develop a joint State–Defense alternative (see FRUS, 1988, pp. 558–559). On November 8, McNamara sent a memorandum to the president laying out the views of the Defense Department. He recommended that Kennedy "commit the U.S. to the clear objective of preventing the fall of South Vietnam to Communism and that we support this commitment by the necessary military actions" (FRUS, 1988, p. 560). McNamara discussed the implications of the fall of South Vietnam and argued that "the chances are against, probably sharply against, preventing the fall by any measures short of the introduction of U.S. forces on a substantial scale" (FRUS, 1988, p. 560). He then noted that the "ultimate possible extent" of the U.S. military commitment would not exceed "205,000 men" (FRUS, 1988, p. 560). Thus, McNamara suggested accepting the Taylor proposals as a first step, fully recognizing that more U.S. troops would be needed (FRUS, 1988, pp. 560–561). McNamara's memorandum served as the basis for the initial draft (November 8) of the State–Defense proposal.

In his recent autobiography, McNamara indicates that he immediately "worried we had been too hasty in our advice to the President" (McNamara, 1995, p. 38). He suggests that increasing awareness of the "complexity" and "uncertainties" of the situation led him to change his mind (McNamara, 1995, pp. 38–39). Regardless of the veracity of McNamara's recent claims, it is clear from the documentary record that Secretary Rusk and his State Department advisers were uncomfortable with the draft proposal. In a November 9 meeting, Rusk "insisted on discussing troop deployment rather than face real issue of troops" (FRUS, 1988, pp. 572–573). Rusk refused to endorse the 8,000-man flood relief force. Thus, the final draft of the State–Defense proposal did not recommend the immediate commitment of any U.S. troops (Johnson to Bundy, November 11, 1961).

As the first key White House meeting approached on November 11, Rostow wrote a memorandum to President Kennedy detailing the need for an immediate U.S. troop deployment to Vietnam. Rostow's proposal evoked the concerns of those who favored immediate intervention. He noted that the rhetoric of the State–Defense proposal was ambiguous, the communists would "interpret our policy by deeds, not words" (FRUS, 1988, p. 574). He also commented on the fact that the South Vietnamese expected a U.S. troop deployment, noting that "Diem would be strengthened if this threshold in U.S. action were passed" (FRUS, 1988, p. 574). He suggested the placement of 5,000 U.S. troops on the 17th parallel to act as a "bargaining counter for a return to the Geneva Accords" (FRUS, 1988, p. 574). Finally, he castigated the State–Defense plan because it "would inhibit U.S. action on our side of the truce lines of the Cold War for fear of enemy escalation," and he performed some interesting motivational analysis: "if he goes to war because of what we do on our side of the line, it does not mean that he went to war because of what we did. It means that he had already determined to face war rather than forego victory in South Viet Nam, and that only our surrender of South Viet Nam could prevent war" (FRUS, 1988, p. 575).

The joint State–Defense proposal was the main document under consideration at the November 11 White House meeting. As noted above, this proposal included many of the recommendations of the Taylor report with the addition of the commitment to use U.S. forces in South Vietnam, if necessary, and the omission of any immediate troop deployment. President Kennedy prepared a list of eight questions that he wished to address at the meeting. The questions focused on the State–Defense proposal, raising issues of effectiveness and implementation and forcing Rusk and McNamara to flesh out ideas, make clarifications, and justify their recommendations (FRUS, 1988, p. 576). During the meeting, Kennedy discussed potential congressional opposition, specifically noting that "We have a congressional prob. Sen. Russell & others are opposed" (FRUS, 1988, p. 577). He also noted that "Troops are a last resort. Should be SEATO forces. Will create a tough domestic problem. Would like to avoid statements like Laos & Berlin" (FRUS, 1988, p. 577). In the end, Kennedy refused to approve the full commitment advocated in the State–Defense paper asking, "Will it mean a war with China? Will not go that far as to approve" (FRUS, 1988, p. 578). He did, however, tentatively approve ten actions providing military, economic, and administrative assistance to the South Vietnamese and the publication of the "Jorden Report" (detailing communist infiltration into South Vietnam) (FRUS, 1988, p. 578). At the close of this meeting, U. Alexis Johnson commented "Line clearly drawn in VN—it was not in Laos" (FRUS, 1988, p. 578).

In the wake of the November 11 meeting, Kennedy's advisers prepared for the final meeting that would take place on November 15. Rostow exchanged memoranda with the president regarding the potential threat of escalation by communist China, should the United States intervene militarily (FRUS, 1988, pp. 578–579, 601–603; see also previous discussion).[11] Averell Harriman submitted a memorandum on November 11 that outlined another "diplomatic-political course of action in Vietnam" (FRUS, 1988, p. 580). Harriman's alternative did not "preclude other actions should it fail" (FRUS, 1988, p. 580). He argued that the administration should use the publication of the Jorden Report as an opportunity for approaching the Soviets. Harriman could then persuade the Soviet Union and the United Kingdom to open negotiations as part of the Geneva conference, and attempt to reach an agreement to cease hostilities and abide by the 1954 accords. He argued that, "Major military commitment as well as possible UN initiative should be held in reserve as long as direct negotiations seemed to be making progress" (FRUS, 1988, p. 582). Finally, McGeorge Bundy sent Kennedy a memorandum on November 15, supporting the military commitment advocated by the initial State–Defense proposal. Bundy argued, "I believe the odds are almost even that the commitment will not have to be carried out" (FRUS, 1988, p. 605).

On November 13, a draft NSAM was circulated within Kennedy's advisory group. The draft NSAM included the recommendations of the State–Defense proposal tentatively approved by the president at the November 11 meeting. On the evening of November 14, Kennedy put forth a number of issues that he wished addressed in the NSC meeting the next day. These included consideration of the Harriman proposal, questions regarding the implementation of the State–Defense plan, and a request to "have someone look into what we did in Greece." Kennedy stressed, "Our actions should be positive rather than negative. . . . concerning Laos—we took actions which made no difference at all. . . . Our actions should be substantial otherwise we will give the wrong impression" (FRUS, 1988, pp. 603–604).

The NSC meeting that took place at 10 a.m. on November 15, was full of contentious debate. The first item on the agenda was the formal commitment and military contingency planning recommendations in the initial State–Defense proposal. Kennedy was concerned with the prospects for Soviet or Chinese intervention and "expressed the fear of becoming involved simultaneously on two fronts on opposite sides of the world" (FRUS, 1988, p. 607). The president also expressed the fear that even members of his own party were "wary of proposed activities in the Far East" (FRUS, 1988, p. 608). He then "returned the discussion to the point of what will be done next in Viet Nam rather than whether or not the U.S. would become involved" (FRUS, 1988, p. 609). At this point, the discussion turned to the issue of breaking the Geneva Accords and Kennedy "delineated a clever plan to charge North Viet Nam with the onus for breaking [the] accords" (FRUS, 1988, p. 609). Kennedy then "asked how he could justify the proposed courses of action in Viet Nam while at the same time ignoring Cuba" (FRUS, 1988, p. 610). Finally, he "again expressed apprehension on support of the proposed action by Congress as well as by the American people. He felt that the next two or three weeks should be utilized in making the determination as to whether or not the proposed program for Viet Nam could be supported. His impression was that even the Democratic side of

Congress was not fully convinced" (FRUS, 1988, p. 610). Kennedy then closed the meeting, indicating that he would discuss the issues with the vice president (FRUS, 1988, p. 610). Later that day, Kennedy approved the ten actions tentatively agreed on at the November 11 meeting, and the first cables of instruction were sent to Ambassador Nolting (Rusk to Nolting, November 15, 1961, 8:59, 9 p.m.). Kennedy did not approve the full commitment or military contingency planning proposals (see the final version of NSAM 111, FRUS, 1988, pp. 656–657).

The above discussion of Kennedy's consideration of the alternatives regarding Vietnam in November of 1961 provides some evidence in support of REF hypothesis 2 (*security-motivated presidents tend to focus on worst-case outcomes and maximum losses*). During the November 11 and 15 meetings, Kennedy focused almost exclusively on the relative costs associated with the various alternatives. He particularly expressed concerns relating to the achievement of his aspiration level: focusing on the chances of failure of the various options to prevent the communist domination of the South, on potential communist Chinese escalation, and on potential negative congressional and public opinion. Of course, we must again be concerned with the possibility of note-taker bias and we must also recognize the limited scope of the documentary record regarding Kennedy's information processing. Once again, there is some nondirect evidence suggesting support for this hypothesis. Both Harriman's plan and Rostow's proposal were promoted as opportunities to take actions that possessed fewer negative consequences, and left the president's future options open. Indeed, even the joint State–Defense proposal was marketed in this manner.

In evaluating REF hypothesis 4 (*security-motivated presidents are likely to behave in a risk-averse manner*) in this case, we must determine whether Kennedy behaved in a risk-averse, risk-seeking, or risk-neutral manner. Based on the evidence presented above, I feel that we may again characterize the course that Kennedy followed—marked by decisional delay and incrementalism—as suggestive of risk-aversion. Kennedy clearly opposed the immediate troop commitments recommended by the Taylor report and seconded by McNamara's November 8 memorandum. He also opposed the formal commitment to the defense of South Vietnam proposed in the joint State–Defense program. On the other extreme, Kennedy rejected the policy reorientation suggested by Bowles, Galbraith, and Senator Mansfield. In the end, Kennedy steered a risk-averse course, refusing to abandon South Vietnam but also refusing to commit U.S. ground troops to its defense (see Hess, 1993, p. 73). Recalling the discussion of "riskiness" in chapter two, Kennedy clearly perceived that the worst-case outcome of a U.S.–Chinese war was possible, and recognized that his advisers were unsure of Chinese intentions, potential domestic reaction, and the potential reactions of U.S. SEATO allies. Once again, Kennedy's tactics of delay and incrementalism allowed future options to remain open, letting events on the ground in Vietnam dictate when new decisions and possibly new commitments would need to be made. (A summary of the findings for this case study can be found in table 4.2.)

Table 4.2 Summary of findings for Vietnam 1961 case study

Aspiration level	
Immediate goal	Preserve the independence of noncommunist South Vietnam under Diem's regime
Constraints on means	Fear of a negative reaction from Democrats in Congress and the fear of potential communist reactions to U.S. initiatives
Commitment reinforced by	Fear that communist success in South Vietnam would lead to the fall of Southeast Asia, concern regarding the need to demonstrate resolve and the credibility of U.S. commitments to the SEATO allies, and fear of a negative reaction from Republicans in Congress who would criticize the administration for "losing" Vietnam
Uncertainty	High uncertainty during both decision periods—three major missions are sent to the region and two separate task forces are created to address the most important issues
Time pressure	Moderate time pressure during October 5–11 period—Sorensen, Bundy, and Vice President Johnson advise caution and deliberation; rainy season limits military activity, but Viet Cong begin offensive in September
	Acute time pressure during November 3–15 period—Taylor/Rostow mission emphasizes severity of situation, Viet Cong offensive leads Diem to urgently request stepped up aid, catastrophic flood offers window of opportunity
Consideration of alternatives	Little evidence of focus on worst-case outcomes and maximum losses during October 5–11 period—Vietnam Task Force report offers balanced analysis of "pros" and "cons"
	Moderate evidence of focus on worst-case outcomes and maximum losses during November 3–15 period—Kennedy's "eight questions" focus on negative outcomes, November 11 and 15 meetings almost exclusively focused on relative costs associated with various alternatives
Final decision	Moderate evidence of delay during October 5–11 period—Taylor mission is dispatched to clear up uncertainty, but no record of Kennedy comments during October 11 meeting
	Moderate evidence of risk averse decision during November 3–15 period—Kennedy rejects extremes on both sides; no large scale intervention, but also no policy reorientation as suggested by Galbraith, Mansfield, and Harriman; approves incremental elements of State–Defense proposal, but rejects full commitment and military contingency planning proposals

Epilogue

As briefly discussed above, Paul Kattenburg calls Kennedy's November 1961 decisions "the most fateful ever made by the United States in Vietnam" (1982, p. 113). Despite the president's aversion to sending U.S. troops to the region, by 1963 his administration had sent 15,500 "advisers" to South Vietnam (Sorensen, 1965, p. 661). The extent to which these advisers participated in the day-to-day conduct of the antiguerrilla campaign was "a vitally important step toward 'Americanization' of the conflict" (Hess, 1993, p. 74). Another byproduct of Kennedy's November decisions was the fact that Vietnam would increasingly become a military problem, with the State Department playing a more and more limited role in the policy making process. Kennedy's risk-averse balancing act resulted in a policy of gradualism[12] and minimum commitment that leaves us to speculate as to what would have been the result, had Kennedy served a second term. Sorensen suggests that Kennedy "was simply going to weather it out, a nasty, untidy mess to which there was no other acceptable solution" (1965, p. 661). And so, Kennedy has been criticized from both sides: by the hawks who argued that Kennedy unreasonably restrained the military and the doves who argued that Kennedy started the United States on the slippery slope to war.

IV.   Congo 1962

Overview

On June 30, 1960, the Belgian Congo became the Republic of the Congo (Hilsman, 1967, p. 235), one of the largest newly independent states in Africa. The Belgian government agreed to the swift decolonization of the Congo, despite the fact that the Congolese political elites had little experience governing. The "Belgian gamble" (Mahoney, 1983, p. 36) focused on the hope that the Congolese would have to continue to rely on Belgian civil servants and military officers. Belgium could therefore defuse anti-colonial sentiment in the region, while maintaining de facto control over the new republic. The Belgian gamble failed on July 5, when the "Force Publique" (the Congolese Army) mutinied against its white officer corps. As the revolt continued, reports of rape, pillaging, and murder by mutinous soldiers began to reach the outside world (see "Analytical Chronology," 1961, p. 4). As Belgian reinforcements began to arrive in the Congo on July 11 (a Belgian military contingent was already in the Congo), Moise Tshombe, the Premier of Katanga (the Congo's richest region), announced the secession of his province and asked Belgian troops to intervene to "restore order" ("Analytical Chronology," 1961, p. 6). Congolese officials, Foreign Minister Justin Bomboko and Vice Premier Antoine Gizenga, asked for U.S. intervention on July 12. A second request for assistance was sent to the UN on July 13 when President Joseph Kasavubu and Prime Minister Patrice Lumumba returned to Leopoldville ("Analytical Chronology," 1961, p. 7). The Eisenhower administration deferred to the UN and the U.S. Air Force began to transport more than 10,000 UN troops into the region. Over the next three years, the "Congo Crisis" would become a significant part of the Cold War between the United States and Soviet Union.

The main objective of the Eisenhower administration was to keep the Soviets from taking advantage of the chaos in the Congo (see Mahoney, 1983, p. 37). As time passed, the administration began to view Patrice

Lumumba as pro-communist and actively sought to remove him from power (see Mahoney, 1983, pp. 40–41). On September 5, 1960, President Kasavubu set off a series of coups and countercoups when he dismissed Lumumba and asked Joseph Ileo to form a new government. On September 12, Colonel Joseph Mobutu announced a temporary military takeover to calm the situation (Mahoney, 1983, p. 48). During the last four months of the Eisenhower administration, the United States battled with the Soviet Union in the UN while the various factions consolidated their positions in the Congo. At the end of 1960, Mobutu and Kasavubu were in control of the central government in Leopoldville, Antoine Gizenga and his pro-Lumumbists were in control of Stanleyville and most of Orientale province, Moise Tshombe and his European mercenaries controlled Elisabethville and Katanga province, and Patrice Lumumba was imprisoned. This volatile situation was inherited by John F. Kennedy, when he was inaugurated on January 20, 1961.

The first major Congo event to "rattle" the new administration occurred on February 13, when Kennedy was notified of the death of Patrice Lumumba. The news hurt the administration in the UN and domestically as race riots rocked U.S. cities (Mahoney, 1983, p. 72). Despite the negative implications of Lumumba's death, it did provide an opportunity for a review of Congo policy, which resulted in an attempt to reconvene the Congolese parliament and reconcile the contending factions. In mid-July, a conference was held at Louvanium University where parliamentary representatives would elect a unity government. Pro-Lumumbist parliamentarians from Orientale province attended the conference, but Tshombe refused to let his Katanganese representatives participate. The United States supported Cyrille Adoula, a trade leader, for prime minister. When Adoula's hopes began to fade and Gizenga's representatives were prevailing, the Kennedy administration resorted to bribery to secure an Adoula government (Weissman, 1974, p. 149). "Wearied by isolation, fearful of another Mobutu coup, and finally undone by bribery, the Lumumbists struck a deal: they would support Adoula as premier in exchange for half the ministries in his new government" (Mahoney, 1983, p. 87). On August 1, 1961, Cyrille Adoula became the new prime minister. The Kennedy administration would now focus on maintaining the Adoula government and dealing with Tshombe's secession.

Domestic Congolese support for the Adoula government hinged upon its ability to end the secession of Katanga (Weissman, 1974, p. 153). This put the Kennedy administration in a difficult position because support for Adoula in ending the Katanga secession ran directly against the policies of America's NATO allies—Great Britain, France, and Belgium. The administration attempted to balance these contending interests by supporting UN military action against Katanga and yet preventing the UN from ending Tshombe's secession (see Mahoney, 1983, pp. 98–123; Weissman, 1974, pp. 152–183). Through two "rounds" of conflict, UN military success resulted in negotiations, compromise, and broken promises.

By the fall of 1962, events in the Congo were coming to a head. The Adoula government, fearing U.S. disengagement, began to consider soliciting Soviet assistance (Mahoney, 1983, p. 149). The pending withdrawal (in February 1963) of the Indian contribution to the UN effort contributed to the urgency of the situation (Hilsman, 1967, p. 263). Kennedy called for a reappraisal of the administration's Congo policy in October, but the Cuban Missile Crisis put off any major policy overhaul until November (Mahoney, 1983, pp. 149–150). The president and his advisers considered variations on two basic alternatives: disengagement and military intervention (Weissman, 1974, p. 183). In the key NSC meetings on December 14 and 17, Kennedy decided to send a "military survey mission" to the Congo, provide requested military equipment to the UN, and approved planning regarding the deployment of a U.S. Air Squadron to the Congo (FRUS, 1994b, pp. 750–752). At this point, events on the ground in Katanga overtook events in Washington. On December 24, the UN activated "Operation Grandslam" and, without further assistance from the United States, ended Tshombe's secession by mid-January (Mahoney, 1983, p. 155).

Aspiration Level

As noted above, the president's "aspiration level" is expected to comprise a set of minimum level goals that the president hopes to achieve or surpass. In order to evaluate REF hypothesis 1 (*presidents tend to evaluate outcomes relative to an aspiration level rather than an overall value level*), we must infer the elements of President Kennedy's aspiration level (regarding the Congo) from the documentary record. We need to find descriptions of acceptable/ desirable outcomes/objectives in this case. Thus, we need to find relevant documents that address Kennedy's goals, desires, hopes, needs, and/or requirements in this case.

Based on the evidence presented below, I believe that President Kennedy's immediate goal in the Congo was the reintegration of Katanga into the Republic of the Congo in order to solidify the position of Cyrille Adoula's government and forestall communist intervention in the region. The means available for achieving this goal were constrained by the fear of a negative reaction from the European allies of the United States and by the fear of a negative domestic reaction, particularly from senators associated with the powerful Katanga lobby. The president's commitment to achieving or surpassing his immediate goal was reinforced by his fear that communist success in the Congo would lead to communist influence in the rest of Central Africa, his concern regarding the need to demonstrate the credibility of U.S. commitments to the leaders of other African states, and by his fear that a failure in the Congo would have a negative impact on the future role of the UN in regional peacekeeping. And so again, a complex combination of goals and constraints formed the aspiration level that guided Kennedy's decision making. President Kennedy's aspiration level was well articulated and the documentary evidence supports REF hypothesis 1.

As in the Laos and Vietnam cases, it is useful to first consider the goals of the Eisenhower administration and the impact they had on the formation of President Kennedy's aspiration level. Ernest Lefever argues that "there was no significant difference between Eisenhower and Kennedy in the assessment of the [Congo] crisis, or the nature of American interests in Central Africa" (1967, p. 76). He suggests that each president "wanted to frustrate Soviet subversion, to avoid civil war, and to integrate Katanga peacefully" (1967, p. 76; see also Mahoney, 1983, p. 35). I would add that the differences that did exist between the administrations' policies focused more on means and levels of commitment. Eisenhower was more careful in dealing with the European allies, and more likely to overstate the Soviet threat in the region. Kennedy was more careful in dealing with potential African allies, and more sensitive to the effect of the "crisis" on the UN.

The Eisenhower administration's policy in the Congo was based on the assumption that "Moscow, not Brussels" was "the chief threat to independence" (Lefever, 1967, p. 76). Thus, the effort to reintegrate Katanga was not about anticolonialism, but rather about anticommunism. In the debate over the initial UN resolutions on the Congo, the United States prevented the "Communist effort to brand Belgium as an aggressor" (Lefever, 1967, p. 78). In fact, although the Congolese initially requested U.S. aid, Eisenhower and Dulles decided to channel U.S. aid through the UN to prevent a direct Soviet role in the region (Lefever, 1967, pp. 78–79; Mahoney, 1983, p. 37). The Eisenhower administration's impressions of Patrice Lumumba were formed by CIA reports that alleged he had been "bought by the Communists" (Mahoney, 1983, p. 38). Finally, in August of 1960, when Lumumba accepted Soviet military assistance, Eisenhower is believed to have approved his assassination by the CIA (see Mahoney, 1983, pp. 40–41). As the end of Eisenhower's term drew near, his administration focused on supporting Mobutu within the Congo, and within the UN. The U.S. policy in the Congo was immediately put under review by the incoming administration (Mahoney, 1983, pp. 62–63). Under Kennedy, the Congo was identified as one of the four "crisis" areas requiring its own task force.

Very early in his administration, Kennedy publicly discussed the overall policy concern of the United States in the Congo. In a news conference on February 15, 1961, the president expressed his concern "at what appears to be a threat of unilateral intervention in the internal affairs of the Republic of Congo" (Kennedy, "Public Papers," 1962, p. 91). This statement came the day after Gizenga's (ostensibly) pro-communist government in Stanleyville was recognized by the United Arab Republic (UAR), and the same day that East Germany, Ghana, and Yugoslavia followed suit (Hilsman, 1967, p. 235). This policy concern represents a degree of continuity between the Congo policies of the Eisenhower and Kennedy administrations. The overriding U.S. policy objective in the Congo was to keep the communists from taking advantage of the chaos in the region (see Hilsman, 1967). This concern was expressed throughout the "crisis" by members of the Kennedy administration, *both privately and publicly.*

On the public side, in a toast to Prime Minister Adoula on February 5, 1962, Kennedy noted that the United States was "vitally interested in the success of the Congo because we believe the success of your country is essential to the success of a free Africa" (Kennedy, "Public Papers," 1963, p. 108). Also, in an address in Los Angeles on December 19, 1961, Under Secretary of State George Ball set forth the administration's position—calling the Congo the "keystone" of Central Africa (1961, p. 1). In describing the administration's long-term objectives, Ball stated that they desired "a stable society under a stable and progressive government" that "may be 'non-aligned' in its international policies" (1961, p. 2). He also noted that the administration wished "to insulate the African continent from the kind of military intervention by the Sino–Soviet bloc that has created such problems in other parts of the world" and that the United States "could, of course, not sit idly by in the case of such a direct intervention" (1961, p. 3). Finally, in a rhetorical flourish undoubtedly intended for public consumption, Ball noted that, in the event of Soviet intervention, the United States "would be compelled to act even at the risk of a direct confrontation between the free world and the bloc—a confrontation that could lead to another Korean war, that could, in fact, blow the flames of a brush-fire conflict into the horrible firestorm of nuclear devastation" (1961, p. 3).

Private correspondence between the relevant administration officials also indicates that the fear of communist intervention was paramount. In an attachment to a memorandum from Secretary Rusk to Kennedy, U.S. objectives are clearly stated:

> Our aim in the Congo is the consolidation of the country with an essentially pro-Western orientation. Premier Adoula is the best available man to achieve this since he has the necessary intelligence, will power, nationwide stature and the appropriate political predilections. To succeed he has to overcome the secession of Katanga, the threat of ultra-nationalist anti-Western politicians whether in Stanleyville or elsewhere and the virtual breakdown of the national economy. A defeat of Adoula would make civil war inevitable and open the country to Communist penetration. (FRUS, 1994b, p. 270)

This concern with the potential for communist penetration of the Congo is further expressed in two intelligence estimates regarding Soviet intentions. (Both of these estimates were found in the president's National Security Files that were used during the crucial decision-making period of December 1962.) These estimates (one from the CIA/Office of National Estimates (ONE), the other from the State Department/Bureau of Intelligence and Research) note that the Soviets were unlikely to undertake a major unilateral intervention if the UN failed in the Congo, but they also suggest that "a more radical regime [than Adoula's] could expect to receive significant assistance from both African and Soviet sources" (CIA/ONE, December 11,

1962, p. 2; see also Hilsman/INR, December 7, 1962). Finally, it appears that the degree to which the estimates of Soviet intentions were accurate became an issue of contention in the key White House meetings on December 14 and 17.[13] Kennedy was concerned that the "sense that the alternatives to Tshombe and Adoula were sufficiently adverse to U.S. interests to justify American military intervention did not exist" (FRUS, 1994b, p. 735). He wondered "What could we do to create it?" (FRUS, 1994b, p. 735). Clearly, keeping the Sino-Soviet bloc from intervening in the Congo was a major concern of President Kennedy. And yet despite the overall significance of this immediate goal, other U.S. interests constrained the means available for achieving this goal and reinforced the president's commitment to this goal.

Roger Hilsman (1967; see also Schlesinger, 1965) provides an excellent discussion of the contending forces that shaped Kennedy's thinking on Congo policy. Within his own inner circle, Kennedy was faced with an emerging "New Africa" group that viewed the Congo as a test of the administration's policy in Africa (Hilsman, 1967, p. 246). They believed that, if the UN failed in the Congo because of a lack of U.S. support, the United States "would be on the wrong side of history in African eyes; our influence throughout black Africa would be all but destroyed; and the Congo would be only the first of many defeats" (Hilsman, 1967, p. 246). On the other side of the issue, an "Old Europe" group agreed that the administration should favor an independent and unified Congo, but disagreed with the means and urgency advocated by the "New Africa" group. The "Old Europe" group put relations with the North Atlantic Treaty Organization (NATO) allies first, they felt that the administration should not endanger these positive long-term relationships over internal African disputes (Hilsman, 1967, p. 247). Another constraint on Kennedy's policy was the powerful Katanga lobby run by Michael Struelens, who was associated with Belgian mining interests, and supported by Senator Thomas Dodd of Connecticut. A final administration interest focused on the effect of the Congo mission on the prestige of the UN (see CIA/ONE, December 11, 1962). Kennedy was acutely aware of the effects that failure in the Congo would have on future UN peacekeeping efforts and on the status of the UN Secretariat (Hilsman, 1967, p. 244).

Uncertainty and Time Pressure

As noted above, I expect that *presidential perceptions of high uncertainty and a lack of valid information will interact with presidential risk predispositions and affect the output of the decision process* (REF hypothesis 7). In the Kennedy cases, if the president perceives high uncertainty and inaccurate information but does not perceive acute time pressure, I expect to observe decisional delay and an expanded search for information (REF hypothesis 7a). If the president perceives high uncertainty and inaccurate information and also perceives acute time pressure, I expect to observe incrementalism (REF hypothesis 7b).

As the evidence presented below suggests, President Kennedy's perception of high uncertainty persisted across the various phases of the Congo "crisis." The president sent two major missions to the region, continually sought advice from the relevant European allies, and established a special "Task Force" to consider Congo policy. Indeed, the minutes of the crucial December meetings indicate that the president felt certain about very few of the issues relating to this case. From July to November of 1962, Kennedy's perception of time pressure became increasingly acute as the Kitona accords failed, as Adoula's regime continued to falter, and as it appeared that UN military strength in the region would decline following the withdrawal of Indian peacekeepers. As suggested by REF hypothesis 7a, when President Kennedy perceived high uncertainty but little (or moderate) time pressure, he delayed the consideration of U.S. intervention in order to gather more accurate information. But by November of 1962, when Kennedy perceived acute time pressure and persistent uncertainty, he engaged in incrementalism as suggested by REF hypothesis 7b, providing military material requested by the UN but withholding final approval of the deployment of a U.S. air squadron until another military survey mission could be completed.

Perceptions regarding uncertainty and time pressure had a significant impact on President Kennedy's decision making during the "Congo Crisis." In the crucial White House meetings on December 14 and 17, Kennedy raised concerns about Tshombe's behavior in negotiations, about potential U.S. domestic criticism if he decided to intervene militarily, about the amount of U.S. military force needed to affect outcomes in the Congo, about the severity of the Soviet threat, and about the strength of Adoula's government (FRUS, 1994b, pp. 734–737, 747, 750–752). Despite the vast quantity of critical policy papers and intelligence estimates (discussed below), Kennedy remained unconvinced of the accuracy of the information presented to him (particularly since much of it was contradictory). Also, despite his desire to take action to end the Katanga secession, Kennedy withheld final approval on the deployment of a U.S. air squadron to the region, pending the results of talks with British Prime Minister Harold Macmillan, Belgian Vice Premier and Foreign Minister Paul-Henri Spaak, UN Secretary General U Thant, and Adoula, and the results of a "military survey mission" headed by Lieutenant General Louis W. Truman. The indeterminacy of Kennedy's decision making during this period is best emphasized by the minutes of a White House Staff Meeting on December 20, 1962, where several top White House aides commented on the logical gaps and inconsistencies in the decisions Kennedy had reached (FRUS, 1994b, pp. 768–769).

The importance of time pressures as a factor in Kennedy's Congo decision making cannot be overstated. During the year between the signing of the Kitona accords (which ended Round 2 of the UN-Katanganese conflict) and Kennedy's December 1962 decisions, time pressures were often noted by Kennedy and his advisers. In a July 23, 1962 news conference, Kennedy stated "time is not running in favor of the Adoula Government" (Kennedy, "Public Papers," 1963, p. 572). In fact, in a letter received in the State

Department on July 24, Adoula lamented "I am becoming pessimistic, if not desperate" (FRUS, 1994b, p. 517). By September, the Adoula–Tshombe negotiations over a proposed "National Reconciliation Plan" had clearly reached an impasse, and George Ball wrote to Kennedy, "All evidence indicates that—barring some new major effort—our plans for the Congo are slowly sinking into the African ooze" (FRUS, 1994b, p. 594). In light of this perception that his Congo policy had stalled, Kennedy called for a major reevaluation of U.S. Congo policy and sent the Under Secretary of State for Political Affairs George C. McGhee to the Congo in a final attempt to encourage Adoula and Tshombe to accept the National Reconciliation Plan (for the report of McGhee's mission, see FRUS, 1994b, pp. 635–638).

By early November, the president concluded that he was "near or at a decisive point in the Congo situation" (FRUS, 1994b, p. 646) and approved increased pressures on Tshombe (in the form of economic sanctions) and further contingency planning (FRUS, 1994b, pp. 653–656). During the crucial decision period in early to mid-December, Kennedy focused on Adoula's tenuous hold on power in Leopoldville, reports that Tshombe was bolstering his forces in Katanga, and the knowledge that Indian UN peacekeepers would soon be returning home—thereby undermining UN military strength in the region (see FRUS, 1994b, pp. 686–690). Convinced that he needed to make a significant decision, but fearful of the uncertainty associated with the alternatives under examination, Kennedy hedged. At the crucial late afternoon meeting on December 17, Kennedy agreed to provide the UN with military material that it had requested, and he also expressed a willingness to deploy a U.S. air squadron given certain conditions, but he withheld final approval of the air squadron deployment pending receipt of the report of the Truman mission (FRUS, 1994b, pp. 750–752). Within the next two weeks Kennedy's cautious incrementalism paid off, the UN (surprising Kennedy's advisers) successfully ended Operation Grandslam and Tshombe's secession.

Consideration of Alternatives and Final Decision

As noted earlier, I expect that President Kennedy (identified as a security-motivated president) will tend to focus on worst-case outcomes and maximum losses when considering alternatives (REF hypothesis 2). I also anticipate that President Kennedy is likely to behave in a risk-averse manner in making final decisions (REF hypothesis 4).[14] In order to evaluate these hypotheses, we must examine the manner in which alternatives were considered, and the decisions that were reached during crucial periods in the cases. For the Congo case, one period is worthy of careful scrutiny—December of 1962.

The Kennedy administration did not seriously consider U.S. military intervention in the Congo until early December 1962. At that point, it was noted that the president had the Congo "much on his mind" (FRUS, 1994b, p. 717). As time pressures mounted and Kennedy recognized the growing need for new decisions, he requested that George Ball and other State Department officials develop policy papers considering the various "alternative possibilities" (FRUS, 1994b, p. 717). In preparation for the first White House meeting on December 14, Ball provided a package of papers for Kennedy and his top advisers to use as background material. These papers included memoranda and policy appraisals by Director of the Bureau of Intelligence and Research Roger Hilsman, Jr., a memorandum by Chester Bowles, a memorandum and policy appraisal by Assistant Secretary of State for African Affairs G. Mennen Williams, and a defense department memorandum and report from Deputy Assistant Secretary of Defense for International Security Affairs William Bundy and the Joint Chiefs of Staff (see FRUS, 1994b, pp. 727–728, FN1–2).[15] Ball's covering memorandum attached to the packet noted that the papers "all move in the direction of a hard line on the Congo" (FRUS, 1994b, p. 728, FN2). The final policy paper, developed by State Department officials—Director of the Office of United Nations Political and Security Affairs Joseph J. Sisco, Deputy Director of the Office of United Nations Political and Security Affairs William B. Buffum, and Assistant Secretary of State for International Organization Affairs Harlan Cleveland—and titled "New Policy on the Congo" was presented at the beginning of the December 14 meeting, and was the main focus of the discussion (FRUS, 1994b, pp. 729–737).

Carl Kaysen forwarded the packet of papers to president Kennedy along with a covering memorandum that focused the president's attention on Hilsman's appraisal of the alternatives. Kaysen offered three criticisms of Hilsman's analysis: that it overstated the Soviet threat, that it overestimated the costs of continuing the present policy, and that it underemphasized "the importance of limiting the objectives of forcible action" (FRUS, 1994b, pp. 727–728). In an interesting style of argumentation, Kaysen artfully illustrated the costs of continuing the administration's current policies, but noted that the current policy would not lead to the least favorable outcomes of Soviet intervention or the "spectacular outbreak of civil war" (FRUS, 1994b, p. 728). I note that Kaysen's argument was "interesting," because he framed the costs of staying the course as "not as bad" as Hilsman suggested, but provided no discussion of any positive benefits associated with maintaining the administration's policy. He did not suggest that maintaining the current policy was the "best" available option, only that it was not the "worst."

The analysis found in Hilsman's appraisal of the alternatives and estimate of the prospects of Soviet military intervention was very similar to the conclusions found in the official State Department proposal that Ball presented at the December 14 meeting (see FRUS, 1994b, pp. 729–733; Hilsman/INR, December 7, 1962; and Hilsman/INR, December 11, 1962). Hilsman argued that the current administration policy was failing. Adoula's future was uncertain, Tshombe's strength was growing, a bloc military presence was now a "distinct possibility," and the UN could not "field an effective force in the Katanga much longer" (Hilsman/INR, December 11, 1962,

p. 1). He then discussed several alternatives that had been proposed in the State Department meetings but were rejected out of hand: the matter could not be turned over to African states, Adoula and his Leopoldville government could not be bought off to accept Tshombe's secession, and Tshombe could not be backed as "the unifier of the Congo" (Hilsman/INR, December 11, 1962, p. 1). Hilsman, therefore, only seriously discussed two options—disengagement and forced integration.

Hilsman argued that the task of administration policy should be to make "secession less palatable for Tshombe than association with the Central Government" (Hilsman/INR, December 11, 1962, p. 2). He doubted that the current attempt to apply economic sanctions would be effective, and argued that "Probably Tshombe will be moved only by the credible threat of military coercion" (Hilsman/INR, December 11, 1962, p. 2, emphasis in original). Hilsman then delineated five requirements for the successful implementation of the suggested policy: an immediate decision should be made, preparations must move forward quickly, consultations with the UN and the Belgians should produce a specific plan of coordinated action, if active force is required the United States should move swiftly, and Tshombe must be given an opportunity to give in at any stage (Hilsman/INR, December 11, 1962, pp. 3–4). In analyzing the costs and risks associated with forced integration, Hilsman noted that if "our action is carefully planned the costs would be reasonably small," but there existed the "very real risk" that UN military coercion would have to "run its full and destructive course" (Hilsman/INR, December 11, 1962, p. 4). Thus, U.S.–Belgian relations would be strained, the administration would face domestic criticism, and Katanga would be a mess (Hilsman/INR, December 11, 1962, p. 4). Hilsman concluded that if "these risks are thought to be unacceptable, there remains in our view only one alternative—disengagement" (Hilsman/INR, December 11, 1962, p. 5).

In discussing the disengagement alternative, Hilsman argued that any withdrawal would have to take place on a piecemeal basis. He suggested ending military aid to the UN immediately and then supporting a Congolese or African solution to the problem. He stated that the administration "could only expect to postpone the time when our policy reversal became fully apparent" (Hilsman/INR, December 11, 1962, p. 5). In analyzing the costs of disengagement, Hilsman noted that they were "relatively high": Adoula or a successor would "almost certainly" become more radical, the Soviets would expand their position, the bloc would have further influence in Angola, and the UN would either be crippled or forced to rely on Communist bloc assistance (Hilsman/INR, December 11, 1962, pp. 6–8). A final conclusion (which would later influence other members of the administration) focused on the extent to which disengagement from the Congo could be permanent. Hilsman argued that, if events deteriorated further, "a policy of disengagement would result in renewed engagement under difficult, and probably unfavorable circumstances" (Hilsman/INR, December 11, 1962, p. 9). In a parallel to Kaysen's comments (discussed above) Hilsman

focused almost exclusively on comparing the relative costs of the two alternatives, neglecting to consider the potential benefits of either strategy. Once
again, the indirect evidence provides support for REF hypothesis 2,
Hilsman's analysis suggests a focus on worst-case outcomes and maximum
losses.

The other papers provided in the Ball packet supported most of
Hilsman's assumptions, but several disputed the need to move immediately
to the policy of forced integration assisted by direct U.S. military aid.
Chester Bowles agreed that Adoula was the administration's only hope, and
further suggested that if the UN failed, the administration would be faced
with several possible developments "all of them unfavorable to us," but he
maintained that Congolese unification could still be "achieved by a combination of economic strangulation of Katanga and of negotiation, with the
risks of major military action held to a minimum" (Bowles, December 12,
1962, p. 2). G. Mennen Williams agreed with Bowles, arguing that the best
alternative was to "support dramatically the existing UN efforts to achieve
national reconciliation" (Williams n.d., p. 7). George McGhee saw recent
developments (Tshombe had agreed to allow some *Union Miniere de Haut
Katanga* tax payments to be made to Adoula's government) in a positive light,
and advocated a renewed attempt at negotiation. He suggested that U.S.
military force be used only in the "last analysis" (McGhee, December 13,
1962, p. 3). On a contrary note, a paper prepared by the JCS advocated the
deployment of a Composite Air Strike Unit if it was necessary to keep
Adoula's government in power (FRUS, 1994b, pp. 718–720). Generally,
Kennedy's advisers agreed with the basic assumption that a new policy on
the Congo was needed. They disagreed about the severity of the current
situation and the necessity of direct U.S. military involvement. The crucial
meetings with the president on December 14 and 17 would focus on this
disagreement.

George Ball's presentation at the December 14 meeting combined
several of the strategies advocated by his State Department colleagues. He
argued that the most significant current policy problem was the "absence of
a U.S. decision as to what we would do, in the final analysis, to prevent
chaos, large-scale massacres, and/or a major Soviet presence called in by
radical successors to Adoula" (FRUS, 1994b, p. 731). In an argument similar
to that of Hilsman's (see Hilsman/INR, December 11, 1962, p. 9), Ball
noted that "we may eventually have to use United States, and perhaps other
western forces to clean up a very messy state of affairs" (FRUS, 1994b,
p. 731). He further argued "we can use the possibility of our fuller intervention later to accomplish our purposes with less intervention now"
(FRUS, 1994b, p. 731). Thus, Ball advocated: the buildup of UN forces, the
proroguing of the Congolese parliament by Adoula, the vigorous pursuit of
acceptance by Tshombe of the National Reconciliation Plan, and the
deployment of a U.S. fighter unit. In an interesting (if not completely logical
argument), Ball suggested a "build-up of U.S. military forces under a U.N.
umbrella, *for the purpose of avoiding the use of force* to reintegrate the Katanga"

(FRUS, 1994b, p. 732, emphasis in original). Thus, the deployment of U.S. forces was conceived in the State Department principally as a political and psychological instrument.

At the December 14 meeting, Kennedy expressed uncertainty over the seriousness of the current situation. He was also concerned with how U.S. public opinion, the Congress, and the European allies would react to this increased U.S. commitment. Kennedy was especially adamant about not putting the proposed U.S. unit under direct UN control. He also wondered about the reaction of Secretary General U Thant. Chief of Naval Operations Admiral George W. Anderson stressed that "what we had was a political rather than a military, problem in the use of force . . . It was the political part that required a U.S. force" (FRUS, 1994b, pp. 735–736). By the end of the meeting, Kennedy "decided that we should undertake to put in an air squadron" (FRUS, 1994b, p. 736), but only after consultation with U Thant and Adoula. Another meeting was planned for December 17 to reconsider the plan of action in light of these consultations.

Secretary General U Thant was initially skeptical (see FRUS, 1994b, p. 738, FN 1–2) of the U.S. plan, instead suggesting that the United States expand its support by providing the UN with an assortment of military material. But at the conclusion of a meeting with Ambassador to the United Nations Adlai E. Stevenson, U Thant "warmed" to the U.S. proposal, suggesting that it might be better if Adoula made the request to the UN (FRUS, 1994b, p. 742). Throughout the meeting, U Thant downplayed the need for immediate action, asking the U.S. ambassador to give UN plans time to work (U Thant was undoubtedly aware of the stepped-up military activity currently being planned by his UN commanders).

The December 17 meetings focused on an "Operating Plan for the Congo" (FRUS, 1994b, pp. 743–746) that detailed the specifics of the policy changes agreed upon at the December 14 meeting. In the first December 17 meeting at 10 a.m., Kennedy questioned whether the United States would have increased control over UN military action and "whether the proposed U.S. squadron would be sufficient" (FRUS, 1994b, p. 747). Secretary Rusk wondered whether, if the proposed actions failed, "we would go in further with whatever force is needed? Or how do we get out?" (FRUS, 1994b, p. 747). Concerned by these questions, Kennedy "approved provision of the military equipment Secretary-General U Thant had requested and discussion of the proposed air squadron with Spaak, Adoula, and the U.N. leadership" (FRUS, 1994b, p. 747). Kaysen noted in his minutes of the meeting that Kennedy was willing to go ahead with the air squadron "if [it] adds any substantial chance of success" (FRUS, 1994b, p. 747). Once again nagged by persistent uncertainty regarding the possibility that U.S. action would result in the negative consequences discussed above, Kennedy steered a middle course of decisional delay and incrementalism.

Prior to the evening meeting, Kennedy received an analytical memorandum from Kaysen. Kaysen noted that "this morning's discussion did not bring out clearly the alternatives to the proposed course of action. The real question is whether any of them is less likely to result in an unacceptable situation in the Congo which will call for U.S. intervention on a larger scale at a later date" (FRUS, 1994b, p. 748). Kaysen starkly summarized the alternatives for Kennedy:

> We can take a risky step now which, by general agreement, has the best chance of moving the Congo problem from its present posture as a Congo–Katanga war to an internal political problem within a nominally unified federal Congo. However, that chance is probably not better than 50–50. The other alternative is immediate withdrawal of the UN and U.S. from the operation. This involves immediate losses of UN and U.S. prestige and may require at some future date, a year or so, from now, renewed U.S. intervention, because of the danger of Soviet involvement in a continuing Congo–Katanga struggle. It will certainly result in a change from the present moderate to a radical Leopoldville Government, and the loss of all European support for the Central Government. (FRUS, 1994b, pp. 748–749)

The structure and wording of Kaysen's presentation suggests that he was asking Kennedy to decide on which was the "least negative" alternative, rather than which was the "best."

At the late afternoon meeting on December 17, Kennedy expressed uncertainty regarding the necessity of deploying the U.S. air squadron. Secretary Rusk opposed the deployment and again suggested that Kennedy simply approve the provision of the military material requested by U Thant. Kennedy "declared that he did not want to get into a fight unless it could be won" (FRUS, 1994b, p. 751). He noted that providing the military material requested by the UN "would not make much impact but might be a useful interim step" (FRUS, 1994b, p. 751). Finally, he decided that he "wanted a military appraisal to provide fresh input" (FRUS, 1994b, p. 751). He also decided that further consultations with Spaak, Macmillan, Adoula, and U Thant should be conducted, before the deployment of the air squadron would be approved. If the consultations and military appraisal were positive, Kennedy would approve the air squadron, if not, he and his advisers would start to "think how we get out" (FRUS, 1994b, p. 751). In a White House meeting on December 19, Kaysen noted that "the President's mind is definitely made up on making some kind of a U.S. military move in the Congo *for the purposes of political demonstration only*; he has certainly, however, not made up his mind on the wisdom of actual involvement of U.S. forces. I am aware of the logical gaps which this leaves, but there it is." (FRUS, 1994b, p. 769 FN1, emphasis in original) In the week after the December 17 White House meeting, Secretary General U Thant reconsidered his position and rejected the offer of the U.S. air squadron (FRUS, 1994b, pp. 777–778). By December 28, General Truman returned from the Congo with a reinforcement plan that McGeorge Bundy termed "feckless"

(FRUS, 1994b, p. 787). Kennedy was saved from making further decisions, when the "third round" of confrontation began in Katanga and the UN troops routed Tshombe's forces.

This discussion of Kennedy's decision making during the "Congo Crisis" provides some support for REF hypothesis 2 and a greater degree of support for REF hypothesis 4. The limited amount of direct Kennedy statements from the meetings on December 14 and 17 (see FRUS, 1994b, pp. 734–737, 747, 750–752), constrains the rigorous evaluation of the REF hypotheses related to patterns of information processing. Generally Kennedy focused more on potential costs, neglecting the potential benefits of the alternatives under consideration. But while this suggests that he may have been engaged in "bottom-up" processing, it may also simply be the result of Kaysen's note-taking biases. There is some nondirect evidence that bears on these hypotheses—Hilsman and Ball's policy papers almost exclusively focused on costs (as noted above) and neglected discussions of benefits. And yet, I would rather not characterize Kennedy's own process of information processing by relying on nondirect sources of evidence. Interestingly, in Hilsman's analysis of Soviet intentions, he discussed the inducements and inhibitions that would affect Kremlin thinking regarding intervention in the Congo. He argued that the Soviets would not intervene in any large-scale, unilateral manner because "they are aware that the Congo is a morass and, at that, one in which they have no vital or even secondary interests" (Hilsman/INR, December 7, 1962, p. 6). Surprisingly, none of the adminis-tration officials involved in the Congo decisions advocated similar inhibi-tions to prevent U.S. intervention.

In evaluating REF hypothesis 4 in this case, we must determine whether Kennedy behaved in a risk-averse, risk-seeking, or risk-neutral manner. In my view, the course that Kennedy followed—marked by decisional delay and incrementalism—is again suggestive of risk-aversion. Hilsman notes that, while he and his colleagues associated significant risks with the forced integration policy, "disengagement contained even greater risks" (Hilsman, 1967, p. 266). Hilsman also writes that "George Ball felt much the same— the notion of getting out was tempting he said, but when you thought it all through the risk was just too great" (1967, p. 266). Indeed, Kennedy attempted to only cautiously engage in the forced integration policy: pro-viding the UN with the requested military equipment, but delaying the decision to commit U.S. troops until he was more certain of what their impact would be. In following this policy, Kennedy avoided both the imme-diate costs of disengagement, and the potential risks associated with the intro-duction of U.S. forces. Recalling the discussion of "riskiness" in chapter two, it appears from the documentary record that Kennedy was concerned with the worse-case outcomes associated with both the disengagement and forced integration options. He was also concerned with the high level of uncertainty that persisted throughout the December decision period. Once again, Kennedy steered a middle course between risky options. He also left future options open, letting events in the Congo dictate when new decisions would need to be made. (A summary of the findings for this case study can be found in table 4.3.)

Epilogue

While Kennedy's admirers have applauded his performance in this case (quoted in Mahoney, 1983, pp. 155–156), others have criticized him for

Table 4.3 Summary of findings for Congo 1962 case study

Aspiration level	
Immediate goal	Reintegration of Katanga into the Republic of the Congo in order to solidify the position of Cyrille Adoula's government and forestall communist intervention in the region
Constraints on means	Fear of a negative reaction from the United States' European allies and the fear of a negative domestic reaction, particularly from Senators associated with the powerful Katanga lobby
Commitment reinforced by	Fear that communist success in the Congo would lead to communist influence in the rest of Central Africa, concern regarding the need to demonstrate the credibility of U.S. commitments to the leaders of other African states, and fear that a failure in the Congo would have a negative impact on the future role of the UN in regional peacekeeping
Uncertainty	High uncertainty during both decision periods—two major missions are sent to the region, a task force is created to address the most important issues, and the European allies are continually consulted
Time pressure	Moderate time pressure during the July to October period—pressures mount on Adoula government, National Reconciliation Plan negotiations reach an impasse, but time available for McGhee mission
	Acute time pressure during December period—Adoula regime falters, looming withdrawal of Indian peacekeepers, Tshombe bolstering forces in Katanga
Consideration of alternatives	Moderate evidence of focus on worst-case outcomes and maximum losses during December period—Kennedy's comments at December 14 and 17 meetings focus on potential costs associated with alternatives, policy papers by Hilsman and Ball focus almost exclusively on costs, Kaysen memorandum frames choice as selection of least bad alternative
Final decision	Strong evidence of delay during July to October period—McGhee mission dispatched to clear up uncertainty, European allies consulted, waiting for Tshombe's next move
	Mix of delay and incrementalism during December period—approval of military aid for U.N. forces; willingness to deploy U.S. air squadron, but final decision withheld pending Truman mission report

undue caution. Stephen Weissman writes:

> The extremism of Kennedy's caution was responsible for some of the tottering, the ambiguity, and the blind alleys of American diplomacy; it was one reason why events—even the most fortuitous events—had such a determinative influence on policy. I am not suggesting that compromise and moderation should be excluded from the making of American foreign policy. I am merely saying that thoughtful compromise entails a modification of ends and a consequent tailoring of means and that it is the result of dispassionate analysis, not fear. Too often Kennedy left the ends confused or untouched and the means confused or inadequate. Too often they were the product of pure caution. (1974, p. 192)

V. Conclusions

The documentary evidence presented in the Laos, Vietnam, and Congo case studies provides empirical support for several of the hypotheses that compose my REF. Table 4.4 summarizes the findings for the three Kennedy case studies. Hypotheses 1 and 1a (relating to the president's aspiration level) are supported by the vast amount of evidence demonstrating that, in each case, President Kennedy perceived a complex and well-articulated combination of goals and constraints. I also found ample evidence of the aspiration level guiding decision making—as outcomes were often framed as

Table 4.4 Degree of support for REF hypotheses across cases and decision periods

	Laos		Vietnam		Congo	
Decision period	1[a]	2[b]	1[c]	2[d]	1[e]	2[f]
Hypotheses						
1	S	S	S	S	S	S
1a	S	S	S	S	S	S
2	W	M	A	M	NA	M
4	NA	W	NA	M	NA	M
6	NA	NA	NA	NA	NA	NA
7a	NA	NA	M	NA	S	M
7b	S	NA	NA	S	NA	S

Key: S = strong, M = moderate, W = weak, A = evidence runs against hypothesis, NA = hypothesis not applicable.

[a] March 9–April 1, 1961
[b] April 26–May 3, 1961
[c] October 5–11, 1961
[d] November 3–15, 1961
[e] July–October 1962
[f] December 1962

departures from particular goals. Based on these case studies, I feel that this part of the REF is on the right track.

REF hypothesis 2 (relating to how security-motivated presidents process information) is only somewhat supported by the evidence presented above. I was able to find little direct evidence of "on-line" information processing by President Kennedy, although the limited evidence that was found does support this hypothesis. In different periods of each case I was also able to find substantial nondirect evidence supporting this hypothesis, but I cannot claim that this evidence is anything more than "suggestive." Another concern is that note-taker bias might also influence the results obtained from what little direct evidence there was. I envision revising the REF in this area, both to deal with evidentiary problems, and to consider other ways in which individual risk predispositions might affect information processing (see chapter five).

REF hypothesis 4 (*security-motivated presidents are likely to behave in a risk-averse manner*) was moderately supported by the evidence found in the case studies. Although the president sometimes failed to make a final decision in these cases, the Laos and Vietnam case studies certainly suggest that President Kennedy tended to avoid options that were perceived to be "risky." The comparative definition of "riskiness" presented in chapter two, does well to capture the empirical fact that both intervention and disengagement alternatives were perceived as "risky" in the three cases. I also feel that the pattern of delay and incrementalism, so common in these cases, provides substantial evidence of risk-aversion. Finally, the careful analysis (and in some cases over-analysis) of the potential policy alternatives in each case suggests a president reluctant to take undue risks.

The REF hypotheses that receive the greatest support are 7a and b (regarding uncertainty and time pressure). When President Kennedy perceived high uncertainty and low or moderate time pressure, he consistently delayed making significant decisions in each of the cases. When President Kennedy perceived high uncertainty and acute time pressure he engaged in incrementalism, basically doing more of the same in Vietnam and the Congo. The picture that emerges from these case studies reveals a cautious president that generally allows events on the ground to determine the pace of decision making, avoiding difficult value trade-offs until time pressures force a decision period upon him. In terms of revising the REF, I will consider refining hypotheses 7a and b, to capture the fact that incrementalism and delay may be a mixed response under certain conditions. In these cases, there were several instances where Kennedy delayed making a major decision, but did make minor decisions that resulted in incremental policy changes.

Overall, I feel that my REF is quite capable of explaining President Kennedy's risk behavior in these cases. Obviously certain elements require refinement, but the empirical accuracy of the other elements is quite encouraging. In the next chapter, I first consider the Truman and Kennedy cases in a comparative manner—analyzing the strengths and weaknesses of the REF across the six cases. I then suggest a number of refinements of the REF, in order to eliminate the identified flaws and increase its explanatory power. Finally, I consider the limits of this project and propose new avenues of research for expanding and refining the REF—in the hopes of developing a *theory* of presidential risk behavior.

CHAPTER FIVE

Conclusion

I.   Overview

At the end of chapters three and four, I discussed the results of the process-tracing analysis within each presidential administration. This concluding chapter begins with a summary discussion of those results, followed by a between-administration comparison of my empirical observations. I then consider the significance of these empirical results in the context of the theoretical, conceptual, and methodological issues discussed in chapters one and two. In the next section, I discuss potential explanations for the negative results obtained in particular cases and decision periods. In section VI, I propose a revised model that may someday serve as the foundation for a process-oriented theory of presidential risk behavior, and suggest a research agenda for exploring the utility of the revised model. Finally, in section VII, I discuss the implications of the results of this project and certain restrictions on the scope of its findings.

II.   Case Study Results

President Harry S. Truman and many of his foreign policy advisers felt that the Soviet Union was bent on world domination, but they did not know how quickly or how openly the Soviets would pursue that objective. Eventually, they concluded that Soviet actions in Iran, Greece, Korea, and elsewhere were designed to capitalize on nationalist movements that hoped to extinguish vestiges of Western imperialism. The Kremlin and their allies probed the periphery looking for weak points that might be exploited, testing the military capabilities and resolve of the United States, Britain, and France. These areas were valued for their possession of raw materials and strategic position, but more importantly as symbols in the struggle between communism and capitalism. The "rotten apple" metaphor, offered by then Under Secretary of State Acheson during the Greek Crisis, conveyed the crucial significance of areas that otherwise might simply be written-off. Viewed objectively and in isolation, communist control of these countries would not affect the balance of power in a significant manner. Viewed subjectively and in *context*, the "loss" of these countries could lead to the defeat of capitalism and enslavement of the "free world."

The framing of the situation adopted by President Truman and his advisers severely constrained the alternatives under consideration in the Iran, Greece, and Korea cases. Conciliatory gestures would be viewed as a sign of weakness by the adversary, and would be met by more demands. Overt large-scale military intervention in Iran or Greece risked a direct confrontation with Soviet forces at a time when the atomic monopoly of the United States may not have been enough to counter the Soviet advantage in conventional forces. There could be no appeasement of the Soviet Union, but the Truman administration did not yet wield the military capability or domestic support it would need to successfully wage World War III. The dearth of options considered by President Truman and his advisers in these cases reflects the fact that they felt compelled by the situation to undertake particular courses of action. The decision-making process that resulted can be characterized as a search for what "must be done." This did not trouble President Truman, a man comfortable with his responsibilities and seldom known to voice regret or agonize over what might have been.

And yet, President Truman was not immune to the impact of uncertainty and time pressure. He did not rush blindly forward when questions about Soviet or allied motives suggested the need for a pause, and the pace of events allowed one. He relied heavily on the advice of ambassadors and special representatives whose knowledge of the situation might clear up ambiguities, and was willing to send trusted men on special missions when he felt he was not fully informed. In the Iran and Greece cases, periods of leisurely reflection were interspersed with short bursts of crisis decision making. In the Korea case, where events of the ground moved much more quickly, Truman and his advisers still took the time to reflect on alternative frames of the situation and approve only limited military actions. "Give 'em hell Harry" tended to have visceral reactions to problems that drove him to favor quick action, but that "gut" reaction was often tempered by his advisers' or his own sense of uncertainty.

Of the three Truman administration cases, Korea offers the clearest conclusion. The "loss" of Korea was intolerable, given Truman's aspiration level. When MacArthur reported that the time for a final decision was at hand, Truman selected the only alternative under consideration capable of producing a desirable outcome. The Iran and Greece cases are more complex because the communist forces in those countries never quite reached the brink of victory. Truman could engage in delay, deliberation, and incrementalism because his aspiration level in these cases was never severely threatened. Unfortunately (for the purposes of this project), in Iran and Greece, we never witness the moment where the level of the president's commitment to his aspiration level is ultimately revealed. It is, however, illustrative that President Truman had at least formally committed to his aspiration level in public statements and private comments. If Teheran or

Athens had been on the brink of collapse, it is highly likely that Truman would have committed U.S. troops to prevent the loss of these areas to communism.

In a number of ways, the geo-strategic situation facing President John F. Kennedy had not changed much since Truman's day. Berlin was still a flashpoint, communist inroads in Asia were still a threat to Japan and Australia, China was a looming menace, and the Soviets supported nationalist movements in the periphery (now fighting to fill the power vacuum that followed decolonization). However, recent changes were reshaping the strategic environment and setting the stage for the upheaval of the 1960s. Stalin was dead and Khrushchev appeared to be a more reasonable adversary, the U.S. nuclear monopoly was gone and the balance and quality of conventional forces were once again important, Mao appeared to be steering China on a more independent course and Eisenhower had followed Truman's policy of expanding U.S. commitments in the periphery. For the Kennedy administration, the Soviet Union was clearly a competitor bent on ideological and territorial expansion, but communist world domination was no longer a likely goal or outcome. In the Laos, Vietnam, and Congo cases, the immediate goal remained the prevention of ultimate communist victory, but the constraints on the means used to achieve the president's objectives were much more important (despite the rhetoric of Kennedy's inaugural address).

In the early months of Kennedy's presidency, an effort was made to reevaluate the commitments made by the Eisenhower administration (particularly after the Bay of Pigs debacle). While Eisenhower had described Laos as the "cork in the bottle" of Southeast Asia and had pushed for a pro-Western "neutrality," Kennedy and his advisers eventually settled on a more manageable goal. A "truly neutral" Laos was more doable given the significant constraints on the means available to achieve the president's objective. Kennedy felt pressure to avoid the "loss" of Laos, but he also knew that there was little support for an attempt to "win."

Unfortunately for the president, the ambiguous resolution of the Laos case acted as a constraint on his aspiration level in Vietnam. Kennedy and his advisers felt compelled to act to avoid the fall of a second domino in the region, disregarding the concerns of Senator Mansfield and Ambassador Galbraith. In the Congo case, the administration once again was able to revisit the decisions made by Eisenhower. Support for Cyrille Adoula's government offered an opportunity to avoid surrendering the Congo to Gizenga's leftist forces, while at the same time reducing support for Mobutu's military solution.

In each case, the aspiration level adopted by Kennedy and his advisers severely limited the options under consideration. But within these limited sets of options, Kennedy had choices that differed in degrees of risk. Given the high levels of uncertainty that persisted across the cases and the lack of crucial "moments of decision" where the president would have to take risks or accept losses, Kennedy was prone to choose delay or incrementalism over large-scale intervention and formal commitments. The various task forces and special missions sent to examine events on the ground in these cases reflect the president's continuing uncertainty. The hope seems to have been that the next mission would find the situation to have changed for the better, or would come up with the "silver bullet" solution that others had ignored. Clearly President Kennedy and his advisers had great confidence in their ability to think through the situation and develop creative alternatives (or to reach that point through trial and error). Indeed, in contrast to the Truman administration, Kennedy and his advisers seemed occasionally to overanalyze policy alternatives causing decisional paralysis. Kennedy also appears to have agonized over each decision, becoming deeply involved in the process of information management and analysis.

Of the three Kennedy administration cases, Vietnam offers the clearest conclusion. Having compromised in Laos, Kennedy could not accept the "loss" of South Vietnam to communist aggression. As time pressure became acute in the fall of 1961, Kennedy felt compelled to escalate the U.S. involvement, but even then Kennedy refused to formally commit to the defense of South Vietnam and rejected the military contingency planning proposals offered in the State–Defense proposal. The president was unwilling to take steps that would irrevocably bind the fate of South Vietnam to a successful U.S. military intervention. In the Laos and the Congo cases, it is more difficult to characterize Kennedy's "final decisions." Despite acute time pressure toward the conclusion of each case, the president's aspiration level was not severely threatened. In Laos, the cease-fire and Geneva conference obviated the need for further decisions, in the Congo the surprising success of the UN's military efforts ended the threat posed by Katanga's secession. And yet, I feel that Kennedy's commitment to his aspiration level in Laos and the Congo was fragile. In May of 1961, coming off the disastrous Bay of Pigs operation, Kennedy did not trust his military advisers and his meetings with Eisenhower, Rockefeller, and the legislative leaders suggested there was no domestic support for a significant U.S. intervention in Laos. Kennedy would have continued to engage in limited actions, but he was not ready to send 60,000 U.S. troops to save Vientiane. Similarly, Kennedy was reluctant to approve the deployment of the U.S. air squadron to the Congo, even in December of 1962, and never seriously considered a large-scale U.S. intervention. Despite the rhetoric of George Ball's speech in Los Angeles a year earlier, Kennedy was not ready to accept the "risk of a direct confrontation between the free world and the bloc—a confrontation that could lead to another Korean war, that could, in fact, blow the flames of a brush-fire conflict into the horrible firestorm of nuclear devastation" (1961, p. 3).

III.   A Comparison of the Truman and Kennedy Case Studies

By evaluating the REF hypotheses through six case studies across two presidential administrations, I was able to observe commonalities and differences in the manner in which each president approached risky decisions. In particular, I noticed differences in their approach to uncertainty and faith in the efficacy of U.S. initiatives. I noticed commonalities in their sensitivity to time as an element of the decision process, in the generic structures of their aspiration levels, and in their responses to the perception of high uncertainty and low time pressure. The commonalities and differences discussed above are summarized in tables 5.1 and 5.2.

I observed two major differences in the manner in which each president confronted risky decisions—their approach to uncertainty and faith in the

Table 5.1   Observed commonalities in approach to risky decisions by Truman and Kennedy

	Commonalities between Truman and Kennedy
Response to acute time pressure	External events contribute to perception of acute time pressure
	Perception of acute time pressure: increases issue salience, increases presidential involvement in the. decision-making process, restricts length of decision period
Generic structure of aspiration level	Aspiration level focused on: potential response of adversary, worthiness of ally, potential response of other allies, possibility of U.S. overcommitment, desire to demonstrate resolve and credibility of U.S. commitments, "domino" fears, desire to generate positive congressional and public opinion
Response to perception of high uncertainty and low time pressure	Search for new information through "special missions" to region led by "objective" outside observers (military officers or trusted presidential advisers)

Table 5.2   Observed differences in approach to risky decisions by Truman and Kennedy

	Truman	*Kennedy*
Approach to uncertainty	Willing to update perceptions upon receipt of new information from field or revised analyses by advisers	Skeptical of incoming information Questioned analyses provided by advisers Reluctant to update perceptions
Faith in efficacy of U.S. initiatives	Convinced of efficacy of U.S. diplomatic and military instruments Success during World War II indicative of U.S. ingenuity and will	Skeptical of efficacy of U.S. diplomatic and military instruments Soviets and Chinese viewed as experienced and resourceful adversaries capable of thwarting U.S. initiatives

efficacy of U.S. initiatives. Truman and Kennedy were both highly sensitive to uncertainty and inaccurate information in the decision process, but Truman was much more willing to accept the judgments of his advisers and revise his perceptions. For Truman, uncertainty about Soviet intentions was cleared up by advice from State Department officials in Moscow (in the Korea case), by direct "evidence" of Soviet behavior (in the Iran case), or by "objective" observations by outside analysts (in the Greek case). Kennedy was much more skeptical of incoming information and required more evidence before he would reach a conclusion. In the Laos and Vietnam cases, Kennedy was reluctant to accept his advisers' judgments regarding the possibility of Chinese intervention despite supportive reports from the Central Intelligence Agency (CIA) and Joint Chiefs of Staff (JCS). In the Congo and Vietnam cases, Kennedy perceived lingering uncertainty even after the Truman and Taylor military survey missions. Indeed, in the Vietnam case, three special missions and two special task forces could not reduce Kennedy's perception of high uncertainty.

In terms of the presidents' faith in the efficacy of U.S. initiatives, Truman was much more convinced of the U.S. ability to obtain positive outcomes. Flushed with perceptions of strength in the aftermath of the victory over Germany and Japan, President Truman placed a great deal of trust in the abilities of the diplomatic and military services. Thus, he seldom questioned the chances for success of the alternatives placed before him. For a country that had saved Western Europe and the Pacific Rim from the Axis Powers, communist insurgents in Iran, Greece, and Korea appeared to be minor obstacles. While the Soviet Union was clearly perceived to be a substantial threat, President Truman appeared to be more concerned with winning congressional and public approval of his foreign policy. President Kennedy was much less sanguine regarding the efficacy of U.S. diplomatic and military instruments of power. China (particularly after the U.S. experience in Korea) loomed as a strong and experienced adversary in Southeast Asia, and the Soviets possessed the resources to influence events in the Congo. Clearly, the Bay of Pigs fiasco also contributed to Kennedy's discounting of the assessments provided by the CIA and JCS. Finally, the disappointment with the Geneva conference regarding Laos called into question the efficacy of diplomatic initiatives.

Despite the differences between the administrations discussed above, I was able to discern a number of commonalities: their sensitivity to time as an element of the decision process, the generic structures of their aspiration levels, and their responses to the perception of high uncertainty and low time pressure. Both presidents perceived time pressure as an important factor in the decision process. Indeed, the presence of acute time pressure was almost a requirement before a final decision was made in these cases. This suggests that both presidents were generally reactive in formulating their foreign policy. In almost every case, events on the ground in the region dictated the pace of administration activity: Soviet troop movements contributed to the Iran "crisis" in March of 1946, the DPRK invasion of South Korea forced President Truman's return to Washington on June 25, 1950, the fall of Muong Sai forced the consideration of intervention in Laos in May of 1961, and the Viet Cong offensive in the fall of 1961 led to Kennedy's November decisions. In the Greece and the Congo cases, the withdrawal of external aid contributed to the perception that time was of the essence: Truman and his advisers were forced to react to the British aide-memoire of February 21, and Kennedy feared the pending withdrawal of UN peacekeepers in early 1963. Given the multiple problems that they were dealing with at any given time, Truman and Kennedy often avoided policy decisions that were not immediately required. Their personal influence on U.S. policy was thus most apparent during "crisis" situations.

Another interesting commonality that emerged from these case studies was the shared generic structure of the presidents' aspiration levels. In general, the presidents' aspiration levels focused on the potential response of the adversary, the worthiness of the ally, the potential response of other allies, the possibility of U.S. overcommitment, the desire to demonstrate resolve and the credibility of U.S. commitments, "domino" fears, and the desire to generate positive congressional and public opinion. To the extent that these commonalities exist, we may consider whether a common "Cold War in the periphery" structure of beliefs was shared by Truman and Kennedy. We may also consider whether a "generic intervention" aspiration level might be found in other cases outside of the Cold War context. It may be that the imperatives discussed above are basic interests that all U.S. presidents perceive in similar situations (see discussion below).[1]

A final commonality that emerged from these case studies is the presidents' responses to the perception of high uncertainty and low time pressure. Generally, when faced with perceptions of high uncertainty and low time pressure, the presidents would delay their decisions and search for new information. More interestingly, this search for new information often took the form of a special mission to the region. Truman and Kennedy frequently sought the advice of an "objective" outside observer to evaluate the seriousness of the situation—as usually communicated by State Department officials. The leaders of the missions were often military officers (although they did not always favor the intervention alternatives). These missions included: Major General Chamberlin's trip to Greece, General MacArthur's trip to Korea, General Taylor's trip to South Vietnam, and Lieutenant General Truman's trip to the Congo. There were also nonmilitary missions that involved sending a trusted adviser to the region (like sending George McGhee to the Congo). In three of the four cases where a military mission was sent to the region, the reports of those advisers played a significant role in the president's final decision. The reports of these detached "objective" observers were used to validate the information obtained from those directly involved in the situation. Unfortunately, these trips were often of short duration and did little to probe beneath the surface.

IV.   Theoretical, Conceptual, and Methodological Significance

The empirical results presented in chapters three and four provide support for a number of the REF hypotheses and also suggest that the domain-sensitive orientation to the study of risk behavior (discussed in chapters one and two) may be successfully employed by researchers interested in studying presidential decisions regarding military intervention. This research has demonstrated that assuming the "riskiness" of particular types of alternatives (as is done in Vertzberger, 1995a, 1997) ignores the subjectivity and inherently comparative nature of the concept. It has shown that theories that neglect personal predispositions and those that simply associate "risk-taking" behavior with the "domain of losses" (such as Farnham, 1992; Huth et al., 1992; Kahneman and Tversky, 1979; or McDermott, 1992), cannot explain the observed variation in risk propensity found in these cases. It suggests that Truman and Kennedy were not concerned so much with final asset positions (as would be suggested by expected-utility theory), but rather with departures from an aspiration level (as suggested by the literature dealing with reference dependence). And finally, it shows that attempts to rigorously and reliably develop quantitative measures of subjective utility and probability estimates in the "real world" are potentially futile and are not necessary for the successful development and testing of process-oriented models of risk behavior.

As noted in chapter two, much of the current research on risk behavior in foreign policy either assumes the "riskiness" of a particular alternative (e.g., Vertzberger, 1995a, 1997), or assumes that only policy change involves a high degree of risk (e.g., Huth et al., 1992). In an attempt to retain the comparative nature of the classical notion of "riskiness" (i.e., based on the comparison of the utilities and probabilities associated with various outcomes), and yet also reflect the difficulties in measuring utilities and probabilities in the "real world," I offered the following definition: Comparatively riskier options are characterized by: (a) more numerous and extremely divergent outcomes, (b) the perception that extreme negative outcomes are at least possible, and (c) recognition that estimates of potential outcomes and the probabilities associated with the occurrence of those outcomes are potentially flawed and may, in fact, be totally incorrect. The cases presented above, particularly those from the Kennedy administration, demonstrate the usefulness of my formulation of the concept.

President Kennedy often viewed policy inertia as a *risky* choice and perceived *variation* in the riskiness of different forms of military intervention. Thus, in the Congo case, both the disengagement and full intervention alternatives were perceived to be *more risky* than incremental escalation. In the Vietnam case, the disengagement alternative was, quite possibly, perceived to be the most risky of the options under consideration—it could result in the loss of all Southeast Asia, the loss of U.S. prestige, and the decline of Kennedy's political fortunes at home. Likewise, in the Greece case, Truman perceived almost as much risk associated with the nonintervention alternative as the risk associated with the intervention alternative. These cases all show that "riskiness" is an inherently comparative construct. Conceivably, a decision maker could even imagine that nuclear war was less risky than another alternative if that alternative offered the serious prospect of outright annihilation. So long as we view "riskiness" as a subjective construct, we cannot ignore the variability and context-dependent nature of risk estimates.

The most significant theoretical contribution of the case study results is the ability of the REF to explain risk-aversion in cases where the outcomes were framed as losses. Recall that Kahneman and Tversky's (1979) "reflection effect" (subjects tended to prefer the less risky option when the problem was framed as a gain, and the more risky option when the problem was framed as a loss) has been the main finding utilized by political scientists. A simple application of the Kahneman and Tversky theory to these cases would suggest that risk-acceptance should have been observed in every case.[2] Only by considering the interactive effect of personal predispositions and situational constraints can we explain risk-averse/acceptant behavior in either domain. The results reported in chapters three and four suggest that the aspiration level did have an impact on the alternatives that were actively discussed, but beyond this point personal predispositions provide a more complete explanation of risk behavior.

In the Vietnam case, Kennedy did not seriously consider the nonintervention alternative, because it was viewed as incapable of achieving or surpassing his aspiration level. But when he selected between the different intervention alternatives, he favored incremental escalation over the more risky alternative pushed by the State and Defense Departments, and the Vietnam Task Force. In Laos, Kennedy rejected the do-nothing option out of hand, but then chose to engage in diplomacy and coercion rather than assume the risks of full-scale intervention (favored by Rostow and the JCS). These cases show that the REF is capable of explaining decisions that would fall in the "off-cells" of Kahneman and Tversky's (1979) experimental research. While these results are not conclusive, they do suggest the potential usefulness of synthetic models that capture both situational and personal factors.

Another significant result of this research is the empirical support for the notion that decision makers are not concerned so much with final asset positions (as would be suggested by expected-utility theory), but rather with departures from an aspiration level (as suggested by the literature dealing with reference dependence). This result should be very troubling for scholars that focus on expected-utility models of risk behavior (see Alpert, 1976; Bueno de Mesquita, 1981, 1985; Bueno de Mesquita and Lalman, 1992; Morrow, 1987). Much of the effort expended by the presidents in these cases was focused on the construction of an aspiration level. The aspiration level then served as the yardstick to measure the value of the outcomes associated with the alternatives under consideration. The presidents appeared to implicitly discount the value of outcomes that fell below the aspiration level, while simultaneously privileging outcomes that fell above the aspiration level. This sensitivity to departures from the reference point also contributed to the tabling of alternatives that offered little hope of achieving or surpassing the aspiration level.

At the very least, researchers from the "expected-utility" tradition should consider the addition of "reflection points" to their utility curves. The use of "reflection points" can capture the reference dependence phenomenon (see Kahneman and Tversky, 1979), showing that perceptions of utility are sensitive to departures from an aspiration level. Of course, the multidimensionality of my formulation of the aspiration level construct contributes a measure of complexity and would require the modeling of multiple utility curves and a persuasive theory of value trade-offs. Even then, the methodological issues discussed in chapter two (and below), would limit the applicability of these models in the domain of foreign policy decision making.

A final significant contribution of this research is that it demonstrates (as does my previous work, see Boettcher, 1995) that attempts to rigorously and reliably develop quantitative measures[3] of subjective utility and probability estimates in the "real world" are potentially futile, and further, are not necessary for the successful development and testing of process-oriented models of risk behavior. The data presented in the case studies reveals that numerical representations of utility and probability seldom entered into the decision-making process. At best, we can use the qualitative data available to develop ordinal rankings of utility and probability, but we cannot then attempt to enter those rankings into any sort of mathematical expected-utility calculation.

Beyond these negative conclusions, this research suggests that "qualitative process validation" (see Guetzkow and Valadez, 1981; Hermann, 1967) provides an appropriate criterion for evaluating models of presidential risk behavior. Since the context of the domain prevents us from competitively testing mathematical models of decision making, we must take a closer look and tease out what these models have to say about the process of decision making. Rather than exclusively focusing on the ability of different models to produce accurate outcome predictions, this project shows that we may successfully evaluate models based on their ability to explain the "nuts and bolts" of decision making: the role of personality, situation, uncertainty, and time pressure.

V.   Potential Explanations for Negative Results

As noted in chapters three and four, the REF hypotheses were not supported in certain cases/decision periods. Figure 5.1 summarizes the hypotheses while tables 5.3 and 5.4 recap the results for the Truman and Kennedy case studies (with the negative results underlined and in boldface). Overall,

H1: Presidents tend to evaluate outcomes relative to an aspiration level rather than an overall value level.

    H1a: The president's aspiration level (acting as a situational constraint) is likely to preclude the consideration of options that are viewed as incapable of achieving (or surpassing) the aspiration level in a particular case.

H2: Security-motivated presidents tend to engage in "bottom-up" processing— (i.e., focusing on worst-case outcomes and maximum losses).

H3: Potential-motivated presidents tend to engage in "top-down" processing— (i.e., focusing on best-case outcomes and maximum gains).

H4: Security-motivated presidents are likely to behave in a risk-averse manner.

H5: Potential-motivated presidents are likely to behave in a risk-acceptant manner.

H6: If there is only one alternative capable of achieving the aspiration level, that alternative is likely to be selected regardless of its level of risk.

H7: Presidential perceptions of high uncertainty and a lack of valid information will interact with presidential risk predispositions and affect the output of the decision process.

    H7a: If time pressures are not acute, both risk-averse and risk-acceptant presidents are likely to delay the moment of decision. (The rationale is that the presidents will use this added time to reduce uncertainty and collect more valid information.)

    H7b: If time pressures are acute, risk-averse presidents are likely to engage in incrementalism.

    H7c: If time pressures are acute, risk-acceptant presidents are likely to engage in bolstering.

Figure 5.1 Summary of REF hypotheses

my "REF" performs rather poorly in the Iran case and in the later decision periods of the Greek case. It is not my intention here to defend the REF against the evidence, but rather to discuss certain factors that contributed to the negative results obtained.

During the decision periods mentioned above, it was difficult to find direct evidence of President Truman's decision making. There is almost no evidence of President Truman's "on-line" processing of information. Thus, I was forced to rely on indirect evidence that may not fully reflect Truman's perceptions. The evaluation of REF hypothesis 3—*potential-motivated presidents tend to engage in "top-down" processing—(i.e., focusing on best-case outcomes and maximum gains)*—is particularly hampered by this lack of data. I cannot claim that President Truman engaged in "best-case" processing because his advisers produced policy papers that included balanced analyses of potential costs as well as benefits. It is possible that Truman ignored the discussions of potential costs and "worst-cases," but there is no evidence to support or oppose this conclusion. Unfortunately, when faced with a dearth of evidence, I was often forced to judge the REF hypotheses in a negative manner.

These negative findings may also be the result of violations of the case selection criteria discussed in chapter one. In the second decision period regarding Iran, and the second decision period regarding Greece, President Truman was clearly less involved in the decision-making process than I would have liked. These decisions did not achieve "crisis" stature and the president did not engage in extensive policy deliberations. In these decision periods, the president was less of an active player in the policy process, simply approving the alternatives recommended by his advisers. M. Hermann has noted that a leader's personality is more likely to have an impact "when the situation the nation faces is a crisis and likely to involve high-level officials; and when the situation is ambiguous and demands definition" (1984, p. 53). Unfortunately, neither of these criteria were met in these decision periods.

Table 5.3 Degree of support for REF hypotheses across Truman cases and decision periods

	Iran		Greece			Korea
Decision period	1[a]	2[b]	1[c]	2[d]	3[e]	1[f]
Hypotheses						
1	S	M	S	S	S	S
1a	S	M	S	S	S	S
3	**A**	W	M	**A**	**A**	S
5	NA	NA	NA	**A**	NA	NA
6	NA	W	S	NA	NA	S
7a	NA	NA	NA	NA	W	S
7c	**A**	**A**	NA	**A**	NA	NA

Key: S = strong, M = moderate, W = weak, **A** = evidence runs against hypothesis, NA = hypothesis not applicable.

[a] December 1945–May 1946
[b] June–December 1946
[c] February 21–March 12, 1947
[d] August–November 1947
[e] December–June 1948
[f] June 24–June 30, 1950

Table 5.4 Degree of support for REF hypotheses across Kennedy cases and decision periods

	Laos		Vietnam		Congo	
Decision period	1[a]	2[b]	1[c]	2[d]	1[e]	2[f]
Hypotheses						
1	S	S	S	S	S	S
1a	S	S	S	S	S	S
2	W	M	**A**	M	NA	M
4	NA	W	NA	M	NA	M
6	NA	NA	NA	NA	NA	NA
7a	NA	NA	M	NA	S	M
7b	S	NA	NA	S	NA	S

Key: S = strong, M = moderate, W = weak, **A** = evidence runs against hypothesis, NA = hypothesis not applicable.

[a] March 9–April 1, 1961
[b] April 26–May 3, 1961
[c] October 5–11, 1961
[d] November 3–15, 1961
[e] July–October 1962
[f] December 1962

VI.   A Revised "Risk Explanation Framework" and a Research Agenda for the Future

Clearly, tables 5.3 and 5.4 indicate that the weakest results were obtained for the REF hypotheses dealing with the presidents' processing of information. While I found some direct and indirect evidence of a concern with "worst-case" outcomes and maximum losses in the Kennedy administration, I found little evidence of a concern with "best-case" outcomes and maximum gains in the Truman cases (with the exception of the Korea case). As noted above, this may be partially explained by the lack of evidence for the Iran and Greece cases. I feel, however, that this is also the result of applying Lopes' expectations regarding individual behavior to what is, in part, a group decision.

In chapter two, I indicated my rationale for treating these six cases as individual decisions. I am now less willing to accept the treatment of the inputs to the decision process as exogenous information. Particularly with respect to this hypothesis, the president's advisory structure clearly mitigates the impact of his personality. In the Iran and Greece cases, President Truman may have wanted to ignore the potential costs of the options under consideration, but his advisers would not allow it. In the Greece case, the president's military advisers made sure that Truman received analyses that countered those of Ambassador MacVeagh and Governor Griswold. Given these observations, I feel that I can no longer avoid the extensive effort of translating an individual model of risk behavior into a model that takes some account of group dynamics. Thus, I intend to explore the literature on group risk behavior further in order to at least identify the circumstances when an individual model of risk behavior is more or less appropriate.

One other REF hypothesis consistently performed poorly in the Truman cases. Hypothesis 7c—*if time pressures are acute, risk-acceptant presidents are likely to engage in bolstering*—clearly understates the effect of uncertainty on the decision maker. Contrary to this hypothesis, President Truman engaged in delay and incrementalism in the two decision periods of the Iran case and in incrementalism during the second decision period of the Greece case. I believe that these results are due to the fact that the high uncertainty per-ceived during these decision periods was focused on a central element of the president's aspiration level—the fear of a Soviet response to U.S. initia-tives. Uncertainty regarding an issue of such centrality could not be ignored. Thus, President Truman did not engage in bolstering.

The above discussion leads to three major potential revisions of the REF: the identification of more specific conditions regarding applicability, the expansion of the model to include a limited number of small-group process variables, and the development of a more nuanced understanding of the impacts of uncertainty and time pressure. I discuss these three areas of revision below, suggesting future research modes for pursuing empirical tests of the revised model.

I remain reluctant to limit my research to the study of "crisis" decision making, yet I still feel that a high level of presidential involvement is a necessary condition for the successful performance of the REF. As suggested above, if we can only assure these levels of involvement through the study of crises, then we may have to follow that path.[4] We should also attempt to identify specific issue areas that are highly salient to the president under study (see Hermann, 1984, p. 77). In this project, I assumed that decisions regarding potential military intervention would be highly salient to U.S. presidents, and yet that assumption appears to be questionable in at least two decision periods. Finally, we might also consider whether particular geographic regions are less important in a president's mind. Of the cases examined, the Congo and Iran appeared to be areas that generated somewhat less presidential interest and involvement.

In my effort to include a limited number of small-group process variables in the REF, I am mainly interested in exploring processes that are treated as exogenous in the current model. As noted in section IV (see above), the most interesting question facing researchers studying reference dependence is: how are aspiration levels constructed by the decision maker? The Kennedy and Truman case studies suggest that the president's aspiration level is the product of the president's own views altered (or combined) by (or with) the views of his advisers. Given the importance of the president's aspiration level to the overall decision process, advisers may compete to influence the president's interpretation of the situation (see McDermott, 1992). I am currently developing a study of Truman's Korea decision that focuses on the role of advisers in shaping the president's aspiration level. I intend to concentrate exclusively on the development of the president's aspiration level, attempting to identify the point at which each element entered the decision process. I am interested in knowing whether the aspiration level that emerged was the product of a consensus among decision makers, of conflict among decision makers, or of some more basic process. In this book, I simply attempted to identify the presidents' aspiration levels. In my future work, I plan to examine the process that led to a particular aspiration level, and further, to suggest a more generic model of aspiration level formation.

I am also interested in the process by which the inputs to the decision process are formed (a second process that was treated as exogenous in the current model). In the Kennedy cases, the president played a significant role in interpreting raw intelligence, developing alternatives, and estimating potential costs and benefits. Conversely, Truman played the role of a consumer of information developed by his advisers. Since the effects of reference dependence are often contingent on the manner in which alternatives are constructed, any revision of the REF should explore the role of the advisory group in shaping alternatives and developing estimates of success or failure. I can tentatively suggest that: given less consensus between the president and his advisers, we should expect to observe less of an impact of the president's personality on the shaping of alternatives and the development of estimates of success or failure. Conversely, given a greater degree of consensus between the president and his advisers, we should expect to observe more of an impact of the president's personality on the shaping of alternatives and the development of estimates of success or failure. Of course, this issue extends beyond the scope of this project. I can only say that I intend to explore this subject through both case studies and laboratory experimentation.

In terms of revising REF hypothesis 7c—*if time pressures are acute, risk-acceptant presidents are likely to engage in bolstering*—I feel that we must consider the circumstances in which bolstering or incrementalism should be expected. Based on the Truman case studies, we should expect to observe incrementalism when the president perceives high uncertainty regarding one or more elements of the aspiration level. Since the elements of the aspiration level are accorded special status in the decision process, it is unlikely that a president would select an alternative that may seriously endanger the achievement of their objectives. Even in the Korea case, President Truman acted somewhat cautiously until the end of the week when he was more confident of Soviet intentions. I remain confident that bolstering *will* occur when the president perceives high uncertainty that is not directly related to one or more elements of his aspiration level. This discussion suggests a greater sensitivity to the specific character of perceived uncertainty.

Beyond the potential revisions to the REF discussed above, I also envision future experimental research in order to provide empirical validation for my risk-predisposition index. This research could investigate whether the effects attributed to presidential personality are due to an overall predisposition toward risk (as I suggest in chapter two) or to individual personality characteristics (like belief in ability to control events or conceptual complexity taken alone). I plan to use Kowert and Hermann's (1995) reformulation of the Kogan and Wallach (1964) social choice dilemma questionnaire to examine this question.[5] Subject responses to the social choice dilemma questionnaire can provide information regarding individual risk orientation that can then be correlated with measures of the individual personality characteristics, and the risk-predisposition index. This research could provide a much more refined understanding of the relationship between individual personality and risk behavior.

Despite the negative results and potential REF revisions discussed above, I remain optimistic about the utility of this research. The REF hypotheses performed well in the Kennedy cases, and the hypotheses regarding the presidents' aspiration levels performed consistently well across both administrations. I am particularly encouraged by the results for REF hypotheses 1 and 1a. Overall, Truman and Kennedy did "*tend to evaluate outcomes relative to an aspiration level rather than an overall value level*" and options were tabled that were "*viewed as incapable of achieving (or surpassing) the aspiration level in a particular case.*" The strong empirical support for these hypotheses demonstrates the relevance of the notion of reference dependence to the study of foreign policy decision making. Hypotheses 6—*if there is only one alternative capable of achieving the aspiration level, that alternative is likely to be selected regardless of its level of risk*—and 7a—*if time pressures are not acute, both risk-averse and risk-acceptant presidents are likely to delay the moment of decision*— also received empirical support when they were applicable. Indeed, I found no evidence against these hypotheses in any case/decision period.

I should also point out that, out of fifty-three opportunities to test the REF hypotheses in these cases, I found strong support for the hypotheses thirty times, moderate support ten times, and weak support five times. I found evidence against the hypotheses only eight times. Given the overall success of the empirical evaluation, I feel that by pursuing the additional research discussed above I may someday develop a more comprehensive theory of presidential foreign policy risk behavior. As I pointed out in chapter two, this research program can only advance through rigorous empirical studies—both in the laboratory, and in the "real" world.

VII.   Implications

Given the scope conditions discussed in chapter two, the results of this research can only be viewed as *suggestive* rather than *generalizable*. I simply hoped to demonstrate that it is possible to at least partially explain presidential risk behavior through the use of the "REF." With these caveats in mind, I feel that I can now claim to have successfully accomplished this task. While the case studies produced certain negative results discussed above, the strength of support for the REF hypotheses in a number of the cases contributes to my optimism regarding the future of this research program. The attempt to meld the literatures on reference dependence, personal predispositions, and uncertainty and information accuracy is in its early stages. This research agenda can only advance through fits and starts, successes and failures. The case studies presented in this book provide a firm empirical foundation on which to build revisions of the proposed model. It is hoped that future research in the laboratory and "real" world will contribute to a context-sensitive *theory* of presidential risk behavior based on the refined REF discussed above. This study has shown that aspiration levels matter, that personal predispositions have an impact, and that presidential perceptions of uncertainty and time pressure can moderate or accentuate risk behavior. We may now begin to investigate the specific contextual conditions that interact with these factors to produce risk-averse or risk-acceptant decisions.

NOTES

Chapter One

1. Defensive realists note that one of the advantages of a bipolar world is the lack of intra-alliance military interdependence. According to Waltz (1979, p. 169), the losses of China (once by the United States and once by the Soviet Union) "were accommodated without disastrously distorting, or even much affecting, the balance between America and Russia." Clearly, the "loss" of any (or even all) of the states discussed above would be less significant. Of course Waltz also argued that "with only two world powers there are no peripheries" (1964, p. 882) and that a bipolar system would be characterized by constant zero-sum competition and counterpressure (see Rosecrance's critique 1966, p. 316). Defensive realists tend to follow the first interpretation or simply acknowledge that Waltz's theory makes indeterminate predictions here.

2. For an offensive realist view of balancing, buck-passing and appeasement see Mearsheimer (2001, pp. 147–164). For Mearsheimer, Truman's decisions reflect prompt and efficient balancing behavior (2001, p. 329); but earlier discussions of "the primacy of land power" and "the stopping power of water" suggest that Truman might have declined to intervene because the chances of U.S. victory in these distant theaters was quite low. For an overview of the debate between defensive and offensive realism see Taliaferro (2000/01).

3. The central objective of this project is to identify factors that lead to risk-taking or risk-aversion in cases of foreign policy decision making by U.S. presidents. Two observations serve as foundations for this research: (1) studies of risk behavior have generally focused on either individual or situational factors—eschewing a more integrative approach, and (2) experimental research on risk behavior has largely focused on laboratory studies of gambling preferences—resulting in theories that are not easily generalizable to other domains of human behavior. A significant portion of the literature on risk behavior relies on the analysis of subjects' responses to gambling problems. A key concern is whether the knowledge gained through this type of experiment is generalizable to human behavior when confronted with different types of problems. Paul Slovic reflects that, when asked to provide insight regarding the domain of human response to natural hazards, "we realized that our laboratory studies had been too narrowly focused on choices among simple gambles to tell us much about risk-taking behavior outside the laboratory" (Slovic, 1992, p. 117). The extent to which the foreign policy domain is different from the domain of gambling argues against our automatic acceptance of results obtained from experiments in the gambling milieu. Only by identifying these differences, considering whether these differences might alter the observed behavioral regularities, and developing domain-sensitive means for evaluating the validity of the relevant findings in the area of foreign policy decision making, can we begin to produce research that provides insight into risk behavior in foreign policy decision making.

4. The study of *risk behavior* should not be confused with the process of *risk analysis* or *assessment*. In this book, I focus on the decision-making process through which presidents deal with risk and uncertainty. I do not examine how estimates of risk are formulated in the intelligence community, nor do I advocate a particular procedure for developing risk estimates. Readers interested in risk analysis or assessment can refer to the work of Coplin and O'Leary (1983), Haendel (1979), or Nagy (1979).

5. This critique of defensive realism does not apply to recent extensions developed by Taliaferro (see 2000/01, 1998).

6. Classical realists (Morgenthau, 1985; Schweller, 1994, 1996) discuss revisionist states and status-quo states leaving open the possibility for variation in risk propensity. Offensive realists view "states as

more gain seeking and assumes they are never satisfied short of hegemony" (Goldgeier and Tetlock, 2001, p. 70), suggesting persistent risk-acceptance.

7. Please note here that risk-aversion does not equal policy inertia.

8. Bueno de Mesquita's indicator of a state government's risk propensity (developed in Bueno de Mesquita, 1981, 1985) focuses on security/vulnerability, but does not include an autonomy term.

9. See Berejikian, 2002a,b; Bueno de Mesquita et al., 2001; Davis, 2000; Elms, 2004; Fanis, 2004; Farnham, 1992; Haas, 2001; Huth et al., 1992; Jervis, 1988; Levy, 1987; Levi and Whyte, 1997; Maoz, 1990; McDermott, 1992, 1995, 1998; McDermott and Kugler, 2001; McInerney, 1992; Mintz and Geva, 1998; Stein and Pauly, 1993; Taliaferro, 1998, 2004; Whyte, 1993, 1998; and Whyte and Levi, 1994.

10. See Adomeit, 1982; Boettcher, 1995, 2004a,b; Bueno de Mesquita and McDermott, 2004; Goldgeier, 1997; Goldgeier and Tetlock, 2001; Jervis, 1992, 2004; Kanner, 2004; Kowert and Hermann, 1995; Levy, 1992b, 1995, 1996, 1997a,b, 1998; McDermott, 2001, 2004a,b; O'Neill, 2001; Schaub, 2004; Shafir, 1992; and Vertzberger, 1995a, 1997, 1998.

11. The notion of *framing* or *reference dependence* is also important to researchers concerned with "problem representation" (see particularly Beasley, 1996; and also Sylvan and Thorson, 1992; Sylvan and Voss, 1998). These scholars view the foreign policy decision-making process in terms of developing solutions to ill-structured problems. Research on problem representation explores the origins of perceived problem frames (or states), operators, and constraints (Voss, 1998, p. 3). A more complete discussion of the relevance of this research tradition is found in chapter two.

12. The notion of loss aversion should not be overextended to suggest that decision makers will always take risks to recoup losses. Decision makers often make capability calculations and may decline to take excessive risks. More research is needed to calibrate referent-dependent models of risk behavior. If "losses loom larger than gains," how much larger do they loom? At what point will decision makers accept limited losses to avoid larger ones?

13. For discussions of this debate, see Houts et al., 1986; and Backteman and Magnusson, 1981.

14. The literature attempting to draw a direct link between subject personality traits and risk-aversion/acceptance is confusing and contradictory. Most of these studies fail to observe statistically significant correlations between the traits identified by the researchers and subject risk behavior. Clearly, this is due to the fact that situational factors also affect subject responses. The REF advances the individual literatures discussed in this section by combining them. While it rejects the simple assumption that risk behavior is determined solely by situational factors, it also rejects the suggestion that risk behavior can be associated with a single or small set of personality traits. As Lopes (1995) argues, security-motivated individuals may take great risks when reference dependence or concerns about information accuracy, time, and uncertainty limit the range of options open to decision makers.

15. It is, perhaps, unfortunate that Lopes has chosen to use the expressions "bottom-up" and "top-down" to describe the alternate ways in which information is processed by security/potential-motivated individuals. Social psychologists use these phrases to describe data-driven versus conceptually/theory-driven information processing (see Fiske and Taylor, 1991, p. 98). It is important to note that Lopes' use of these terms is not intended to be directly related to their traditional usage by social psychologists. For Lopes (1995, p. 202), "bottom-up" and "top-down" simply refer to the different aspects of the decision problem that are most salient to decision makers.

16. One of the seminal works on this subject is Janis and Mann's *Decision Making: A Psychological Analysis of Conflict, Choice and Commitment* (1977). Their "conflict model" of decision making is one of the best explications of the manner in which stress affects decision makers. Their work introduced many of the concepts discussed here (and in George, 1980). (See also Hermann, 1979; Holsti, 1979; and Mann, 1992.) For a more complete review of these works, refer to section III, chapter two.

17. Incrementalism also promotes "reality-testing" and allows for adaptation during "crises." As clearly exhibited in Davis (2000, pp. 60, 63), skilled decision makers have often relied on subtle policy shifts to explore the capabilities and/or intentions of their adversaries.

18. A more detailed description of the theoretical origins of each hypothesis may be found in chapter two (section V).

19. Complete coding rules are available from Hermann upon request.

20. The reader should note that the "risk predisposition index" that results simply reveals variation in styles of information processing. It does not claim to identify individual presidents that will *always* take or avoid risks. Instead of directly forecasting outcomes, this index suggests particular decision-making processes will be followed (i.e., best-case or worst-case analysis). These processes will

interact with situational factors including reference dependence, uncertainty, information accuracy, and time pressure to produce risk-averse/acceptant behavior.

21. A more complete discussion of this method and a table including the actual risk index scores for each of the presidents is found in chapter two.

22. Clearly, other scholars interested in risk behavior agree with this assertion—see Farnham, 1992; McDermott, 1992; Taliaferro, 1994, 1995; Vertzberger, 1995a.

23. An obvious omission in the list of cases under consideration is the Cuban Missile Crisis. Given the extensive literature on this case (including the recent prospect theory-based examination by Haas (2001) and Whyte and Levi's (1994) study of the group process) and the fact that it would clearly violate a number of the case selection criteria, this case was eliminated at an earlier stage of the research design.

24. I do not claim to have identified the universe of potential cases across the Truman and Kennedy administrations. I have instead attempted to identify the most significant cases (i.e., high profile, significant stakes, crisis atmosphere) from each administration, and then further limited the pool of cases to enhance their comparability. I am confident that these cases were selected in a systematic manner, despite the fact that they may not be a strictly representative sample of the entire pool of potential cases. In this regard, I am willing to sacrifice some methodological rigor in exchange for the ability to focus on more interesting and relevant cases.

Chapter Two

1. Kahneman (2000, p. x) noted that he and Tversky took 13 years to extend prospect theory to multioutcome choice under uncertainty and that "the extension was not at all straightforward."

2. Vertzberger puts forth a distinction between "real risk . . . the actual risk resulting from a situation or behavior, whether decision-makers are aware or unaware of it," "perceived risk . . . the level of risk attributed to a situation or behavior by the decision-makers," and "acceptable risk . . . the level of risk representing the net costs that decision-makers perceive as sustainable, and are willing to bear, in pursuit of their goals" (1995a, pp. 355–356, see also 355 FN6). Risk-seeking is suggested to occur when perceived risk ≤ acceptable risk, while risk-aversion occurs when perceived risk > acceptable risk. Vertzberger uses the relationship between real risk and perceived risk to indicate when misperceptions may have their greatest impact. In the more traditional conception, risk-seeking occurs when an option is chosen with (a) a higher probability of a negative outcome, and (b) equal or lower expected-utility; while risk-aversion occurs when an option is chosen with (a) a lower probability of a negative outcome, and (b) equal or lower expected-utility (see Kahneman and Tversky, 1979).

3. Davis (2000) is one of the only recent researchers to truly examine decision making in both domains. McDermott (1998) looks at decision making when a president is "in" the domain of gains, but the actual outcomes facing the president are in the domain of losses.

4. Schweller (1996) provides an interesting discussion of the status-quo bias in the neorealist literature. Jervis strongly cautions prospect theorists: "it should be stressed that prospect theory does not deny that actors may want to change the status quo . . . Actors will take some risks to improve their situations even if they are risk-averse for gains" (1992, p. 195).

5. The analytical value of introducing *real risk* seems to lie in the ability to attach a normative judgment to the decision maker's choice (Vertzberger, 1995a, p. 357, table I). Since normative evaluation of decision-maker choice is not a goal of this project, I am comfortable with rejecting Vertzberger's distinction between *real* and *perceived risk*. I also reject this distinction on the grounds of practicality, and the fact that we may debate whether *real risk* actually exists apart from *perceived risk*. Vertzberger suggests that two "realities" exist—one subjective and perceived by the decision maker, the other objective and observable by the researcher (1990, p. 37). In defending this epistemological orientation, he argues that: "Indeed, reality as defined by the researcher cannot represent perfect objectivity. Yet since we are dealing with a soft science, we must rest content with qualified objectivity, that is, the researcher's perception of reality, and not allow this to deter us from dealing with the subject and making the best of it" (1990, p. 37). While I do not characterize myself as a "post-positivist" (see Smith et al., 1996), I find that I disagree with Vertzberger's epistemological perspective. Given that the researcher can only approach "qualified" objectivity, does it make sense to suggest that the researcher's estimate of risk is more truthful or accurate than the subjects? In terms of probability theory, can we actually discriminate between veridical and inaccurate perceptions of risk (even if we

are allowed to benefit from hindsight)? When the weather forecaster predicts a 40 percent chance of snow for Tuesday, March 8 and it rains instead, was his estimate of the risk of snow wrong? These practical and epistemological problems lead me to focus on "perceived risk" and avoid notions of "real risk" altogether. (See Sylvan and Thorson, 1992 for a similar discussion regarding the "accuracy" of problem representations and decision frames.)

6. The term "negative outcome" describes the outcomes that are least preferred by the decision maker. This category should therefore include perceived opportunity losses as well as perceived losses. By possible, I mean that the decision maker's subjective estimate of the probabilities associated with extreme negative outcomes exceed .05 (if represented numerically).

7. Vertzberger (1995a, 1997) avoids developing a general operational definition of risk-acceptant/averse behavior. He focuses on a particular policy instrument—military intervention—and associates risk-taking behavior with the use of this instrument and risk-averse behavior with a decision not to use this instrument. This perspective is far removed from the explicitly comparative view of risk-acceptant/averse behavior preferred by most decision theorists. I feel that it is a mistake to measure the "riskiness" of options in an objective, isolated manner. One may easily construct hypothetical cases where military intervention may be the least risky option under consideration.

8. Savage's (1954) subjective expected-utility (SEU) theory is used somewhat less extensively. (A notable use of SEU in research on risk behavior in international relations may be found in Alpert, 1976.)

9. Kahneman (2000, p. x) noted that he and Tversky "considered a treatment of risky choice in terms of regret, but we eventually abandoned this approach because it did not elegantly accommodate the pattern of results that we labeled 'reflection' . . . ."

10. Daniel Kahneman recently received the Nobel prize in economics for this and other contributions to the field.

11. Kahneman (2000, p. x) noted "The goal we set for ourselves was to assemble the minimal set of modifications of expected utility theory that would provide a descriptive account of everything we knew about a severely restricted class of decisions: choices between simple monetary gambles with objectively specified probabilities and at most two nonzero outcomes. Without additional assumptions, prospect theory is not applicable to gambles that have a larger number of outcomes, to gambles on events, or to transactions other than choice; it does not even specify a selling price for monetary gambles."

12. I have distinct reservations regarding the methods employed in these experiments. One of the strongest findings reported by Kahneman and Tversky (1979) is the "certainty effect." When one of the prospects presented to subjects included a certainty term, the preference reversal phenomenon was more extensive. Unfortunately these prospects did not measure decisions under risk, but rather subjects' choices between certainty and risk. Thus, risk-aversion under these circumstances may be more accurately characterized as risk-avoidance.

13. Kahneman (2000, p. xiv) noted the "initial motivation for introducing editing operations was defensive: they eliminated some foolish predictions to which prospect theory seemed otherwise committed."

14. For a more extensive discussion of prospect theory see Levy, 1992a, 1995.

15. Lopes notes that this notion of security/potential-motivation "is also related to the maximin gain and minimax loss rules that have figured in theories of decision under uncertainty, but it does not share their propensity to be foolishly affected by very small differences" (1990, p. 280).

16. It is suggested that the aspiration level interacts with security/potential motivation so that security-motivated individuals "set more modest aspiration levels than potential-motivated people" (Lopes, 1987, p. 279).

17. Lopes' findings are supported by research in the area of managerial response to risk (see March and Shapira, 1987, 1992).

18. SP/A theory appears, at least intuitively, to have great potential relevance for the study of foreign policy decision making. Lopes' focus on process—how decision makers go about making choices—fits well with a research tradition that has long noted the empirical failure of more normative models of choice. The focus on process presents hypotheses that are *actually* testable in the "real world" of presidential foreign policy decision making (see section IV of this chapter). Also, the emphasis on individual personality should strike a chord with researchers that thus have stressed the importance of leadership and presidential character. Unfortunately, few international relations theorists interested in risk behavior (notable exceptions include Vertzberger, Levy, and Taliaferro) have exhibited even a basic familiarity with this research tradition.

19. It should be noted here that Kowert and Hermann adopt the "individual-by-situation" perspective discussed below. They clearly understand that personality factors interact with situational factors to produce risk behavior. Following this research tradition, the REF asserts that personal predispositions alter the decision-making process. The REF does not, however, posit either a direct or simplistic connection between personality and risk behavior.

20. Davis is representative of other prospect theorists when he writes that "the idiosyncracies of individual decision makers are discussed only insofar as they provide background to the cases and are not accorded causal primacy" (2000, p. 42). And yet his own case studies suggest the relevance of the individual decision makers' risk predispositions.

21. This may be contrasted with George's "defensive" procrastination, which is closer to Janis and Mann's notion of buck-passing.

22. I have intentionally avoided a consideration of Janis and Mann's buck-passing since the cases I have chosen all involve presidential *decisions*.

23. Of course, there are exceptions. Huth et al. (1992) follow Bueno de Mesquita (1981) and use military alliances as an indicator of utility. While this allows for rigorous and replicable measures, the validity of the utility estimates produced is questionable (see Majeski and Sylvan, 1984).

24. Budescu et al., suggest that "people understand words better than numbers" and that "numbers are perceived as conveying a level of precision and authority that people do not associate with their opinions" (1988, p. 281). Erev and Cohen test the hypothesis that the fear of accountability and punishment for being wrong influences the use of verbal versus numerical expressions of probability, but their results are not supportive of this explanation (1990).

25. There is a large amount of evidence that indicates that this has indeed been a significant problem. In 1964, Sherman Kent (the head of the CIA's Board of National Estimates [BNE] from 1952–1967) wrote an essay titled "Words of Estimative Probability" in a vain attempt to rationalize and quantify the use of verbal expressions of probability in National Intelligence Estimates (NIEs) (Steury, 1994; see also Boettcher, 1996). The documentary record for both the Vietnam and Laos cases indicates that the use of these expressions was quite common in memoranda and analytical papers (Foreign Relations of the United States [FRUS]: 1961–1963, Volume I, Vietnam 1961; 1961–1963, Volume XXIV, Laos Crisis).

26. Taliaferro's more recent work (1995) examines how frames are manipulated by advisers. He now views analogical reasoning as "one rhetorical tactic that a manipulator may employ" (personal correspondence with author).

27. The studies by Farnham (1992), McDermott (1992), and McInerney (1992) reveal the extensive amount of data that must be marshaled to convincingly identify the frame adopted by decision makers.

28. Berejikian argues that "peasants living through social-structural transformations that lead, for example, to an increased vulnerability to subsistence crises (market penetration into closed rural villages, regime change, famine, etc.) would view a choice in favor of the status quo not as neutral but as a loss" (1992, p. 653). But surely not all peasants would share this perception (or insight into economic theory).

29. To be fair to McDermott, she clearly demonstrates that she is aware of this problem (1998, pp. 37–38). Unfortunately, I feel that she does not deal with it effectively in her case studies.

30. A study coming at this subject from a different angle has examined the link between domestic political gains/losses and war termination decisions (see Mintz and Geva, 1998).

31. Boettcher (2004a) explores the impact of indirect versus direct framing and finds that indirect frames have no discernible independent impact on subject choices.

32. Most behavioral decision theories assume that some cost–benefit analysis is being conducted, their differences are more stark when they discuss the process by which estimates of utility and probability are constructed and how those estimates are entered into the cost–benefit calculations that result in a decision. Recall that expected-utility theory suggests a process of utility-maximization, where utility is evaluated relative to a decision maker's overall asset level. Prospect theory posits that utility is evaluated relative to a reference point and that perceptions of probability are altered by decision weights. SP/A theory argues that utility is evaluated relative to an aspiration level and that security/potential-motivated decision makers engage in "bottom-up" or "top-down" processing of information.

33. I am well aware of the "as if" assumption and the "predictive accuracy" defense of rational choice models (see Friedman, 1953). I contend that the development of "descriptively accurate" models of choice are essential for accurate prediction (see Kahneman and Tversky, 1979; and Quattrone and

Tversky, 1988, for a discussion of "normative" versus "descriptive" models of choice). I firmly believe that understanding the process by which a decision is made can lead to enhanced predictive power.

34. Deborah Welch Larson (2001, p. 327) argues that: "Experiments provide useful hypotheses about cognitive and motivational influences on human decisions. But precisely because the laboratory is an artificial environment, such hypotheses need to be validated by real-world data."

35. Boettcher (2000, 2004a) demonstrates the extent to which subtle changes in experimental design to more closely reflect "real world" decision making reduce framing effects. Simply allowing subjects to choose between four or six alternatives, instead of the usual two, can produce substantial declines in preference reversals.

36. Bazerman et al. (1984) have demonstrated that escalation of commitment in the face of investment losses occurred for both groups and individuals.

37. Boettcher (2001, 2004a) explores the relationship between problem frames and group polarization. This is one of the first attempts to experimentally study prospect theory in a small group setting using foreign policy decision-making scenarios.

38. I am indebted to Professor Jeffrey Taliaferro for this observation.

39. In his dissertation, J. W. Taliaferro (1997) treats the framing of a problem as endogenous and examines how advisers may manipulate the framing of problems.

40. Kahneman (2000, p. xi) appears to concur, stating that "although it is surely futile to 'test' prospect theory against utility theory in the domain of international relations, the concepts of loss aversion and pseudocertainty are useful tools for understanding strategic decisions. No warranty is implied, of course. The scholars who use the tools to explain more complex decisions do so at their own risk." Bueno de Mesquita and McDermott (2004) advocate building bridges across the "No Man's Land" that divides prospect theorists from expected utility theorists in the field of international relations.

41. A recent empirical attempt to differentiate between "objective" and frame-weighted estimates of verbal probability expressions weakly supports this suggestion (see Boettcher, 1995).

42. Despite their focus on qualitative process validation in Sylvan et al. (1990), these authors view both types of validation (quantitative and qualitative) on an equal footing. They simply argue that the choice of validation strategy should reflect theoretical and empirical concerns.

43. Of course, the president's perceptions of the situational constraints are subject to updating throughout the decision-making process.

44. Deborah Welch Larson (2001) offers an excellent argument (and primer) for careful archival research by political scientists attempting to identify the causal mechanisms underlying foreign policy events.

45. Please recall that one of the goals of this project is to simply *consider* the role of personal predispositions in the foreign policy decision-making process. The difficulty of attempting this through case study research is clearly reflected here. While the development of the risk-predisposition index allows for systematic case selection, the external validity of the index is clearly open to question. The biographical data is supportive of the index, but many of these observers had their own motivations for characterizing the personality of the presidents under examination. This project thus offers a test of the hypotheses relating to security/potential-motivation, but the results are nowhere near definitive. The best venue for testing SP/A theory and prospect theory will continue to be the laboratory, where personality tests can be administered to subjects and the researcher can control the impact of other variables.

Chapter Three

1. Dale Copeland (2000, pp. 159–162) argues that the first evidence of an "active containment" policy by the Truman administration was the deployment of U.S. troops to China from August to September 1945. He suggests that "eight interlocking actions taken in 1945 to restrict Soviet growth in military, economic, and potential power" reveal a new and comprehensive strategy that was being implemented by the Truman administration (2000, p. 149).

2. For a discussion of the offensive nature of Truman administration's grand strategy as exemplified in NSC 20/4 see Mitrovich, 2000, pp. 23–36.

3. The signs of growing U.S. interests in Iran were not ignored by the Soviets or the British. The British viewed the United States as a potential protector of British oil interests in southern Iran,

while the Soviets saw the United States as one more competitor for Iranian oil concessions and a threat to their position of influence in Teheran (see Kuniholm, 1980, pp. 214–216, 270–298).

4. Stalin's "technically accurate" reading of the 1942 agreement allowed allied troops to remain in Iran until six months after the end of the war with Japan (Kuniholm, 1980, p. 272).

5. As noted in chapter two, I view the notion of an aspiration level as a multidimensional concept. For the purposes of this project, I suggest that the president's aspiration level is composed of an immediate goal, constraints on the means available for achieving the immediate goal, and factors reinforcing the president's commitment to achieving or surpassing the immediate goal. The notion of an immediate goal captures the distinction between an "overall value level" and an aspiration level. The focus on constraints on means identifies the situational factors that limit alternatives. Finally, the examination of factors reinforcing the president's commitment to the immediate goal attempts to capture the extent to which the aspiration level approaches a "survival level."

6. As noted above, I expect President Truman to evaluate outcomes relative to an aspiration level rather than an overall value level. In this case, President Truman's desire to eliminate spheres of influence and respect treaty commitments represent "overall value levels." These desires become policy-relevant only through their contribution to Truman's aspiration level. Thus, the aspiration level, rather than the overall value level, provides the metric for evaluating alternatives.

7. Throughout this time period, Ambassador Ala provided assurances of Iran's resolve in order to garner U.S. support. Isolated in the United States, Ala was less affected by Soviet pressure and Iranian politics. He was also more convinced of U.S. resolve because of personal assurances from Secretary Byrnes. Qavam, in Teheran, was subject to the harassment of the Soviet ambassador and the pressure of Tudeh activists. He was less convinced of the U.S. commitment to Iran.

8. For a discussion of the history of this note see Kuniholm, 1980, p. 298 FN243 and Byrnes, 1958, pp. 401–402.

9. Leffler (1992, p. 79) notes, "What the Americans wanted to do was to create a buffer zone between the Soviet Union and the rich oil fields of the Persian Gulf. World War II had underscored the importance of petroleum as a strategic asset as well as an economic resource."

10. Melvin Leffler (1992, p. 110) describes Qavam as "a wily, experienced politician."

11. Qavam's wavering combined with the competing interpretations of Soviet intentions and contributed to President Truman's perception of high uncertainty during this period.

12. Qavam's party was called the "Democratic Party of Iran" in order to steal adherents from the Democrats of Azerbaijan (see FRUS, 1969b, p. 505).

13. Six years later (April 24, 1952), President Truman suggested that he sent an "ultimatum" to Stalin during this period. This document has never been found and many doubt the truth of the president's assertion (see Rosenberg, 1979; Samii, 1987; Thorpe, 1978; Allen, "Mission to Iran" n.d.; Curry to Bennorth, February 2, 1969; George to Lagerquist, June 20, 1969; Henderson, 1973; Rountree, 1989).

14. Recall the exception to this hypothesis: *if there is only one alternative capable of achieving the aspiration level, that alternative is likely to be selected regardless of its level of risk* (REF hypothesis 6).

15. Leffler (1992, p. 506) argues that in this case and others, Truman and his advisers "distorted the importance of the Third World, underestimated the local sources of conflict, and exaggerated the relevance of strategic arms and the conventional military balance in Europe to developments on the periphery." For Leffler (1992, p. 507), "Revolutionary nationalists like Mohammed Musaddiq had no affinity for the Russians. Nor did the Soviets have the capacity, the need, or the will to purchase and transport Persian Gulf Oil."

16. The American observers of the plebiscite were not convinced of the accuracy of the government's figures, but their report was not released publicly (see Alexander, 1982, pp. 209–210).

17. For a more complete and nuanced discussion of Greek politics during this period see Xydis, 1963.

18. The British foreign office regretted the cabinet's decision to withdraw aid to Greece, but Foreign Secretary Ernest Bevin could not convince the economy-minded ministers of the importance of the Greek situation.

19. A second aide-memoire indicated that British aid to Turkey was also about to be discontinued (FRUS, 1971, pp. 35–37).

20. In his oral history, George Elsey, administrative assistant to President Truman, states: "the President was very well informed of what the Soviets were up to in the Eastern Europe. He had no illusions whatsoever about their interests, their activities, and what they were up to in Poland, Hungary, Romania, their zone of Austria, Bulgaria. He knew, our whole government knew that they were trying to subvert the governments of Greece and Turkey and I think he accepted without question

the assessment of the British and our State Department and military departments of what would happen if he didn't act" (1970, p. 354).

21. Leffler (1992, p. 142) writes that, "Eighteen months before, around the time of the Potsdam conference, U.S. officials had decided to oppose a greater Soviet presence in the Turkish straits, the Eastern Mediterranean, and the middle East."

22. Aaron Friedberg (2000, p. 97) argues that "fiscal constraint was the single most important factor pushing the United States toward a strategy of minimum deterrence" from September 1945 to June 1950 (see also Christensen, 1996, pp. 39–43).

23. Leffler (1992, p. 146) comments that after this point "isolationism could still influence the size and configuration of administration programs, but it could not masquerade as a policy alternative."

24. Acheson likened the struggle to that between Rome and Carthage (Jones, 1955, p. 141).

25. Unfortunately, there is a lack of direct evidence for President Truman's perceptions during the August–November 1947 and December 1947–June 1948 decision periods. We may, however, cautiously infer the president's perceptions from the evidence at hand.

26. Recall the exception to this hypothesis: *if there is only one alternative capable of achieving the aspiration level, that alternative is likely to be selected regardless of its level of risk* (REF hypothesis 6).

27. The report also argued that "half-way measures will not suffice and should not be attempted" (FRUS 1971:54), but this language was not approved by the State–War–Navy Coordinating Committee (see FRUS, 1971, p. 57).

28. In his oral history, Clark Clifford notes: "I don't recall President Truman agonizing through the decision as far as the Truman Doctrine was concerned. I think he had begun to feel that we had to face up to Soviet expansionism" (1971, p. 153).

29. Isaacson and Thomas ponder the effect of Truman's speech on a young congressman named Lyndon Baines Johnson (1986, p. 398).

30. These authors note that the use of U.S. operational advisers and advanced weapons (including napalm) to support a shaky right-wing regime against communist rebels is common to both Greece and Vietnam (1986, p. 461).

31. For an excellent discussion of the United Nations role during this period see Stueck (1995, pp. 23–27).

32. I shall leave to others the difficult question of deciding who was "responsible" for the outbreak of hostilities. Bruce Cumings (1990, pp. 568–621) has discussed three "mosaics" pieced together from the existing evidence. Goncharov et al. (1993, pp. 130–167) place responsibility squarely on the shoulders of Kim Il Sung (acting with the approval of Stalin and Mao). Clearly, the Truman administration believed that the North Koreans had embarked on an unprovoked "act of aggression" (see FRUS, 1976, p. 144).

33. As Marc Trachtenberg (1991, pp. 115–116) points out, President Truman and his advisers had by this time developed an "impulse to escalate" that was only constrained by "considerations of expediency." The early decision to limit U.S. aspirations in Korea was thus not a matter of principle, but rather a response to the decline of U.S. military capabilities and the inherent difficulty of military operations in the Korean theater.

34. The analogy with Greece reinforced Truman's commitment to his immediate goal in two ways: (1) it contributed to the interpretation of the North Korean invasion as a Soviet test of U.S. resolve, and (2) it suggested that strong U.S. action would force the communists to back down.

35. Recall the exception to this hypothesis: *if there is only one alternative capable of achieving the aspiration level, that alternative is likely to be selected regardless of its level of risk* (REF hypothesis 6).

36. In his oral history, Secretary Pace suggests that MacArthur's report and discussion with Washington took place on Thursday night, and the decision to intervene was postponed by the president until Friday morning (January 1972, pp. 73–74). Unfortunately, I have been unable to locate independent corroboration of this account.

37. Melvyn Leffler (1992, p. 368) notes that when "Dwight Eisenhower visited the Pentagon on 27 June and lunched with the president on 6 July, he was dismayed by the complacency he witnessed."

38. Leffler (1992, pp. 368–369) argues that Truman and Acheson "do not seem to have found this an agonizing or painful decision despite the previous reservations expressed by Johnson, Bradley, and Army Secretary Frank Pace."

39. Leffler (1992, p. 502) suggests that Truman and his advisers were: "Prudent officials taking calculated risks. Operating on given sets of assumptions and beliefs and with finite information, they seek to advance national interests and avoid worst-case scenarios." Elsewhere (1992, p. 503) he states, "Prudent men aware of the wealth and power of the United States could not allow such worst-case

scenarios to unfold." I would argue that these worst-case scenarios did drive the grand strategy of the Truman administration, but that best-case analysis of alternatives often contributed to their risk-taking behavior in the cases under examination.

Chapter Four

1. For a more complete discussion of the Laos crisis see George et al., 1971; Hilsman, 1967; Schlesinger, 1965; Sorensen, 1965; Walton, 1972; and FRUS, 1994a.
2. In his oral history, Dean Rusk noted: "Had it been possible for the Eisenhower administration to support a neutral Laos rather than overreaching to try to convert it into a right-wing Laos, a pro-Western Laos, I think the Laotian situation might have developed on different lines" (Rusk, 1969, p. 21).
3. Various sources disagree on whether President Kennedy remained open to the intervention alternative on May 3. Sorensen (1965) and Hilsman (1967) suggest that Kennedy "bluffed" the Soviets. Schlesinger (1965), based on comments by Rostow (see Newhouse, n.d., p. 28), argues that Kennedy had once again ordered troop movements to the region. I have not found conclusive evidence in either direction, but my considered opinion favors the Sorensen/Hilsman interpretation.
4. Recall the exception to this hypothesis: *if there is only one alternative capable of achieving the aspiration level, that alternative is likely to be selected regardless of its level of risk.*
5. Unfortunately, there is only one brief contemporaneous record of the March 21 meeting (see FRUS, 1994a, pp. 95–96). Schlesinger (1965, pp. 332–333) provides the best account of these meetings, while Hilsman's account (1967, pp. 127–132) combines comments made at different meetings and is thus unreliable.
6. This region of Laos held great significance for Kennedy's advisers because Pathet Lao occupation of the Mekong Valley would threaten South Vietnam and Thailand (see Rostow, 1964).
7. The non-intervention course was somewhat mislabeled as it recommended the introduction of U.S. forces into Thailand and South Vietnam (FRUS, 1994a, p. 167).
8. There is a significant debate over the degree to which the Eisenhower administration's commitment to South Vietnam constrained Kennedy's goals in this case. Kattenburg argues that Kennedy's November 1961 decisions were "extraordinarily fateful" because they broke the MAAG ceilings set by the Geneva accords and altered the U. S.–South Vietnamese relationship from "sharing" to "limited partnership" (1982, pp. 108–109, see also Hess, 1993, pp. 67–68). He suggests that prior to these decisions, the United States could have "disengaged with honor and a minimum of damage" (1982, p. 108). Kennedy's admirers argue that, despite the limited nature of the Eisenhower administration's commitment to South Vietnam, Kennedy "could not go back on the commitments already made" (Hilsman, 1967, p. 420; see also Schlesinger, 1965, p. 536; Sorensen, 1965, p. 651). For my purposes, I am not so much interested in the "objective facts" highlighted by Kattenburg, as I am in the perceptions (in November of 1961) of the president and his advisers regarding the significance of the U.S. commitment. I shall return to this debate below.
9. As suggested by REF hypothesis 7a, when faced with high uncertainty and low time pressure President Kennedy searched for new information regarding the situation in Vietnam.
10. Recall the exception to this hypothesis: *if there is only one alternative capable of achieving the aspiration level, that alternative is likely to be selected regardless of its level of risk.*
11. In terms of the REF hypotheses, Chinese intervention represented the "worst-case" outcome for President Kennedy.
12. In his oral history, Dean Rusk noted, "I think the historian will have a major job in making a judgment as to what might be called the policy of gradualism in our responses to Southeast Asia. In general we were on the strategic defensive in Southeast Asia. We did not want to do more than was necessary to safeguard the area" (December 9, 1969, p. 61).
13. See in particular Deputy Special Assistant for National Security Affairs Carl Kaysen's critique of Hilsman's assessment of the Soviet threat (FRUS, 1994b, pp. 727–728).
14. Recall the exception to this hypothesis: *if there is only one alternative capable of achieving the aspiration level, that alternative is likely to be selected regardless of its level of risk.*
15. Other documents found in the same folder with the aforementioned included a memorandum from George McGhee and a CIA/ONE intelligence estimate (see McGhee, December 13, 1962; CIA/ONE, December 11, 1962).

Chapter Five

1. In my future research, I also intend to consider alternative ways in which aspiration levels can be organized. In my case studies, I focused on immediate goals, constraints on means, and factors reinforcing the president's commitment to achieving or surpassing his aspiration level. We might also view the aspiration level as a hierarchy of primary and subsidiary goals, which would begin to address the question of the relative importance of the various elements.
2. Particularly if the researcher suggested that the presidents were "in" the domain of losses.
3. I am, however, convinced that rigorous *non-quantitative* measurement of these concepts is possible and useful in research evaluating other hypotheses.
4. It is important to note here that I have reached this conclusion through the study of both crisis and non-crisis decisions.
5. I am indebted to M. Hermann for suggesting this avenue of research.

BIBLIOGRAPHY

Books, Articles, Manuscripts

Acheson, D. (1969). *Present at the creation: My years in the State Department*. New York: Norton.

Adomeit, H. (1982). *Soviet risk-taking and crisis behavior*. London: George Allen & Unwin.

Alexander, G. M. (1982). *The prelude to the Truman Doctrine: British policy in Greece 1944–1947*. Oxford: Clarendon Press.

Allais, M. (1979[1952]). The foundations of a positive theory of choice involving risk and a criticism of the postulate and axioms of the American school. In M. Allais & O. Hagen (Eds.), *Expected utility hypotheses and the Allais paradox: Contemporary discussion of decisions under uncertainty with Allais' rejoinder* (pp. 27–145). Boston, MA: D. Reidel.

Alpert, E. (1976). Capabilities, perceptions, and risks: A Bayesian model of international behavior. *International Studies Quarterly, 20*, 415–440.

Anderson, P. (1984). Foreign policy as a goal directed activity. *Philosophy of Social Science, 14*, 159–181.

Atkinson, J. W. (1957). Motivational determinants of risk-taking behavior. *Psychological Review, 64*, 359–372.

Backteman, G., & Magnusson, D. (1981). Longitudinal stability of personality characteristics. *Journal of Personality, 49*, 148–160.

Ball, G. W. (1982). *The past has another pattern*. New York: Norton & Company.

Barnet, R. J. (1968). *Intervention and revolution: The United States in the Third World*. New York: The World Publishing Company.

Bassett, L. J., & Pelz, S. E. (1989). The failed search for victory: Vietnam and the politics of war. In T. G. Paterson (Ed.), *Kennedy's Quest for Victory* (pp. 223–252). New York: Oxford University Press.

Bazerman, M. H., Giuliano, T., & Appelman, A. (1984). Escalation of commitment in individual and group decision making. *Organizational Behavior and Human Performance, 33*, 141–152.

Beasley, R. (1996, June–July). Foreign policy making in groups: A problem representation approach to framing. Paper presented at the annual meeting of the International Society of Political Psychology, Vancouver, Canada.

Bennett, A., & George A. L. (1997a, October). Process tracing in case study research. Paper presented at the MacArthur Foundation Workshop on Case Study Methods, Belfer Center for Science and International Affairs (BCSIA), Harvard University, Cambridge, MA.

Bennett, A., & George A. L. (1997b, October). Research design tasks in case study methods. Paper presented at the MacArthur Foundation Workshop on Case Study Methods, Belfer Center for Science and International Affairs (BCSIA), Harvard University, Cambridge, MA.

Bennett, A., & George, A. L. (2001). Case studies and process tracing in history and political science: similar strokes for different foci. In C. Elman & M. F. Elman (Eds.), *Bridges and boundaries: Historians, political scientists, and the study of international relations* (pp. 137–166). Cambridge, MA: MIT Press.

Berejikian, J. (1992). Revolutionary collective action and the agent-structure problem. *American Political Science Review, 86*, 647–657.

Berejikian, J. (1997). The gains debate: Framing state choice. *American Political Science Review, 91*, 789–805.

Berejikian, J. D. (2002a). A cognitive theory of deterrence. *Journal of Peace Research, 39*, 165–183.

Berejikian, J. D. (2002b). Model building with prospect theory: A cognitive approach to international relations. *Political Psychology, 23(4)*, 759–786.

Bernoulli, D. (1967[1738]). *Exposition of a new theory on the measurement of risk* (L. Sommer, Trans.). Farnsborough Hants, UK: Gregg Press.

Bernstein, B. J. (1977). The week we went to war: American intervention in the Korean Civil War. *Foreign Service Journal, 54(2)*, 8–34.

Boettcher, W. A. (1995). Context, methods, numbers, and words: Prospect theory in international relations. *Journal of Conflict Resolution, 39*, 561–583.

Boettcher, W. A. (1996, April). Risk and reward: Foreign policy decision making by U.S. presidents. Paper presented at the annual meeting of the International Studies Association, San Diego, CA.

Boettcher, W. A. (2000, August–September). Framing effects in the "real world": Evaluating the political psychology adaptation of prospect theory. Paper presented at the annual meeting of the American Political Science Association, Washington, D. C.

Boettcher, W. A. (2001, July 26–28). Prospect framing and choice shifts: The response of advisory groups to semantic manipulations. Paper presented at the Hong Kong Convention of International Studies, Hong Kong, S. A. R., China.

Boettcher, W. A. (2004a). The prospects for prospect theory: An empirical evaluation of international relations applications of framing and loss aversion. *Political Psychology, 25(3)*, 331–362.

Boettcher, W. A. (2004b). Military intervention decisions regarding humanitarian crises: Framing induced risk behavior. *Journal of Conflict Resolution, 48(3)*, 331–355.

Bromiley, P., & Curley, S. (1992). Individual differences in risk taking. In J. Yates (Ed.), *Risk-taking behavior* (pp. 87–132). New York: John Wiley & Sons.

Budescu, D. V., & Wallsten, T. S. (1990). Dyadic decisions with numerical and verbal probabilities. *Organizational Behavior and Human Decision Processes, 46*, 240–263.

Budescu, D. V., Weinberg, S., & Wallsten, T. S. (1988). Decisions based on numerically and verbally expressed uncertainties. *Journal of Experimental Psychology: Human Perception and Performance, 14*, 281–294.

Bueno de Mesquita, B. (1975). *Strategy, risk and personality in coalition politics.* Cambridge: Cambridge University Press.

Bueno de Mesquita, B. (1981). *The war trap.* New Haven, CT: Yale University Press.

Bueno de Mesquita, B. (1985). The war trap revisited: A revised expected utility model. *American Political Science Review, 79*, 156–173.

Bueno de Mesquita, B., & Lalman, D. (1992). *War and reason.* New Haven, CT: Yale University Press.

Bueno de Mesquita, B., & McDermott, R. (2004). Crossing no man's land: Cooperation from the trenches. *Political Psychology, 25(2)*, 271–287.

Bueno de Mesquita, B., McDermott, R., & Cope, E. (2001). The expected prospects for peace in Northern Ireland. *International Interactions, 27*, 129–167.

Byrnes, J. (1947). *Speaking frankly.* New York: Harper & Row.

Byrnes, J. (1958). *All in one lifetime.* New York: Harper & Brothers.

Christensen, T. J. (1996). *Useful adversaries: Grand strategy, domestic mobilization, and Sino-American conflict, 1947–1958.* Princeton, NJ: Princeton University Press.

Clark, D. A. (1990). Verbal uncertainty expressions: A critical review of two decades of research. *Current Psychology: Research and Reviews, 9*, 203–235.

Clark, R. D. (1971). Group-induced shift toward risk: A critical appraisal. *Psychological Bulletin, 76*, 251–270.

Coombs, C. H. (1975). Portfolio theory and the measurement of risk. In M. F. Kaplan & S. Schwartz (Eds.), *Human Judgment and Decision Processes* (pp. 63–85). New York: Academic Press.

Copeland, D. C. (2000). *The origins of major war.* Ithaca, NY: Cornell University Press.

Coplin, W., & O'Leary, M. (1983). *Introduction to political risk analysis.* Syracuse, NY: Public Affairs Program.

Cumings, B. (1990). *The origins of the Korean War: Volume II, the roaring of the cataract 1947–1950.* Princeton, NJ: Princeton University Press.

Davis, J. W. (2000). *Threats and promises: The pursuit of international influence.* Baltimore, MD: The Johns Hopkins University Press.

DeRouen, K. R., Jr. (1995). The indirect link: Politics, the economy, and the use of force. *Journal of Conflict Resolution, 39*, 671–695.

Douglas, M. (1990). Risk as a forensic resource. *Daedalus, 119*, 1–16.

Downs, G. W., & Rocke, D. M. (1994). Conflict, agency, and gambling for resurrection: The principal-agent problem goes to war. *American Journal of Political Science, 38*, 362–380.

Eckstein, H. (1975). Case study and theory in political science. In F. I. Greenstein & N. W. Polsby (Eds.), *Handbook of political science, VII* (pp. 79–138). Reading, MA: Addison-Wesley.

Edwards, W. (1953). Probability-preferences in gambling. *American Journal of Psychology, 66*, 349–364.

Ellsberg, D. (1961). Risk, ambiguity and the savage axioms. *Quarterly Journal of Economics, 75*, 643–669.

Elms, D. K. (2004). Large costs, small benefits: Explaining trade dispute outcomes. *Political Psychology, 25(2)*, 241–270.

Erev, I., & Cohen, B. L. (1990). Verbal versus numerical probabilities: Efficiency, biases, and the preference paradox. *Organizational Behavior and Human Decision Processes, 45*, 1–18.

Etzioni, A., & Dubow F. L. (Eds.). (1970). *Comparative perspectives: Theories and methods.* Boston, MA: Little, Brown.

Fanis, M. (2004). Collective action meets prospect theory: An application to coalition building in Chile, 1973–75. *Political Psychology, 25(3)*, 363–388.

Farnham, B. (1992). Roosevelt and the Munich crisis: Insights from prospect theory. *Political Psychology, 13*, 205–235.

Fischhoff, B. (1983). Predicting frames. *Journal of Experimental Psychology, 9*, 103–116.

Fiske, S., & Taylor S. (1991). *Social cognition.* New York: McGraw-Hill.

Foot, R. (1985). *The wrong war: American policy and the dimensions of the Korean conflict, 1950–1953.* Ithaca, NY: Cornell University Press.

Foyle, D. C. (1997). Public opinion and foreign policy: Elite beliefs as a mediating variable. *International Studies Quarterly, 41*, 141–169.

Freudenburg, W. R. (1992). Heuristics, biases, and the not-so-general publics: Expertise and error in the assessment of risks. In S. Krimsky & D. Golding (Eds.), *Social Theories of Risk* (pp. 229–250). Westport, CT: Praeger.

Friedberg, A. L. (2000). *In the shadow of the garrison state: America's anti-statism and its Cold War grand strategy.* Princeton, NJ: Princeton University Press.

Friedman, M. J. (1953). The methodology of positive economics. In M. J. Friedman (Ed.), *Essays in Positive Economics* (pp. 3–43). Chicago, IL: University of Chicago Press.

Friedman, M., & Savage, L. J. (1948). The utility analysis of choices involving risk. *Journal of Political Economy, 56*, 279–304.

George, A. L. (1979). Case studies and theory development: The method of structured, focused comparison. In P. Lauren (Ed.), *Diplomacy* (pp. 43–68). New York: Free Press.

George, A. L. (1980). *Presidential decisionmaking in foreign policy: The effective use of information and advice.* Boulder, CO: Westview Press.

George, A. L. (1982, October). Case studies and theory development. Paper presented at the Second Annual Symposium on Information Processing in Organizations, Carnegie Mellon University, Pittsburgh, PA.

George, A. L., Hall, D. K., & Simons, W. E. (1971). *The limits of coercive diplomacy: Laos, Cuba, Vietnam.* Boston, MA: Little, Brown and Company.

George, A. L., & Smoke R. (1974). *Deterrence in American foreign policy: Theory and practice.* New York: Columbia University Press.

Gerring, J. (2004). What is a case study and what is it good for? *American Political Science Review, 98(2)*, 341–354.

Goldgeier, J. M. (1997). Psychology and security. *Security Studies, 6*, 137–166.

Goldgeier, J. M., & Tetlock, P. E. (2001). Psychology and international relations theory. *Annual Review of Political Science, 4*, 67–92.

Goncharov, S. N., Lewis, J. W., & Litai X. (1993). *Uncertain partners: Stalin, Mao, and the Korean War.* Stanford, CA: Stanford University Press.

Gosnell, H. F. (1980). *Truman's crises: A political biography of Harry S. Truman.* Westport, CT: Greenwood Press.

Grether, D. M., & Plott, C. R. (1979). Economic theory of choice and the preference reversal phenomenon. *American Economic Review, 69*, 623–638.

Guetzkow, H. S., & Valadez, J. J. (Eds.). (1981). *Simulated international processes: Theories and research in global modeling.* Beverly Hills, CA: Sage Publications.

Haas, M. L. (2001). Prospect theory and the Cuban missile crisis. *International Studies Quarterly, 45,* 241–270.

Haendel, D. (1979). *Foreign investments and the management of political risk.* Boulder, CO: Westview Press.

Harless, D. W., & Camerer, C. F. (1994). The predictive utility of generalized expected utility theories. *Econometrica, 62,* 1251–1289.

Heath, C., Larrick, R. P., & Wu, W. (1999). Goals as reference points. *Cognitive Psychology, 38,* 79–109.

Hermann, C. F. (1967). Validation problems in games and simulations with special reference to models of international politics. *Behavioral Science, 12,* 216–231.

Hermann, M. G. (1979). Indicators of stress in policy makers during foreign policy crises. *Political Psychology, 1,* 27–46.

Hermann, M. G. (1980a). Explaining foreign policy behavior using the personal characteristics of political leaders. *International Studies Quarterly, 24,* 7–46.

Hermann, M. G. (1980b). Comments: On "Foreign policy makers, personality attributes, and interviews: A note on reliability problems." *International Studies Quarterly, 24,* 67–73.

Hermann, M. G. (1984). Personality and foreign policy decision making: A study of 53 heads of government. In D. Sylvan & S. Chan (Eds.), *Foreign policy decision-making: perceptions, cognition, and artificial intelligence* (pp. 53–80). New York: Praeger.

Hermann, M. G., Winter, D. G., Weintraub, W., & Walker, S. G. (1991). The personalities of Bush and Gorbachev measured at a distance: Procedures, portraits, and policy. *Political Psychology, 12,* 215–243.

Herrmann, R. K., & Fischerkeller, M. P. (1996). Counterfactual reasoning in motivational analysis: U.S. policy toward Iran. In P. E. Tetlock & A. Belkin (Eds.), *Counterfactual thought experiments in world politics: Logical, methodological, and psychological perspectives* (pp. 149–167). Princeton, NJ: Princeton University Press.

Hershey, J. C., & Schoemaker, P. J. H. (1980). Prospect theory's reflection hypothesis: A critical examination. *Organizational Behavior and Human Performance, 25,* 395–418.

Hess, G. R. (1974). The Iranian crisis of 1945–46 and the Cold War. *Political Science Quarterly, 89,* 117–146.

Hess, G. R. (1993). Commitment in the age of counterinsurgency: Kennedy's Vietnam options and decisions, 1961–1963. In D. L. Anderson (Ed.), *Shadows on the White House: Presidents and the Vietnam War, 1945–1975* (pp. 63–86). Lawrence, KA: University of Kansas Press.

Hilsman, R. (1967). *To move a nation.* New York: Doubleday.

Holsti, O. (1979). Theories of crisis decision making. In P. Lauren (Ed.), *Diplomacy* (pp. 99–136). New York: Free Press.

Houts, A. C., Cook, T. D., & Shadish, W. R. (1986). The person–situation debate: A critical multiplist perspective. *Journal of Personality, 54,* 52–105.

Huth, P., Bennett, D. S., & Gelpi, C. (1992). System uncertainty, risk propensity, and international conflict among the Great Powers. *Journal of Conflict Resolution, 36,* 478–517.

Isaacson, W., & Thomas E. (1986). *The wise men: Six friends and the world they made.* New York: Simon and Schuster.

Janis, I., & Mann L. (1977). *Decision making: A psychological analysis of conflict, choice and commitment.* New York: Free Press.

Jervis, R. (1976). *Perception and misperception in international politics.* Princeton, NJ: Princeton University Press.

Jervis, R. (1988). War and misperception. *Journal of Interdisciplinary History, 18,* 675–700.

Jervis, R. (1992). Political implications of loss aversion. *Political Psychology, 13,* 187–204.

Jervis, R. (2004). The implications of prospect theory for human nature and values. *Political Psychology, 25(2),* 163–176.

Johnson, R. T. (1974). *Managing the White House: An intimate study of the presidency.* New York: Harper & Row.

Jones, H. (1989). *"A new kind of war": America's global strategy and the Truman Doctrine in Greece.* New York: Oxford University Press.

Jones, J. M. (1955). *The fifteen weeks.* New York: Harvest/HBJ.

Kahneman, D. (2000). Preface. In D. Kahneman & Amos Tversky (Eds.), *Choices, Values and Frames* (pp. ix–xvii). Cambridge, UK: Cambridge University Press.

Kahneman, D., & Tversky, A. (1979). Prospect theory: An analysis of decision under risk. *Econometrica, 47,* 263–291.

Kahneman, D., & Tversky, A. (1982). The Psychology of preferences. *Scientific American, 246,* 160–173.

Kahneman, D., & Tversky, A. (1984). Choices, values and frames. *American Psychologist, 39,* 341–350.

Kameda, T., & Davis, J. H. (1990). The function of the reference point in individual and group risk decision making. *Organizational Behavior and Human Decision Processes, 46,* 55–76.

Kanner, M. D. (2004). Framing and the role of the second actor: An application of prospect theory to bargaining. *Political Psychology, 25(2),* 213–239.

Kattenburg, P. M. (1982). *The Vietnam trauma in American foreign policy, 1945–75.* New Brunswick, CT: Transaction Books.

Keohane, R. (Ed.). (1986). *Neorealism and its critics.* New York: Columbia University Press.

Keyes, R. (1985). *Chancing it.* Boston, MA: Little, Brown.

Khong, Y. F. (1992). *Analogies at war.* Princeton, NJ: Princeton University Press.

Kinder, D. R., & Weiss, J. A. (1978). In lieu of rationality: Psychological perspectives on foreign policy decision making. *Journal of Conflict Resolution, 22,* 707–735.

King, G., Keohane, R., & Verba, S. (1994). *Designing social inquiry.* Princeton, NJ: Princeton University Press.

Kogan, N., & Wallach, M. (1964). *Risk taking: A study in cognition and personality.* New York: Holt, Rinehart and Winston.

Kowert, P. A., & Hermann, M. G. (1995, February). When prospects look dim: Rival hypotheses to prospect theory for risky decision making. Paper presented at the annual meeting of the International Studies Association, Chicago, IL.

Kuniholm, B. (1980). *The origins of the Cold War in the near East.* Princeton, NJ: Princeton University Press.

Kusnitz, L. A. (1984). *Public opinion and foreign policy: America's China policy.* Wesport, CT: Greenwood Press.

Lakatos, I. (1968). Criticism and the methodology of scientific research programmes. *Proceedings of the Aristotelian Society, 69,* 149–186.

Lamborn, A. (1985). Risk and foreign policy choice. *International Studies Quarterly, 29,* 385–410.

Larson, D. W. (2001). Sources and methods in Cold War history: The need for a new theory-based archival approach. In C. Elman & M. F. Elman (Eds.), *Bridges and boundaries: Historians, political scientists, and the study of international relations* (pp. 327–350). Cambridge, MA: MIT Press.

Lefever, E. (1967). *Uncertain mandate: Politics of the U. N. Congo Operation.* Baltimore, MD: Johns Hopkins Press.

Leffler, Melvyn. (1992). *A preponderance of power: National security, the Truman administration and the Cold War.* Stanford, CA: Stanford University Press.

Lenczowski, G. (1968). *Russia and the West in Iran, 1918–1948: A study in big-power rivalry.* New York: Greenwood Press.

Levenson, M. R. (1990). Risk taking and personality. *Journal of Personality and Social Psychology, 58,* 1073–1080.

Levi, A. S., & Whyte, G. (1997). A cross-cultural explanation of the reference dependence of crucial group decisions under risk: Japan's 1941 decision for war. *Journal of Conflict Resolution, 41,* 792–813.

Levy, J. S. (1987). Declining power and the preventive motivation for war. *World Politics, 40,* 82–107.

Levy, J. S. (1992a). An introduction to prospect theory. *Political Psychology, 13,* 171–186.

Levy, J. S. (1992b). Prospect theory and international relations: Theoretical applications and analytical problems. *Political Psychology, 13,* 283–310.

Levy, J. S. (1994, September). Prospect theory, aggregation effects, and survival levels: Implications for international relations. Paper presented at the annual meeting of the American Political Science Association, New York.

Levy, J. S. (1995). Prospect theory, rational choice, and international relations. Unpublished manuscript.

Levy, J. S. (1996, April). Hypotheses on the framing of decisions. Paper presented at the annual meeting of the International Studies Association, San Diego, CA.

Levy, J. S. (1997a). Prospect theory and the cognitive-rational debate. In N. Geva & A. Mintz (Eds.), *Decisionmaking on War and Peace: The Cognitive-Rational Debate* (pp. 33–50). Boulder, CO: Lynne Rienner Publishers.

Levy, J. S. (1997b). Prospect theory, rational choice, and international relations. *International Studies Quarterly, 41,* 87–112.

Levy, J. S. (1998). Loss aversion, framing, and bargaining: The implications of prospect theory for international conflict. In F. P. Harvey & B. D. Mor (Eds.), *Conflict in World Politics: Advances in the Study of Crisis, War, and Peace* (pp. 96–115). New York: St. Martin's Press.

Loomes, G., & Sugden, R. (1982). Regret theory: An alternative theory of rational choice under uncertainty. *The Economic Journal, 92*, 805–824.

Lopes, L. L. (1981). Notes, comments, and new findings: Decision making in the short run. *Journal of Experimental Psychology, 7(5)*, 377–385.

Lopes, L. L. (1987). Between hope and fear: The psychology of risk. *Advances in Experimental Social Psychology, 20*, 255–295.

Lopes, L. L. (1990). Re-modeling risk aversion: A comparison of Bernoullian and rank dependent value approaches. In G. M. Von Furstenberg (Ed.), *Acting under uncertainty: Multidisciplinary conceptions* (pp. 267–299). Boston, MA: Kluwer Academic Publishers.

Lopes, L. L. (1995). Algebra and process in the modeling of risky choice. *The Psychology of Learning and Motivation, 32*, 177–220.

Lopes, L. L., & Oden, G. C. (1999). The role of aspiration level in risky choice: A comparison of cumulative prospect theory and SP/A theory. *Journal of Mathematical Psychology, 43*, 286–313.

MacCrimmon, K. R., & Wehrung, D. A. (1986). *Taking risks.* New York: The Free Press.

Machina, M. J. (1987). Decision-making in the presence of risk. *Science, 236*, 537–543.

Mahoney, R. (1983). *JFK: Ordeal in Africa.* New York: Oxford University Press.

Majeski, S. J., & Sylvan, D. J. (1984). Simple choices and complex calculations. *Journal of Conflict Resolution, 28*, 316–340.

Mann, L. (1992). Stress, affect, and risk taking. In J. Yates (Ed.), *Risk-taking behavior* (pp. 201–229). New York: John Wiley & Sons.

Maoz, Z. (1990). Framing the national interest: The manipulation of foreign policy decisions in group settings. *World Politics, 43*, 77–110.

March, J. G., & Shapira, Z. (1987). Managerial perspectives on risk and risk taking. *Management Science, 33*, 1404–1418.

March, J. G., & Shapira, Z. (1992). Variable risk preferences and the focus of attention. *Psychological Review, 99*, 172–183.

Mazlish, B. (1988). Kennedy: Myth and history. In J. R. Snyder (Ed.), *John F. Kennedy: Person, policy, presidency* (pp. 25–34). Wilmington, DE: Scholarly Resources Books.

McClelland, D. C. (1961). *The achieving society.* Princeton, NJ: Van Nostrand.

McCullough, D. (1992). *Truman.* New York: Simon & Schuster.

McDermott, R. (1992). Prospect theory in international relations: The Iranian hostage rescue mission. *Political Psychology, 13*, 237–263.

McDermott, R. (1995, September). The U.S. decision to launch operation Desert Storm, January, 1991: A prospect theory analysis. Paper presented at the annual meeting of the American Political Science Association, Chicago, IL.

McDermott, R. (1998). *Risk-taking in international politics: Prospect theory in American foreign policy.* Ann Arbor, MI: University of Michigan Press.

McDermott, R. (2001). The psychological ideas of Amos Tversky and their relevance for political scientists. *Journal of Theoretical Politics, 13*, 5–33.

McDermott, R. (2004a). Editor's introduction. *Political Psychology, 25(2)*, 147–162.

McDermott, R. (2004b). Prospect theory in political science: Gains and losses from the first decade. *Political Psychology, 25(2)*, 289–312.

McDermott, R., & Kugler, J. (2001). Comparing rational choice and prospect theory analyses: The US decision to launch operation "Desert Storm," January 1991. *Journal of Strategic Studies, 24*, 49–85.

McInerney, A. (1992). Prospect theory and soviet policy towards Syria, 1966–67. *Political Psychology, 13*, 265–282.

McNamara, R. S. (with VanDeMark, B.). (1995). *In retrospect: The tragedy and lessons of Vietnam.* New York: Times Books.

Mearsheimer, J. (2001). *The tragedy of great power politics.* New York: W. W. Norton & Company.

Mintz, A., & Geva, N. (1998). A prospect-based analysis of war termination. In F. P. Harvey & B. D. Mor (Eds.), *Conflict in world politics: Advances in the study of crisis, war, and peace* (pp. 288–305). New York: St. Martin's Press.

Mitrovich, G. (2000). *Undermining the Kremlin: America's strategy to subvert the Soviet Bloc, 1947–1956.* Ithaca, NY: Cornell University Press.

Morgenthau, H. J. (1985). *Politics among nations: The struggle for power and peace.* New York: Alfred A. Knopf, Inc.

Morrow, J. (1987). On the theoretical basis of a measure of national risk attitudes. *International Studies Quarterly, 31,* 423–438.

Morrow, J. (1994). *Game theory for political scientists.* Princeton, NJ: Princeton University Press.

Morrow, J. (1997). A rational choice approach to international conflict. In N. Geva & A. Mintz (Eds.), *Decisionmaking on war and peace: The cognitive-rational debate* (pp. 11–31). Boulder, CO: Lynne Rienner Publishers.

Nagy, P. (1979). *Country risk: How to assess, quantify and monitor it.* London: Euromoney Publications.

Neilson, W. S. (1992). A mixed fan hypothesis and its implications for behavior towards risk. *Journal of Economic Behavior and Organization, 19,* 197–212.

Nincic, M. (1992). *Democracy and foreign policy: The fallacy of political realism.* New York: Columbia University Press.

O'Neill, B. (2001). Risk aversion in international relations theory. *International Studies Quarterly, 45,* 617–640.

Paese, P. W., Bieser, M., & Tubbs, M. E. (1993). Framing effects and choice shifts in group decision making. *Organizational Behavior and Human Decision Processes, 56,* 149–165.

Paige, G. (1968). *The Korean decision.* New York: The Free Press.

Paterson, T. G. (Ed.). (1989). *Kennedy's quest for victory.* New York: Oxford University Press.

Pauly, L. W. (1993). The political foundations of multilateral economic surveillance. In J. G. Stein & L. W. Pauly (Eds.), *Choosing to cooperate: How states avoid loss* (pp. 93–127). Baltimore, MD: The Johns Hopkins University Press.

Payne, J. W., Bettman, J. R., & Johnson, E. J. (1990). The adaptive decision maker: Effort and accuracy in choice. In R. M. Hogarth (Ed.), *Insights in decision making: A tribute to Hillel J. Einhorn* (pp. 129–153). Chicago, IL: University of Chicago Press.

Payne, J. W., Laughhunn, D. J., & Crum, R. (1980). Translation of gambles and aspiration level effects in risky choice behavior. *Management Science, 26,* 1039–1060.

Pelz, S. (1983). U.S. decisions on Korean policy, 1943–1950: Some hypotheses. In B. Cumings (Ed.), *Child of conflict: The Korean-American relationship, 1943–1953.* Seattle, WA: University of Washington Press.

Plax, T. G., & Rosenfeld, L. B. (1976). Correlates of risky decision-making. *Journal of Personality Assessment, 40,* 413–418.

Preston, J. T. (2001). *The President and his inner circle: Leadership style and the advisory process in foreign affairs.* New York: Columbia University Press.

Quattrone, G. A., & Tversky, A. (1988). Contrasting rational and psychological analyses of political choice. *American Political Science Review, 82,* 719–736.

Rasler, K., & Thompson, W. (1980). Foreign policy makers, personality attributes, and interviews. *International Studies Quarterly, 24,* 47–66.

Renn, O. (1992). Concepts of risk: A classification. In S. Krimsky & D. Golding (Eds.), *Social theories of risk* (pp. 53–82). Westport, CT: Praeger.

Richards, R., Morgan, T. C., Wilson, R. K., Schwebach, V. L., & Young, G. D. (1993). Good times, bad times, and the diversionary use of force: A tale of some not-so-free Agents. *Journal of Conflict Resolution, 37,* 504–535.

Rosecrance, R. N. (1966). Bipolarity, multipolarity, and the future. *Journal of Conflict Resolution, 10,* 314–327.

Rosen, L. D., & Rosenkoetter, P. (1976). An eye fixation analysis of choice and judgment with multiattribute stimuli. *Memory & Cognition, 4,* 747–752.

Rosenberg, P. J. (1979). The Cheshire ultimatum: Truman's message to Stalin in the 1946 Azerbaijan crisis. *Journal of Politics, 41,* 933–940.

Rossow, R., Jr. (1956). The battle of Azerbaijan, 1946. *Middle East Journal, 10,* 17–32.

Rust, W. J. (1985). *Kennedy in Vietnam.* New York: Charles Scribner's Sons.

Samii, K. A. (1987). Truman against Stalin in Iran: A tale of three messages. *Middle Eastern Studies, 23(1),* 95–107.

Savage, L. J. (1954). *The foundations of statistics*. New York: Wiley.

Schaub, G., Jr. (2004). Deterrence, compellence, and prospect theory. *Political Psychology, 25(3)*, 389–411.

Schlesinger, A. M., Jr. (1965). *A thousand days*. Boston, MA: Houghton Mifflin.

Schweller, R. L. (1994). Bandwagoning for profit: Bringing the revisionist state back in. *International Security, 19*, 72–107.

Schweller, R. L. (1996). Neorealism's status-quo-bias: What security dilemma? *Security Studies, 5*, 90–121.

Seibert, S. E., & Goltz, S. M. (2001). Comparison of allocations by individuals and interacting groups in an escalation of commitment situation. *Journal of Applied Social Psychology, 31*, 134–156.

Shafir, E. (1992). Prospect theory and political analysis: A psychological perspective. *Political Psychology, 13*, 311–322.

Sheehan, M. K. (1968). *Iran: The impact of United States interests and policies 1941–1954*. New York: Theo. Gaus' Sons.

Singer, J. D., Bremer, S., & Stuckey, J. (1972). Capability distribution, uncertainty, and major power war, 1820–1965. In B. Russett (Ed.), *Peace, war, and numbers* (pp. 19–48). Beverly Hills, CA: Sage.

Sjöberg, L. (1980). The risks of risk analysis. *Acta Psychologica, 45*, 301–321.

Slovic, P. (1964). Assessment of risk-taking behavior. *Psychological Bulletin, 61*, 220–233.

Slovic, P. (1972). Information processing, situation specificity, and the generality of risk-taking behavior. *Journal of Personality and Social Psychology, 22*, 128–134.

Slovic, P. (1992). Perception of risk: Reflections on the psychometric paradigm. In S. Krimsky & D. Golding (Eds.), *Social theories of risk* (pp. 117–152). Westport, CT: Praeger.

Slovic, P., & Lichtenstein, S. (1968). Relative importance of probabilities and payoffs in risk taking. *Journal of Experimental Psychology Monograph, 78*, 1–18.

Slovic, P., & Lichtenstein, S. (1983). Preference reversals: A broader perspective. *American Economic Review, 73*, 596–605.

Smith, B. (1951). The White House story: Why we went to war in Korea. *The Saturday Evening Post, November 10, 1951*, 22, 23, 76, 78, 80, 82, 86, 88.

Smith, S., Booth, K., & Zalewski, M. (Eds.). (1996). *International theory: Positivism and beyond*. Cambridge: Cambridge University Press.

Snyder, J. (1984/85). Richness, rigor, and relevance in the study of Soviet foreign policy. *International Security, 9*, 89–108.

Snyder, J. (1988). Science and sovietology: Bridging the methods gap in Soviet foreign policy Studies. *World Politics, 40*, 169–193.

Snyder, J. (1991). *Myths of empire: Domestic politics and international ambition*. Ithaca, NY: Cornell University Press.

Sorensen, T. C. (1965). *Kennedy*. New York: Harper & Row.

Stein, J. G., & Pauly, L. W. (Eds.). (1993). *Choosing to cooperate: How states avoid loss*. Baltimore, MD: Johns Hopkins University Press.

Steury, D. P. (Ed.). (1994). *Sherman Kent and the board of national estimates: Collected essays*. Washington, D.C.: Central Intelligence Agency.

Stueck, W. W. (1981). *The road to confrontation: American policy toward China and Korea, 1947–1950*. Chapel Hill, NC: University of North Carolina Press.

Stueck, W. W. (1995). *The Korean war: An international history*. Princeton, NJ: Princeton University Press.

Sylvan, D. (1998). Introduction. In D. Sylvan & J. Voss (Eds.), *Problem representation in foreign policy decision making* (pp. 3–8). New York: Cambridge University Press.

Sylvan, D., & Thorson S. (1992). Ontologies, problem representation, and the Cuban missile crisis. *Journal of Conflict Resolution, 36*, 709–732.

Sylvan, D., & Voss, J. (Eds.). (1998). *Problem representation in foreign policy decision making*. New York: Cambridge University Press.

Sylvan, D., Goel, A., & Chandrasekaran, B. (1990). Analyzing political decision making from an information-processing perspective: JESSE. *American Journal of Political Science, 34*, 74–123.

Taliaferro, J. W. (1994, March). Analogical reasoning and prospect theory: Hypotheses on framing. Paper presented at the annual meeting of the International Studies Association, Washington, D.C.

Taliaferro, J. W. (1995, February). Reference dependence, strategic choice and war. Paper presented at the annual meeting of the American Political Science Association, Chicago, IL.

Taliaferro, J. W. (1997). Cognitive realism: Risk taking and the psychology of loss aversion in foreign policy. Unpublished doctoral dissertation, Harvard University, MA.

Taliaferro, J. W. (1998). Quagmires in the periphery: Foreign wars and escalating commitment in international conflict. *Security Studies, 7*, 94–144.

Taliaferro, J. W. (2000/2001). Security seeking under anarchy. *International Security, 25*, 128–161.

Taliaferro, J. W. (2001). Realism, power shifts, and major war. *Security Studies, 10*, 145–178.

Taliaferro, J. W. (2004). Power politics and the balance of risk: Hypotheses on great power intervention in the periphery. *Political Psychology, 25(2)*, 177–211.

Teuber, A. (1990). Justifying risk. *Daedalus, 119*, 235–254.

Thorpe, J. A. (1978). Truman's Ultimatum to Stalin on the 1946 Azerbaijan crisis: The making of a Myth. *Journal of Politics, 40*, 188–195.

Trachtenberg, M. (1991). *History and strategy*. Princeton, NJ: Princeton University Press.

Truman, H. S. (1956). *Memoirs, Vol. II: Years of trial and hope*. New York: Doubleday.

Tversky, A. (1969). Intransitivity of preferences. *Psychological Review, 76*, 31–48.

Tversky, A., & Kahneman, D. (1981). The framing of decisions and the psychology of choice. *Science, 211*, 453–458.

Tversky, A., & Kahneman, D. (1992). Advances in prospect theory: Cumulative representation of uncertainty. *Journal of Risk and Uncertainty, 5*, 297–323.

Tversky, A., Slovic, P., & Kahneman, D. (1990). The causes of preference reversal. *American Economic Review, 80*, 204–217.

Van Wagenen, R. W. (1952). *The Iranian Case 1946*. New York: Carnegie Endowment for International Peace.

Vertzberger, Y. Y. I. (1990). *The world in their minds*. Stanford, CA: Stanford University Press.

Vertzberger, Y. Y. I. (1995a). Rethinking and reconceptualizing risk in foreign policy decision-making: A sociocognitive approach. *Political Psychology, 16*, 347–380.

Vertzberger, Y. Y. I. (1995b, February). Cognitive, motivational and personality factors in risk taking. Paper presented at the Annual Meeting of the International Studies Association, Chicago, IL.

Vertzberger, Y. Y. I. (1997). Collective risk taking: The decision making group. In P. 't Hart, E. K. Stern, & B. Sundelius (Eds.), *Beyond groupthink: Political group dynamics and foreign policy-making* (pp. 289–316). Ann Arbor, MI: University of Michigan Press.

Vertzberger, Y. Y. I. (1998). *Risk taking and decisionmaking: Foreign military intervention decisions*. Stanford, CA: Stanford University Press.

Vlek, C., & Stallen, P. J. (1980). Rational and personal aspects of risk. *Acta Psychologica, 45*, 273–300.

von Neumann, J., & Morgenstern, O. (1947). *Theory of games and economic behavior*. Princeton, NJ: Princeton University Press.

Voss, J. F. (1998). On the representation of problems: An information-processing approach to foreign policy decision making. In D. A. Sylvan & J. F. Voss (Eds.), *Problem representation in foreign policy decision making* (pp. 8–26). New York: Cambridge University Press.

Walton, R. (1972). *Cold War and counterrevolution*. New York: The Viking Press.

Waltz, K. (1964). The stability of a bipolar world. *Daedalus, 93*, 881–909.

Waltz, K. (1979). *Theory of international politics*. New York: McGraw-Hill.

Weissman, S. (1974). *American foreign policy in the Congo 1960–1964*. Ithaca, NY: Cornell University Press.

Weyland, K. (1996). Risk taking in Latin American economic restructuring: Lessons from prospect theory. *International Studies Quarterly, 40*, 185–207.

Weyland, K. (1998). The political fate of market reform in Latin America, Africa, and Eastern Europe. *International Studies Quarterly, 42*, 645–673.

Whyte, G. (1993). Escalating commitment in individual and group decision making: A prospect theory approach. *Organizational Behavior and Human Decision Processes, 54*, 430–455.

Whyte, G. (1998). Recasting Janis's groupthink model: The key role of collective efficacy in decision fiascoes. *Organizational Behavior and Human Decision Processes, 73*, 185–209.

Whyte, G., & Levi, A. S. (1994). The origins and function of the reference point in risky group decision making: The case of the Cuban missile crisis. *Journal of Behavioral Decision Making, 7*, 243–260.

Wildavsky, A., & Dake, K. (1990). Theories of risk perception: Who fears what and why? *Daedalus, 119*, 41–60.

Wyatt, G. (1989). Decision-making under conditions of risk: Assessing influential factors. *Emporia State Research Studies, 37*, 5–48.

Xydis, S. G. (1963). *Greece and the Great Powers 1944–1947: Prelude to the "Truman Doctrine."* Thessaloniki, Greece: Institute for Balkan Studies.

Yaari, M. E. (1987). The dual theory of choice under risk. *Econometrica, 55*, 95–115.

Yates, J., & Stone E. (1992). Risk appraisal. In J. Yates (Ed.), *Risk-taking behavior* (pp. 49–85). New York: John Wiley & Sons.

Government Documents

Allen, G. V. "Mission to Iran," unpublished manuscript, Chapter I; Mission to Iran folder, Allen papers: Box 1; Truman Library.

"Analytical Chronology of the Congo Crisis," January 25, 1961; Congo, General folder, NSF: Box 27; Kennedy Library.

Ball, G. W. (1961). *The Elements in Our Congo Policy.* Washington, D.C.: U. S. Government Printing Office.

"Blair House Meeting," June 25, 1950; June 25 '50 folder: Box 71; Elsey papers, Truman Library.

Bowles, C. "The Congo Crisis," December 12, 1962; Congo, General, 12/62 folder, NSF: Box 28a; George Ball's Papers, Kennedy Library.

Bowles to Kennedy, "The Developing Situation in Laos," April 26, 1961; Laos, General 4/22/61–4/30/61 folder, NSF: Box 130; Kennedy Library.

Central Intelligence Agency (CIA)/Office of National Estimates (ONE), "Certain Consequences of the Withdrawal of UN Forces from the Congo," December 11, 1962; Congo, General 12/1/62–12/13/62 folder, NSF: Box 28a; Kennedy Library.

Central Intelligence Agency, "Korean Situation," June 29, 1950; June–August 1950 folder, PSF Intelligence File: Box 246; Truman Library.

Central Intelligence Agency, "Korean Situation," June 28, 1950; June–August 1950 folder, PSF Intelligence File: Box 246; Truman Library.

Central Intelligence Agency, "The USSR and the Korean Invasion," June 28, 1950, Memoranda, 1950–52 Folder, PSF Intelligence File: Box 250; Truman Library.

Central Intelligence Agency, "Korean Situation," June 26, 1950, June–August 1950 folder, PSF Intelligence File: Box 246; Truman Library.

CINCFE MacArthur to JCS, June 30, 1950; Korea, June 30 '50 folder: Box 71; Elsey papers, Truman Library.

"Concept for Intervention in Viet-Nam," n.d.; Vietnam, General 10/1/61–10/3/61 folder, NSF: Box 194; Kennedy Library.

"Consequences of US Troop Withdrawal From Korea in Spring, 1949," ORE 3–49, February 28, 1949; Folder 93, Record Group 263; Records of the Central Intelligence Agency, Estimates of the Office of Research Evaluation 1946–1950; Intelligence Publication File: Box 3; National Archives at College Park, MD.

"Consequences of Certain Courses of Action with Respect to Greece," ORE 10–48, April 5, 1948; Folder 43, Record Group 263; Records of the Central Intelligence Agency, Estimates of the Office of Research Evaluation 1946–1950; Intelligence Publication File: Box 1; National Archives at College Park, MD.

"Current Capabilities of the North Korean Regime," ORE 18–50, June 19, 1950; Folder 136, Record Group 263; Records of the Central Intelligence Agency, Estimates of the Office of Research Evaluation 1946–1950; Intelligence Publication File: Box 4; National Archives at College Park, MD.

Curry to Bennorth, "Correspondence," February 2, 1969; Vertical File, Truman Subject File: Iran folder; Truman Library.

Department of State. (1969a). *Foreign Relations of the United States, 1945: Volume VIII, The Near East and Africa.* Washington, D.C.: U. S. Government Printing Office.

Department of State. (1969b). *Foreign Relations of the United States, 1946: Volume VII, The Near East and Africa.* Washington, D.C.: U. S. Government Printing Office.

Department of State. (1969c). *Foreign Relations of the United States, 1946: Volume VI, Eastern Europe; The Soviet Union.* Washington, D.C.: U. S. Government Printing Office.

Department of State. (1971). *Foreign Relations of the United States, 1947: Volume V, The Near East and Africa.* Washington, D.C.: U. S. Government Printing Office.

Department of State. (1974). *Foreign Relations of the United States, 1948: Volume IV, Eastern Europe; The Soviet Union.* Washington, D.C.: U. S. Government Printing Office.

Department of State. (1976). *Foreign Relations of the United States, 1950: Volume VII, Korea.* Washington, D.C.: U. S. Government Printing Office.

Department of State. (1988). *Foreign Relations of the United States, 1961–63: Volume I, Vietnam 1961.* Washington, D.C.: U. S. Government Printing Office.

Department of State. (1994a). *Foreign Relations of the United States, 1961–63: Volume XXIV, Laos Crisis.* Washington, D.C.: U. S. Government Printing Office.

Department of State. (1994b). *Foreign Relations of the United States, 1961–63: Volume XX, Congo Crisis.* Washington, D.C.: U. S. Government Printing Office.

"Draft," n.d.; Korea, June 29 '50 folder: Box 71; Elsey papers, Truman Library.

George to Lagerquist, "Correspondence," June 20, 1969; Vertical File, Truman Subject File: Iran folder; Truman Library.

Hilsman, R./Bureau of Intelligence and Research (INR). "Possible Soviet Military Assistance to the Congo," December 7, 1962; Congo, General 12/1/62–12/13/62 folder, NSF: Box 28a; Kennedy Library.

Hilsman, R./Bureau of Intelligence and Research (INR). "The Congo: An Appraisal of Alternatives," December 11, 1962; Countries, Congo 1959–1963 folder: Box 1; Hilsman Papers, Kennedy Library.

JCS to CINCFE MacArthur, June 30, 1950; Korea, June 30 '50 folder: Box 71; Elsey papers, Truman Library.

JCS to CINCFE MacArthur, June 29, 1950; Korea, June 29 '50 folder: Box 71; Elsey papers, Truman Library.

Johnson (U.A.) To Bundy, "South Viet-Nam," November 11, 1961; Vietnam, General 11/11/61–11/13/61, NSF: Box 195; Kennedy Library.

"J.M. Jones Notes on Acheson's Presentation," February 28, 1947; Truman Doctrine, Important Relevant Papers folder: Box 2; Jones Papers, Truman Library.

Kennedy, J. F. "Statement By The President," March 23, 1961; Laos, General 3/23/61–3/24/61 folder, NSF: Box 130; Kennedy Library.

Kennedy, J. F. "Presidential Statements on Laos. Press Conferences #1–#8"; n.d., Laos, General 3/23/61–3/24/61 folder, NSF: Box 130; Kennedy Library.

Kennedy, J. F. "Handwritten Notes"; n.d., Doodles 1959–1961, 1961:KP70–75 folder, PPF: Box 41; Kennedy Library.

Kennedy, J. F. (1962). *Public Papers of the Presidents of the United States: John F. Kennedy, 1961.* Washington, D.C.: U. S. Government Printing Office.

Kennedy, J. F. (1963). *Public Papers of the Presidents of the United States: John F. Kennedy, 1962.* Washington, D.C.: U. S. Government Printing Office.

Kennedy to Rusk, "Memorandum," November 5, 1962; Congo, General 10/30/62–11/5/62 folder, NSF: Box 28a; Kennedy Library.

Kirk to Acheson, June 25, 1950; June 25 '50 folder: Box 71; Elsey papers, Truman Library.

Landon to Rostow, "Laos and the Indian Ocean Area," February 7, 1961; Laos, General 2/7/61–2/15/61 folder, NSF: Box 130; Kennedy Library.

Mansfield to Kennedy, "The Laotian Situation," January 21, 1961; Laos, General 1/61–3/61 folder, POF: Box 121; Kennedy Library.

McGhee, G. "Recommended Course of Action on the Congo," December 13, 1962; Congo, General 12/1/62–12/13/62 folder, NSF: Box 28a; Kennedy Library.

"Meeting with the President on The Congo, Wednesday, October 31, 1962, 4:00 P.M.," November 1, 1962, Congo, General 10/30/62–11/5/62 folder, NSF: Box 28a; Kennedy Library.

"Memorandum for the President," June 29, 1950; Meetings Discussions, 1950 folder, PSF: Box 220; Truman Library.

"Memorandum for the President," June 30, 1950; Meetings Discussions, 1950 folder, PSF: Box 220; Truman Library.

"Memorandum of Conversation—Meeting of the NSC in the Cabinet Room at the White House," June 28, 1950; Memoranda of Conversation, May-June 1950 folder: Box 65; Acheson papers, Truman Library.

"Memorandum of Conversation—Korean Situation," June 25, 1950; Memoranda of Conversation, May-June 1950 folder: Box 65; Acheson papers, Truman Library.

"Memorandum of Conversation—Korean Situation," June 26, 1950; Memoranda of Conversation, May–June 1950 folder: Box 65; Acheson papers, Truman Library.

Newhouse, N. "Laos"; n.d., Writings, A Thousand Days Background Material, Laos Research, Notes and Memoranda folder: Box W-12; Schlesinger papers, Kennedy Library.

"Notes on Cabinet Meeting," March 7, 1947; Notes on Cabinet Meetings, January 3–December 19, 1947 folder: Box 1; Connelly Papers, Truman Library.

"Notes on Meeting in Cabinet Room at the White House," June 27, 1950; Memoranda of Conversation, May–June 1950 folder: Box 65; Acheson papers, Truman Library.

Oral history interview, Clark M. Clifford, April 19, 1971, Truman Library.

Oral history interview, George M. Elsey, July 7, 1970, Truman Library.

Oral history interview, Thomas K. Finletter, January 20, 1972, Truman Library.

Oral history interview, Loy W. Henderson, June 14, 1973, Truman Library.

Oral history interview, Frank Pace, Jr., January 22, 1972, Truman Library.

Oral history interview, Frank Pace, Jr., February 17, 1972, Truman Library.

Oral history interview, Walt Rostow, April 11, 1964, Kennedy Library.

Oral history interview, William M. Rountree, September 20, 1989, Truman Library.

Oral history interview, Dean Rusk, December 2, 1969, Kennedy Library.

Oral history interview, Dean Rusk, December 9, 1969, Kennedy Library.

Oral history interview, Maxwell Taylor, April 26, 1964, Kennedy Library.

"Persons Present at the President's Meeting," June 27, 1950; Korea, June 27 '50 folder: Box 71; Elsey papers, Truman Library.

"Persons Present at the President's Meeting," June 30, 1950; Korea, June 30 '50 folder: Box 71; Elsey papers, Truman Library.

"Points Requiring Presidential Decision"; n.d., Korea, June 25 '50 folder: Box 71; Elsey papers, Truman Library.

Pravda Observer Article, "Laos Must Be Independent and Neutral," March 27, 1961; Laos, General 1/61–3/61 folder, POF: Box 121; Kennedy Library.

"President Truman's conversations with George M. Elsey," June 26, 1950; Korea, June 26 '50 folder: Box 71; Elsey papers, Truman Library.

"Princeton Seminars," February 13–14, 1954; Princeton Seminars, February 13–14, 1954 folder: Box 90; Acheson papers, Truman Library.

"Public Law 75," May 22, 1947; Greek-Turkish Program folder, PSF: Box 229; Truman Library.

Rostow to Kennedy, "Evolution of Our Policy in Laos," March 9, 1961; Laos, General 3/1/61–3/12/61 folder, NSF: Box 130; Kennedy Library.

Rusk to Nolting, Department of State Telegram, November 15, 1961; Vietnam, General 11/14/61–11/15/61 folder, NSF: Box 195; Kennedy Library.

Shelton, W. "Congress Divided on Military Aid," March 13, 1947; Truman Doctrine, Important Relevant Papers folder: Box 2; Jones papers, Truman Library.

"Teleconference 260355z," June 25, 1950; Korea, June 25 '50 folder: Box 71; Elsey papers, Truman Library.

"Teleconference with MacArthur, 270217z," June 26, 1950; Korea, June 26 '50 folder: Box 71; Elsey papers, Truman Library.

"The Greek Situation," ORE 6/1, February 7, 1947; Folder 9, Record Group 263; Records of the Central Intelligence Agency, Estimates of the Office of Research Evaluation 1946–1950; Intelligence Publication File: Box 1; National Archives at College Park, MD.

Thompson to Rusk, March 10, 1961; Laos, Security 3/1161–3/20/61 folder, POF: Box 121; Kennedy Library.

Truman, H. S. (1963). *Public Papers of the Presidents of the United States: Harry S. Truman, 1947.* Washington, D.C.: U. S. Government Printing Office.

Truman, H. S. (1964). *Public Papers of the Presidents of the United States: Harry S. Truman, 1948.* Washington, D.C.: U. S. Government Printing Office.

Truman, H. S. "White House Press and Radio Conference," June 29, 1950; North Korean Aggression Immediate Evaluation and Response folder (2 of 3), SMOF: Korean War, Box 4; Truman Library.

Webb to Snyder, April 25, 1975; Correspondence folder: Box 456; Webb papers, Truman Library.

Williams, G. M. "Policy Alternatives in the Congo"; n.d., Congo, General, 12/62 folder, NSF: Box 28a; George Ball's Papers, Kennedy Library.

INDEX

DRV, *see* North Vietnam
dual theory of choice, 22
Dulles, Allen (U.S. Director of Central
    Intelligence), 124, 133
Dulles, John Foster (U.S. Secretary of State),
    113, 116, 128, 149
Dunkirk, British retreat from, 74

EAM, *see* National Liberation Front
East Germany, 149, *see also* Germany
Eastern Europe, 53, 55, 58, 70, *see also*
    Europe
Econometrica, 23
economics, academic discipline of
    decision theory and, 27
    expected-utility theory and, 16, 22
    international relations borrows from, 5
    literature of, underlying this study, 46
    prospect theory and, 23, 33–34
    research on risk behavior in, 2, 4,
        15, 17
economists, *see* economics, academic
    discipline of
Eden, Anthony (British Foreign Secretary),
    50–51
EDES, *see* National Republican League
Egypt, 74
Eisenhower, Dwight D.
    confers with Kennedy on Laos, 114, 120,
        127, 135, 167
    personality assessment-at-a-distance
        codings for, 13
    presidential administration of, 113–16,
        126, 128, 134, 146–47, 149, 166
    presidential risk predispostion-index
        score of, 43–44
Ellsberg, D., 22–23
Elsey, George (Truman's administrative
    assistant), 79, 91, 96
Ethridge, Mark (American member, UN
    Commission of Investigation in
    Greece), 73, 76–78
EU, *see* expected-utility theory
Europe, 82, 96, 148–49, 152, 157–58, *see*
    also Eastern Europe; Western Europe
EV, *see* expected-value theory
expected-utility theory
    adding reflection points to, 173
    Bernoullian Tradition of, 16, 21, 29, 33
    cost-benefit model in, 35
    final asset positions in, 6, 23, 171–72
    normative character of, 25

prospect theory vs., 32, 36
recent modications of classical, 22, 24
risk propensity in, 4, 19–20
risk-taking decisions and, 4, 6, 16, 19–25,
    29, viii
standard equation of, 30
expected-value theory, 20–21

"Face the Nation," 12
fanning out hypothesis, 22
Far East
    Democrats wary of U.S. military activity
        in, 133, 143
    Soviet military forces in, 93, 99
    U.S. security interests in, 89, 96
Far East Command, U.S., 95
Farnham, Barbara, 31, viii
Felt, Harry D. (Admiral, U.S. Navy),
    116, 119
Figure 2.1, 38
Figure 2.2, 41–43
Figure 5.1, 173–74
Finletter, Thomas E. (U.S. Secretary of the
    Air Force), 93, 101–02, 104–06
Firuz, Muzaffar (Iranian Interpreter), 55
Fischhoff, B., 24
Fisher, Louis, 74
Formosa
    Chiang and Roosevelt discuss, 88
    Truman fears Communist aggression
        upon, 91, 97, 99, 109
    U.S. Seventh Fleet protects, 93, 104–05
Forrestal, James V. (U.S. Secretary of the
    Navy), 57
"Fortress America," 72
framing, concept of, 23–25, 31–34, 39
France
    actions and policies of, on Congo, 147
    actions and policies of, on Greece, 67
    actions and policies of, on Laos, 120,
        124–25
    defeated in Vietnam, 131
    Soviet Union tests, 164
    Truman fears Communist success in, 70,
        73–74, 87
Free Democratic Government, *see* Greece
Friedman, M. J., 21
Fuchs, Klaus, 97

Galbraith, J. K. (U.S. ambassador to India),
    132, 139, 144–45, 166
game theory, 21